THE HINDI CANON

INTELLECTUALS, PROCESSES, CRITICISM

THE HINDI CANON

INTELLECTUALS, PROCESSES, CRITICISM

MRITYUNJAY TRIPATHI

TRANSLATED BY

SHAD NAVED

 Tulika Books

Published by

Tulika Books
44 (first floor), Shahpur Jat, New Delhi 110 049, India
www.tulikabooks.in

This book by Mrityunjay Tripathi
was originally published in Hindi as
Hindi alochna mein canon-nirman ki prakriya,
by Rajkamal Prakashan Pvt. Ltd., New Delhi, in 2015

First edition (hardback) 2018

ISBN: 978-81-934015-9-0

Printed in India at Chaman Offset, Delhi 110 002

For Tulika

Contents

Preface

The concept for this book was provided by the late Professor Satyaprakash Mishr. With the completion of this work, it is natural to remember Prof. Mishr. Had he been here today, this work could have benefited from his sharp criticism. It took me a long time to articulate the research question behind this book. First, I chose those elements in Hindi criticism which addressed the question of canonization in order to begin the study of the process of canon formation in Hindi. The main difficulties at this point were: first, accessing the primary sources for canon criticism in the west; and second, once available, these debates did not prove very useful for understanding the Hindi context. For example, debates on canon formation in the west have centred on the question of schools and curricula. This was outside the scope of my research topic and I found myself unable to enter these areas of research. Further, African–American studies and women's studies have propelled canon criticism in the west. In the context of the Hindi region, these debates have only just been initiated by feminism and Dalit thought. More discussion needs to happen around the questions raised by these counter-theses to the canon.

The 'process of canon formation' became a guiding term for my search for the canon in the interrelations between different generations of criticism and critics in Hindi. The context here is that in the search for canon formation as a linear history, the thought entered my mind that one could analyse the changes in the bases of canon formation by studying the development of criticism and critical vocabularies. For example, the work of Tulsidas is common to all three critics: George Grierson, Ramchandr Shukl and Ramvilas Sharma. This could be one way of observing the process of Hindi canon formation, but it had the attendant danger that it could obscure the moment of transformation of one canonical standard into another. Therefore I choose to study the structure of critical thought in some exemplary Hindi critics.

Here it feels necessary to acknowledge that I have used the structure of the history of criticism only as a heuristic. Thus many significant critics are not discussed or only cursorily in the pages below, in comparison with those critics whose formulations directly address the question of canonicity. Also, it should be remembered that Hindi criticism is poetry-centric. I have underlined in this book the process of canon formation only in the realm of poetry. These criteria of criticism are being clarified here because this one book is not sufficient to investigate into the vast constituents of Hindi criticism and neither is my critical intelligence. To borrow Tulsi's words, 'my heart and mind are penniless, but my wishes rule me'.

Two other works of criticism have immensely helped me in conceptualizing this book: Pranay Krishn's *Uttar aupniveshikta ke srot aur Hindi sahitya* and Ashutosh Kumar's *Samkalin kavita aur Marxvad*. I am grateful to my DPhil supervisor Surya Narain, Prof. Nityanand Tiwari, Awadhesh Kumar Tripathi, Durga Singh, Kamlakant and Tulika Asthana for their meaningful criticism and advice on this work. Also, I am thankful to the Department of Hindi, University of Allahabad, where my years remain in memory alone, and will always remain there.

Allahabad, 2015   MRITYUNJAY TRIPATHI

Translator's Acknowledgements

I am thankful to Indu Chandrasekhar at Tulika Books for believing in this project and accepting this translation for publication. In translating this work, I have benefited from the unsinkable patience of the author, who is also my friend and colleague, in answering my innumerable queries not just in Hindi, but also Braj and Avadhi. This translation draws on debates, discussions, disagreements I have had with my 'co-investigators', Awadhesh and Mrityunjay, as part of our research project, 'Poetry in the Indo–Islamic Millennium: From Manuscript to Teaching Tools', at the School of Letters, Ambedkar University Delhi. Not being a student of Hindi criticism, I have learned from conversations with and reading the work of Dr Milind Wakankar (especially his book *Subalternity and Religion*) and Prof. Pranay Krishn (especially his study in Hindi, *Uttar aupniveshikta ke srot aur Hindi sahitya*). I remain indebted to my teacher Professor Aamir R. Mufti for inspiring me to think and work beyond English.

The translation also gained from the support of friends and colleagues: Shubhra Nagalia, Sandeep R. Singh, Shelmi Sankhil, Prof. Gopalji Pradhan, Prof. Radha Chakravarty and Madeeha Sadaf.

Dr Awadhesh Kumar Tripathi commented on parts of this translation. All the faults of translation and interpretation remain mine alone.

New Delhi, 2018   SHAD NAVED

Note on Transliteration

The popular convention of transliterating Hindi words into Roman is the adding of a final 'a' at the end of syllables and whole words. This has meant the translation of names such as Gupt, Shukl and Krishn as Gupta, Shukla and Krishna, respectively. This amounts to a distortion of the way these names are pronounced by their bearers and other speakers of the language. I have attempted in this translation to transliterate all Hindi words (including proper names) as they are pronounced in modern standard Hindi. The exceptions to this are the consonant clusters '-tya' and '-rya', which, if written as '-ty' or '-ry', could be mispronounced following the English way ('clarity'). Therefore, I have used *sahitya* and not *sahity*, *saundarya* and not *saundary*, in this translation. Long vowels are marked as double vowels ('aa') only when it is necessary to distinguish against short vowels.

SHAD NAVED

INTRODUCTION

What Is the Canon?

CANON: ORIGIN, MEANING AND HISTORY

In 1999, Namvar Singh gave a talk at the Department of Hindi, University of Allahabad, as part of a lecture series on Nirala, in which he reflected on his famous work in Hindi criticism, *Kavita ke naye pratiman*. During his talk, he discussed the process of determining standards through criticism. In this context, Singh also remarked on the question of the canon and canon formation that gestured towards the status of canon criticism along with its prototypes and problems in Hindi criticism. He reflected on the role of the canon in poetry, history-writing, literary criticism, educational institutions and curricula. He said:

> There is the word 'canon' in English. Through the canon we want to establish 'the hierarchy of values'. The Mishr Brothers constituted a canon in their *Hindi navratn*. How does this process of canonization in literature take place? I want to assert that Hindi criticism is not a part of the history of Hindi literature; rather, the history of Hindi literature is a part of Hindi criticism. Universities and educational organizations are continuously in the process of forming this 'canon'. The history of Hindi literature constitutes a 'canon'. From Tulsi to Nirala and Muktibodh, a 'canon' has taken shape. The paradox of the 'canon' is that it belongs at the same time to the past and is absolutely contemporary. If this were not so, the 'canon' won't remain a 'canon'. Therefore, in discussing the new critical standards for poetry I want to say that the process of 'canon formation' should also be addressed.[1]

The core idea of this book derives from Namvar Singh's statement quoted above.

The word 'canon', derived from western theology, has undergone a continuous process of change in its meaning. In the European world, church-related rules and laws, or ideals and judgements, were based on a few books. Collections of such rules and laws came to be known as the canon. In English–Hindi bilingual dictionaries, we get the following meanings of this word:

1. Secular law, rule or compendium.
2. The basis of a judgement, evaluation or yardstick.
3. Books and the Bible formally approved by the church.
4. Calendar of the feasts of Roman Catholic saints.
5. The validated list of works by an author.
6. A member of a religious group tied to rules and oaths.
7. A musical composition or part of a composition.
8. A measurement of print.
9. A group of priests assigned to a church.
10. Laws related to the church; a rule book for rituals established by committees of the church.[2]

The American critic John Guillory notes that the concept derives from the Greek: '"Canon" descends from an ancient Greek word, *kanon*, meaning a "reed" or "rod" used as an instrument of measurement. In later times *kanon* developed the secondary sense of "rule" or "law"'.[3] In theology, canonization is that process of the Roman Catholic Church through which a person is given the status of a saint. Over the centuries, this process of installation of saints was carried over into the realm of theological exegesis. The decision about which writings of which religious preceptors could become a part of the church's practice became the process of canonization in the Roman Catholic Church. In our context in India, the theological prehistory of canon-making builds up to a *modern* conception of literature in which religion may not have played a recognizably theological role, but the religious connotations of the canon were kept alive in an apparently non-European context through the propagation of the 'vernaculars' in colonial India by Christian missionaries and the enthusiastic adoption of canon-thinking by early nationalists who used religion as a category of social differentiation.

The Hindi poet Neelabh sets up the meanings of the canon in the following way:

> Both the words ['canon' and 'canonization'] . . . come from the core vocabulary of the Christian Catholic sect and they are related to religious law. This law is the 'ecclesiastical law', i.e. it relates to the internal working of the Christian church, that entire process which organizes all extra-worldly matters. A

complete hierarchical system operates this process beginning with priests at the bottom, then bishops, archbishops, cardinals and finally the pope on top. Whatever remains is the realm of the secular or the temporal and it constitutes the everyday realm of the followers of Christianity, i.e. the laity. 'Canon' or a list of books meant to be read is made primarily and solely for that class of priests who are in charge of the internal affairs of the church. The ordinary people can choose to believe in it or not. Similarly, the process of canonization of saints is an extremely complex and codified process in which ordinary people do not participate in any obvious way. Against the example of India, where considering someone a saint or not is based primarily on popular opinion, in the Christian church this special authority is vested solely with the priestly class. Later even ordinary people accept the decisions of the priests. Mere faith or belief in someone's sanctity is not enough to declare that person a saint.[4]

Neelabh turns to the literary meaning of the word:

'Canon', the definitional term of the Catholic sect, has entered literary criticism. In its basic sense, the word 'canon' means a *fatwa*, especially a list of books on canon law which are considered sacred and essential reading, and also a list of saints of the church. 'Canonization' means including someone formally and on authority into the list of saints. But between 'sacred and essential readings' and list of 'saints' there is no specification of a category common to both. It is implied through these select lists that those books or persons not found in them are not considered 'essential reading' or 'saintly'. But the church does not make any adverse comments against them either. Moreover, there seems to be no comment on the degrees of excellence implied in these lists of books and saints, that one book on the list is superior to another or that a saint is greater than another.[5]

In the words of the Hindi writer too, the importance of the prehistory of the canon in theology is underscored. Neelabh is right in pointing out that in the Christian definition, the non-canonical works of theology were not dismissed or condemned by the Church. In fact it can be argued that works really condemned by the church achieved a greater historical prominence than works in the canon. Similarly, the term 'canon' was used to translate the authority of the scriptures of other religions, such as Buddhism. In the context of Hinduism, it was much later in the nineteenth century that a religious canon was specified, often through the same writers and intellectuals who were interested in defining the languages and literatures of India. These writers or, as Edward Said calls them, 'Orientalists', are studied in Chapter One below.

THE CANON IN LITERARY CRITICISM

One thesis of this book is that in the world of Hindi criticism, the language and vocabulary of criticism developed in direct relation with considerations on the canon. Even when writers do not use this word or its correlatives explicitly, the history of modern Hindi criticism, in large part, is also a history of canon formation. The appearance of the word 'history' in both these domains implies that literary history is the third term that underwrites the development of the Hindi canon and Hindi criticism. As we will see in the chapters below, literary periodization, such as the Bhakti period, determines the scope and objectives of individual critical projects and schemas.

While western critics such as John Guillory have emphasized that the process of canon formation is not simply based on the selection or rejection of individual authors, but is founded rather on social processes of access to language and education, succinctly termed 'cultural capital',[6] in Hindi, the selection of canonical authors is not simply a matter of producing a list of authors. Names of poets – for the Hindi tradition in its pre-colonial past is exclusively made up of writers of poetry – represent polemical positions in relation to such crucial issues of cultural debate as religion, secularism, beauty, simplicity, popularity and excellence. In this procedure of cultural canonization, many times the same literary work was canonized through two opposing arguments. In Hindi, Kabir, Tulsi and similar poets are canonical poets, but the bases of evaluating them are in each case different.

Since objective criteria in support of the canon were hard to come by, critics who were zealous supporters eventually took refuge in belief. But they were not able to give a materialist or rationalist explanation, on the level of first principles, for their belief. This begged the question: how did these critics arrive at the notion of greatness in a literary work? Incontestable criteria for greatness are apocryphal. Another feature of pro-canon critics is their transcultural and omni-temporal judgements. In this way they created a transcendental world of aesthetics. Some of these critics are discussed in Chapter Four below. This is a world that does not brook any disagreement or contestation. Liberal critics have always argued against this tendency of pro-canon criticism. They emphasize that any critical evaluation is located in a group, time and location. Therefore, this transcendentalizing claim to objectivity and globality is hardly defensible.

We are now in a position where we cannot wholly negate either aesthetic categories or the social positionality of the canon-givers. To question the concept of judgement itself in the process of canon formation is a false start. Therefore, the choice of a literary work for preservation is a procedure of judgement that operates from complex psychological and sociological reasons. Value judgement is a component of the process of canon formation, but is not sufficient for its execution. Almost all the critics discussed in this book agree implicitly or explicitly with this view. The value judgement of a person about the greatness of a work of art has no significance because only institutions make possible the reproduction of a work and its reintroduction to later generations.

In comparison with western discussions of the canon, Hindi criticism has remained somewhat unselfconscious in using the principle of canon formation. In the backdrop of colonialism, we cannot help but notice the pressures of comparison with the English tradition among early writers of Hindi criticism. Also, due to the acrimonious Hindi–Urdu controversy, the pressure of establishing and stabilizing the Hindi canon through critical and literary–historical means is visible everywhere in the Hindi canon debates. Guillory is right that the true face of canon formation is not the roster of writers chosen or excluded, but is based on other social processes. Some of these processes for the Hindi context are the establishment of a linguistic tradition, describing and securing a historical past not just for the language but for society at large, and engaging with the emerging forms of the nation and nationalism. Marxist criticism, which had become the dominant trend in Hindi criticism by the mid-twentieth century, raises these questions to the level of social emancipation and social transformation.

The logic of selection in canon formation in Hindi displays the dialectic of social and aesthetic criteria. The beginnings of Hindi criticism display an anxiety about the difficulty in pinning down any one logic of selection. The early selections were based on the literary anthology format. Although the anthology tradition is not popular in Hindi, unlike in the west, some literary compendiums were published under this category. In these compendiums, the canon is formulated by the editor according to his own understanding, which is the sole determinant for the selection of writers. A similar logic of selection can be found in the historical treatises of writers before the work of Ramchandr Shukl, which he calls 'anecdotal', and in Shukl's own literary history of Hindi. Neelabh cites examples from both Hindi and English of this process:

> In these selections, two examples of fixing criteria are worth mentioning. The first comes from English literature. For a long time, John Donne, the significant seventeenth-century poet, was either not included in the early editions of two important anthologies of English poetry – Palgrave's *The Golden Treasury* and *The Oxford Book of English Verse* – or included only as a minor poet. This was

despite the fact that his contemporaries such as Ben Jonson were his admirers. It was only in the nineteenth century, due to the efforts of Samuel Taylor Coleridge and Robert Browning, that Donne was rehabilitated into English poetry. The second example is of the Hindi collection *Kavita aur kavita* [Poems and Poems], edited by Indranath Madaan and published in 1967, which did not include Bhartendu Harishchandr, Maithilisharan Gupt and Ayodhya Singh Upadhyay. Madaan defends his selection principle thus: 'The purpose of preparing this selection is to present those poems which, from the viewpoint of composition, are tightly woven or which bear very few cracks. In selecting these poems, I have come to realize that from *Chhayavad* or before we get famous poets; only famous poems after it. Bhartendu Harishchandr, Maithilisharan Gupt, Ayodhya Singh Upadhyay and other famous poets were left out because, even on searching, their poems could not be found.'[7]

The introduction to the Hindi selection reveals Madaan's conception of the haloed list of poets, and the process by which a canon comes into being. One anxiety here seems to be about the definition of authorship (i.e. great authorship). How is the work of the individual to be spoken of in terms of literary critical standards? Will the present crop of poets be as recognizably individual as the great names from the past?

Literary historians in the west have established that schools in the ancient period began the process of canon-making in order to disseminate knowledge about writing and reading. In order to achieve this goal, research scholars and teachers were busy searching for appropriate texts and preserving them. The foundation of Fort William College in Calcutta in the early years of modern Hindi literature can be understood accordingly. In the colonial context, the historical situation was that the old educational procedures were on the way out or were dominated by a narrow, elite group. The colonial rulers decided to start their own educational institutions to train their officers. Undoubtedly the aim was to strengthen their own rule. As happened later with colonial modernity in South Asia, the methodology of the school continued alongside the feudalist rituals of education. The present debates on the Hindi canon still struggle with the question of feudalism and the medieval past.

It is essential to determine the writer's or the literary work's reach into the various classes of society. Neelabh touches on this issue in relation to Hindi literary history and criticism: 'the final reason is – consent. The most fundamental basis of consent is the curriculum. On becoming part of the curriculum and finding other elements in its favour, Shukl's literary history has today truly become the canon of canons.'[8] Namvar Singh addresses the issue thus: 'universities and education institutions are continuously in the process of producing this canon'.[9] Neelabh again turns to Shukl's literary history in discussing this process. Shukl writes in his celebrated work on the importance of literary history in Hindi: 'In the recent past as Hindi higher education is being established in universities, both students and teachers have experienced the need for a chronological history of its literature.'[10] In relation to this canon-making demand, Neelabh raises the provocative question: why is Shukl's literary history placed on a higher pedestal than any writer's work, when anywhere in the world the status of the literary historian is lesser than the writer's? He elaborates on this question:

> No author in any language of the world has been bestowed with the honour that he is more important than all the writers in that language and its literature. You can ask the greatest scholar of English literature who can marshal a list of the greatest writers, even of the greatest critics, but he would give only academic importance to historians of the English language and its literature. In their field, the principles of literary theory and theorists are considered important, but not literary historians so much.[11]

This problem belongs to Hindi uniquely. Neelabh's formulation of this problem incites us to enquire after the conditions of Hindi canon formation, and draws our attention towards the colonialist pressures on Hindi criticism and the efforts to counteract these under historical conditions. Both these questions will be posed and discussed in the following chapters.

The first chapter of this book engages with the making of 'modern' Hindi literature at its centre. It is a historical fact that the first testimonies of modernity in Hindi came from the west in the form of Orientalist writing. Scholars such as Garcin de Tassy, John Gilchrist and George Grierson are the ones who established the name of the language we now know as Hindi through their writings and organizational endeavours. A mixed language that was in existence from pre-modernity and which was known by several different names was now divided into two apparently distinct languages. This was also the moment of emergence of the process of canon formation in Hindi criticism. Hindi was eager to be cast into a new fashion in contrast with its prior literary and linguistic forms. Bhartendu Harishchandr announced in 1873 that Hindi was now cast in a new mould. The language problem was markedly different prior to this announcement. Only in this period of history did the problem take on the form that we know of today as the Hindi–Urdu debates. To borrow the words of the Urdu poet Jigar Moradabadi: 'that which was solved, I complicate that conundrum again'. The first chapter begins with this period of complications.

The early literary-historical writings of Garcin de Tassy (*Histoire de la littérature hindoui et hindoustani*, 1839) and George Grierson (*The Modern Vernacular Literature of Modern Hindustan*, 1889), which announced a separate language called Hindi, also established its nascent canon. Further, these literary histories, written in opposition to earlier pre-colonial forms such as *varta* (in Hindi) and *tazkira* (in Urdu), established the early terms of literary criticism in Hindi. The point of view of these writers was undeniably western and colonial, as they were in search of the intellect and creativity of the 'natives', and in the process they aimed to propose a canon for their literatures. On the one hand, they produced criticism of the old literatures; on the other, they were writing textbooks to teach these languages to officers of the empire. As an example of their comparative thinking, on the one hand they connected Tulsidas with the notion of religious 'catholicity', and on the other, they were sifting poems by Surdas, Mir Taqi and Sauda that, according to their western standards, were obscene. By analysing these phenomena in criticism, Chapter One argues that there is a continuum between the standards proposed by early western critics and the succeeding generation of Indian critics writing on canon formation. Although the Indian critics were pioneers of nationalist thought and stood firm on the ground of anti-colonialism, the influence of the early western critics of Indian literatures is clearly visible in the latter's writings.

The second chapter tries to understand the standards of canon formation in the period of consolidation of Hindi criticism in the early twentieth century. Hindi criticism has been deeply responsive to social transformations. With the consolidation of the nationalist movement, its effects were visible in Hindi criticism too. In this period the Hindi writer aspired not for the language of 'the tattered, chintz bodice of Braj full of holes' but a 'national language'.[12] However, the phenomenon of consolidation of the national language took place gradually, and the connection with Braj Bhasha and other related languages was severed equally slowly. The critics who stand at the cusp of this transformation are the Mishr Brothers. In Hindi criticism, the Mishr Brothers were the first to propose a canon. They chose the nine jewels of Hindi poetry, ranging from old Braj–Avadhi to modern-day Bhartendu Harishchandr. Their area of engagement was split into two. While they were affiliated with the project of nation-building of their time, they were also firmly ensconced in the old poetic tradition of Braj–Avadhi. Mirza Ghalib would have expressed their position thus: 'the Ka'bah is behind me, the church, before me'. It was Ramchandr Shukl who took on the responsibility of nation formation in criticism by systematizing the principles of criticism derived from the previous generation of critics and literary historians. His canon was established using the driving forces of anti-colonialism and the intellectual demands of nation formation. In this canon, Tulsidas, Surdas and Malik Muhammad Jayasi are on top, in descending order. Tulsi's exertions in the cause of 'social bliss', Sur's diverting poetry for the sake of 'social bliss', and Jayasi's harmonization of Hindu and Muslim interests within his earthy poetry are the reasons given for their canonical eminence. For Shukl, only that poetry is beneficial for the people which inspires them towards effort [*lokmangal ka prayatn paksh*]. The poetry that diverts and entertains their hearts is in the second place. As a representative of contemporary intellectual thought, Shukl is determined on the external front (i.e. he is anti-colonial), but no clear position emerges in his criticism on the internal front (i.e. against feudalism in Indian society). These contrasting positions are evident in his canon-thinking as well. A vacillation about the definition of the nation is therefore noticeable throughout Shukl's critical writings on the canon. Nanddulare Vajpeyi, who was writing at the time of the maturation of Hindi literature and poetry (in the form of the romanticist *Chhayavad* trend), questions the usefulness of some of Shukl's principles. Vajpeyi offers oppositional definitions of some of Shukl's favourite terminology such as 'the principle of *ras*', 'epic quality', 'social bliss', 'anti-mysticism', on which he bases his canon criticism. Nevertheless, Vajpeyi himself is not consistent in his principles of canon criticism. He canonizes Jaishankar Prasad's novel *Kankal* [Skeleton] on the principle of its realism [*yatharthvad*], but is unable to recognize that same quality in the work of Premchand whom he condemns as a 'propagandist'. Finally, the criticism of Hazari Prasad Dwivedi belongs to that period of post-Shukl thought when Indian nationalism had crossed a milestone of anti-colonialism, and was confronted by new debates on social and national identity. The anti-colonial struggle is unable to fully accommodate either the minority question or the question of caste. Within this background, Dwivedi makes a genuine contribution to the 'discovery of India' by reinterpreting the category of culture itself. These two projects inform his critical canon, at whose centre is the medieval poet Kabir.

Hindi criticism, until this period, had developed around discussions on Bhakti or medieval devotionalism. The progressive critics who focused on their contemporary modern literature, and are discussed in Chapter Three, continued this emphasis on Bhakti. Through fierce debates with each other, Marxist Hindi critics expanded the field of Hindi criticism. By positing anti-imperialism and anti-feudalism as the basis of his critical canon, Ramvilas Sharma offers not just a revaluation of the literature of his times but of the entire literary tradition. His main goal is to bring together different traditions of the past that would make India into a modern nation. He does this by giving critical readings of the question of 'Hindi nationality' and the modern moment of the Hindi reawakening in the nineteenth century. This becomes the basis of his canon for Hindi, which includes Premchand, Nirala, Mahavir Prasad Dwivedi, Bhartendu and, reaching back in time, Tulsidas. Gajanan Madhav Muktibodh debates with Ramvilas Sharma and other critics of the time to make a case for the deployment of class as a category of analysis in criticism. For him, the evaluation of tradition involves a project of 'civilizational critique' which emerges from his dream of a happy, beautiful and exploitation-free man. Muktibodh witnesses the class bases and aspirations in the poetry of his contemporaries forming under the pressure of Cold War politics, and dispels the fog pervading new poetry [*nayi kavita*] by giving a sociological explanation for the psychological perception of artistic beauty in new poetry. Namvar Singh includes new poetry in his canon by developing a critique of *Chhayavad* and post-*Chhayavad* poetry, and announces Muktibodh himself as its exemplary poet. The chapter ponders over the differences between Namvar Singh's principle behind Muktibodh's canonization and Muktibodh's own understanding of that principle, in order to illustrate not just the complexities in canon formation but the changeability of its criteria.

In Chapter Four, we witness an alternative definition of modernity from critics who were writing in opposition to the Marxist position, on the question of new poetry in particular. The first writer, Vijaydev Narayan Sahi, rejects the 'western' notions of modernity, history and progress, and builds a critique based on indigenous modernity, the concept of the 'insignificant man', depth of intellectual argument in poetry and tragedy. The category of individuality is central to Sahi's thought; he declares that the present must not be sacrificed at the altar of futurity in the name of attaining idealistic goals. Following his sense of history, Sahi considers the medieval poet Jayasi, whom he places at the centre of his canon, to be the exemplar of his theories. Again, in disagreement with the human-centric thought of Europe, Nirmal Verma considers the category of the nation-state to be a cultural one. In opposition to the preceding generation of Marxist critics, Verma argues for the search of Indianness that was disrupted as a cultural tendency by colonialism. In his discussion of Premchand's *Godan*, Verma notes the disruptiveness of colonialism but does not engage with the social contradictions of pre-colonial society. He rejects the genre of the novel as unsuitable for Indian realities and offers instead the Indian epic tradition. The question of genre becomes central in this debate on the Hindi canon.

Finally, Chapter Five takes note of the uprising against the Hindi canon in the form of feminist criticism and Dalit thought in recent decades. The main streams of canon formation in Hindi, i.e. nationalist, Marxist–progressive and modernist, are revealed in all their weaknesses and exclusivity by these critical trends. The latter trends displace the categories of nation, class and individuality from the horizon of criticism, and, using examples from women's writing and Dalit thought and literature, they propose new standards of literary evaluation and new canons based on them. On the one hand, from the poetry of Hira Dom to the poetry of 'Bangmahila' (Rajendrbala Ghosh) there have been several attempts to reimagine not just the canon but also 'literature' as part of feminist and Dalit critiques; on the other, new readings are being proposed for canonical writers ranging from Premchand to Kabir by intellectuals affiliated with these streams of criticism.

THE USE OF 'CANON' IN HINDI

Unlike in the west, there is no substantial tradition in Hindi of discussions on the canon *per se*; its advent in Hindi is comparatively recent. Although fierce debates have happened in Hindi on standards of criticism, these have not been conscious of their implications for canon formation. Shivdan Singh Chauhan's essay, '*Alochna ke maan*' [The Standards of Criticism], which was delivered as a lecture on 16 December 1957 at a writers' conference at the University of Allahabad, focuses on the responsibility of criticism and its relation to contemporary realities. The key point of this essay is visible in the following quotation:

> The point is to elevate and enrich human consciousness. If he keeps this in mind, the critic can at least help develop a composite viewpoint through his knowledge of literature and as much as possible from experiences from life. The success a critic achieves in this attempt will be proportionate to his special contribution and achievement in the discovery of truth. This is the only remedy for the current anarchy in the field of criticism.[13]

Generally, we can derive some criteria of canon formation from such debates on critical principles, but arguments of criteria and value do not necessarily help in the study of the canon and the processes of its formation.

In Hindi, the following words are used to signify the canon: *maan* (standard), *mulya* (worth), *pratiman* (criteria) and *manak* (model). But none of these words bears the conceptual meaning of canon. '*Maan*' and '*mulya*' are closer to the English meaning of 'value'. Their usage leans towards social norms of aesthetic merits and demerits, and political economy. In the world of ideas, these words signify essence. Similarly, '*pratiman*' and

'*manak*' convey the sense of 'standard/s' rather than of canon. The problem
of accommodating and using vocabulary from other languages within
criticism is not unique to Hindi. For example, Aristotle's notion of catharsis
is borrowed from medicine. Literary criticism solves the problem by arguing
that the entry of a word into a new domain produces new possibilities of
meaning. But this is possible really only within the same linguistic context.
The problem of the word 'canon' in Hindi signifies an impossibility. The
historical-intellectual trajectory of the word 'canon' in the west cannot
be replicated in terms like *mulya, maan, pratiman* and *manak*. When this
word moved into the secular world of literary criticism from its theological
origins, it did not completely lose its theological significance because the
latter was a part of its history. The greatest difficulty in translating this word
into Hindi is precisely that history. Therefore, in this entire book the word
'canon' [*kainan*] is retained and left untranslated.

NOTES

[1] Quoted in Neelabh (2005), p. 134.
[2] For standard definitions of canon, see Howatson (1989), p. 114; Murfin and Ray
(2003), p. 46; Cuddon (1981), p. 108.
[3] Guillory (1995), p. 233.
[4] Neelabh (2005), p. 14.
[5] Ibid., p. 135.
[6] Guillory (1993).
[7] Neelabh (2005), p. 144.
[8] Ibid.
[9] Ibid., p. 139.
[10] Shukl (1997), p. 4.
[11] Neelabh (2005), p. 144.
[12] Pant (2008), pp. 23–24.
[13] Chauhan (2002), p. 51.

CHAPTER ONE

The Colonial Canon

THE BRITISH COLONIAL PROJECT: FORT WILLIAM COLLEGE

'The college must stand, or the empire must fall.'
– From the personal correspondence of Marquess Wellesley with his friend
David Scott (12 August 1802)[1]

Fort William College was the second-most important British colonial
institution, after the Asiatic Society founded by William Jones (on 15
January 1774), in the field of education. This institution, it is widely believed,
organized modern education for the first time in India. Established and
planned by Marquess Wellesley, the College kept functioning for almost
fifty years (1800–54) in the field of education. In studying the College we
not only come across the perspective of the British towards modern Indian
education, but also encounter the origins of modern prose and language-
related policies which later on played a part in canon construction.

The form of modernity that the British brought with them was not
founded on industrial transformation, nor on the class contradictions that
could have emerged from such industrial transformation in India; rather, it
was produced by the compulsions to make India fit for colonial exploitation.
The modernity established here took different forms. While debating with
Edward Said about Marx's statement that British rule in India was 'an
unconscious tool of history', Aijaz Ahmad places the statement in its fullest
panorama and writes, 'after the experience of the history that Britain in
fact made, *who* could possibly *want* an "unconscious tool" of that sort?'[2]
He goes on to say, 'Now, it is obviously true that colonialism did not bring
us a revolution. What it brought us was, precisely, a non-revolutionary

and retrograde resolution to a crisis of our own society which had come to express itself, by the eighteenth century, in a real stagnation of technologies and productivities'.[3]

In his study *Acharya Ramchandr Shukl aur Hindi alochna* [The Great Teacher Ramchandr Shukl and Hindi Criticism], the Hindi critic Ramvilas Sharma rehearses Ahmad's conception in these words: 'Any evaluation of Indian literature if based on the view that the British came and produced a social revolution for the first time in an India of untransformed village societies, there would be no other choice but to reject it.'[4] Sharma is here not only establishing his opposition to colonialism, but attempting to place the relations between tradition and modernity on a new footing.

At the turn of the nineteenth century, the British felt the need for new administrative tools to strengthen their rule. When the governance of Bengal came into their hands, their linguistic troubles increased. Persian, which till then had continued as the official language, proved to be insufficient for British rule and its expansion. In this situation, due to the political exigency of learning the people's language, there arose the need for an institution to train British officials. This became the cornerstone of the education-related activities of British rule in India. On 10 July 1800, Wellesley wrote in his Notes about the establishment of the College, clearly underlining its fundamental purpose:

> To dispense justice to millions of people of various languages, manners, usages and religions; to administer a vast and complicated system of revenue throughout districts equal in extent to some of the most considerable kingdoms in Europe; to maintain civil order in one of the most populous and litigious regions of the world; these are now the duties of the larger proportion of the civil servants of the Company. . . . The Company's investment [can never] be conducted with the greatest possible advantage and honour to themselves, or with adequate justice to their subjects, unless their commercial agents shall possess many of the qualifications of statesmen. . . . The manufacturers, and other industrious classes, [their] productive labour is the source of the investment. . . . They [the Company servants] shall be conversant in the native languages, and in the customs and manners of the people, as well as in the laws by which the country is governed. . . . The Civil servants of the English East India Company, therefore, can no longer be considered as the agents of a commercial concern. They are, in fact, the ministers and officers of a powerful sovereign. . . . Their studies, the discipline of their education, their habits of life, their manners and morals should, therefore, be so ordered and regulated as to establish a just conformity between their personal

consideration, and the dignity and importance of their public stations, and to maintain a sufficient correspondence between their qualifications and their duties. . . . To this foundation should be added an intimate acquaintance with the history, languages, customs and manners of the people of India, with the Mahommedan and Hindoo codes of law and religion, and with the political and commercial interests and relations of Great Britain in Asia. . . . Finally, their early habits should be so formed, as to establish in their minds such solid foundations of industry, prudence, integrity, and religion, as should effectually guard them against those temptations and corruptions with which the nature of this climate, and the peculiar depravity of the people of India, will surround and assail them in every station, especially upon their first arrival in India. The early discipline of the service should be calculated to counteract the defects of the climate and the vices of the people, and to form a natural barrier against habitual indolence, dissipation, and licentious indulgence.[5]

First, we get to know from this quotation the British government's view of India and its people. This is the same point of view according to which the west is the publicist for the virtues of justice, civilization and truth, and India the land of indolent, licentious, depraved, corrupt and backward people. Without apology Wellesley wants to fashion the College and education in the interests of the empire. The desiderata of 'industry, prudence, integrity, and religion' required for ruling over a country such as India, of strange corruption and vices, could be provided by the College. Through this ideological basis of its establishment, the College was to develop not just the 'modern' form of our language, but also critical 'prose'. This form of 'modernity' could not have been at that time otherwise, as we can see now in hindsight. That is why the voices of nationalist intellectuals–critics, while discussing these issues, fill up with ironic sarcasm, and time and again they register their disagreements on the role of Fort William College in the formation of Hindi modernity. For example, they register their opposition to the view that the College was the pioneer of 'new prose texts' and Khari Boli prose. The latter position is obviously unpalatable for a viewpoint that wants to establish the currency of 'our' language.

Lakshmisagar Varshney writes in this regard: 'Before the production of Khari Boli Hindi texts under the supervision of the College, prose texts in Khari Boli were already in existence in Hindi.'[6] Varshney's statement is not the first of its kind. Ramchandr Shukl too prominently presented this view in his monumental *Hindi sahitya ka itihas* [History of Hindi Literature]: 'It is not correct to say that it was only inspired by the British that Hindi Khari Boli prose came into existence.'[7] In the backdrop of this unease, another of

Shukl's remarks, which he makes sarcastically in the context of early 'makers of prose', is worth quoting here: 'Munshi*ji* [Sadasukh Lal] composed this prose neither inspired by some British officer nor on a given template.'[8] We can make out clearly the importance Shukl attaches to works inspired by British officials. But the problematic lies elsewhere. Despite this conclusion about the birth of modern Hindi prose, when the discussion turns to the question of Hindi–Urdu, two versions of the same linguistic tradition, Shukl does not tire of praising the Sanskritized Hindi of the Christian missionaries. Similarly, at some places Varshney calls the College the symbol of modernity, while at others he praises Wellesley, both of which do not accord with the conclusions emerging from his own well-researched book. He writes, for example, 'The symbol of British rule and modernity in India, Fort William College holds an important place in Indian history.'[9] And in praise of Wellesley he writes, 'If anyone gains fame in world history for the gift of knowledge in any form, then Wellesley partakes of it completely. The seed that he sowed to realize his deeply heartfelt plan, there was a huge banyan hidden within it.'[10] This praise heaped on Wellesley, British rule and Christian missionaries is part of an extraordinary problem that is often expressed in different ways in the canons of criticism.

At the time of its establishment, John Gilchrist was the head of the Department of Hindustani at Fort William College. Before the formal inauguration of the College, he was training Britishers at the Oriental Seminary in Bengal. Thus, alongside teaching Persian, he took on the task of fulfilling the colonial demand for teaching the Indian languages to officers of the empire. The concern was the same: making the empire durable and cohesive through the medium of education. In the context of Urdu, Aijaz Ahmad highlights the intentions of Gilchrist and the College:

> [M]any – though by no means all – of those prose narratives of the opening decades of the nineteenth century were written and published for the simple reason that a certain Scotsman, John Gilchrist, had argued within his own circles that employees of the East India Company could not hope to administer their Indian possessions on the basis of Farsi alone, and certainly not English, so that Fort William College was established in 1800 for the education of the British in Indian languages. For some time Farsi remained the most popular of all the languages taught at the College, but Gilchrist fancied himself as a scholar and exponent of the indigenous vernaculars, Urdu among them. He hired some of the most erudite men of his time and got them to write whatever they wanted, so long as they wrote in accessible prose.[11]

Towards fulfilling the demands of colonial rule, Gilchrist had texts and textbooks produced in 'Hindustani'. Through these, Gilchrist also realized his conception of language which was a part of his self-styled colonial language policy. This is the same Gilchrist who, in his book *Oriental Linguist* (1802), asserts his linguistic ideas thus:

> Hindoostan is a compound word, equivalent to *Hindoo*-land or *Negro*-land. . . . It is inhabited chiefly by Hindoos and Moosulmans; whom we may safely comprise, as well as their language, under the general, conciliating, comprehensive term of Hindoostanee, and which 1 have adopted for the above and following reasons. . . . That the natives and others call it also *Hindee*, Indian, from Hind, the ancient appellation of *India*, cannot be denied; but as this is apt to be confounded with *Hinduwee, Hindooee, Hindvee*, the derivative from *Hindoo*, I adhere to my original opinion, that we should invariably discard all other denominations of the popular speech of this country, including the unmeaning word *Moors*, and substitute for them *Hindoostanee*, whether the people here constantly do so or not: as they can hardly discriminate sufficiently, to observe the use and propriety of such restrictions, even when pointed out to them. *Hinduwee*, I have treated as the exclusive property of the Hindoos alone; and have therefore constantly applied it to the old language of India, which prevailed before the Moosulman invasion.[12]

The vocabulary of such bullish authority used by Gilchrist, and in which 'Hindoostan' always stood at the receiving end, has been answered by the Urdu critic Shamsur Rahman Faruqi in these words:

> Notice how cheerfully and confidently Gilchrist Bahadur assumes the right to decide for the natives, since they themselves have no discrimination, and don't know what's good for them. If the Hindustanis call their language Hindi then so be it, but British sagacity says that Hindi connotes 'Hindu' and that is why this name is not apposite. The state of Gilchrist's knowledge is such that it not only declares 'Hindavi' to be the special property of the Hindus, but he considers it to be the language that was prevalent before the invasion of Hindustan by the Muslims. (He does not specify before which invasion by the Muslims.) Also he perpetrates a canard on Persian, and Persian speakers, by saying that in Persian 'Hindu' means 'Negro'. . . . He does not seem to realize that 'Hindavi' is not a separate language, but is another name for 'Hindi/ Hindustani'. And neither is this language related to the Muslim conquerors.

But the British had to bring about their rule in this country. They adhered to its realities, but only to the extent that their political goals and beliefs were not countered. Efforts to proclaim 'Hindi' as Hindustani and placing Hindi/ Hindavi in the Hindu camp were going on since before Gilchrist's time. The only difference is that Gilchrist's notions were made popular thanks to Fort William College.[13]

Gilchrist himself became the head of Fort William College, and this prepared an ideological ground for the textbooks he got prepared in the people's language, which later came to be viewed as the first books in modern prose by the speakers of those languages (Hindi, Urdu and Bengali being the most prominent). In this regard, mention must be made of Lallu Lal's *Prem sagar* [Ocean of Love] (a Hindi rendering of some narratives from the *Bhagvat puran*), because its language was made 'according to the wishes of the Sahib'. This is also mentioned in Lallu Lal's autobiography: 'Once Sahib said that if there be a nice tale in Braj Bhasha, say it in the language of Rekhta.'[14] This is the same language that, according to Faruqi, 'was equally popular in the north as "Rekhta" and "Hindi" as the name of our language'.[15] As witness to this usage, we can consider the following couplet from a *ghazal* by Qa'im Chandpuri (1724–1795):

> I, Qa'im, said ghazals in the mixed style, otherwise
> A feeble thing it was in the language of the Deccan.[16]

Even if we ignore the other debates around this couplet, it goes to show that 'Rekhta' was the literary language of north India. Gilchrist instructed Lallu Lal to write in *this* language, as recorded by the latter.

The language of the texts written before *Prem sagar*, which are under discussion here, is characterized decisively as 'Urdu' by Ramchandr Shukl. Thus, according to his argument, the British gave eminence to Urdu, but at the same time he is marginally satisfied with the language used in *Prem sagar* as it does not draw on 'foreign' words. This text was also written as part of the same process as the four other early Hindi books including *Madhav vilas*, whose language Shukl disapproves of. If seen through Shukl's reasoning, the British were in favour of Hindi over Urdu at the time of the writing of *Prem sagar*. Shukl praises this effort of the British but criticizes their counter-effort even as both these promotions of two strains of the *same* language attest to the deliberate language strategy adopted by the British.[17]

In this light, it was through the Fort William College that Gilchrist articulated the totality of colonial thought, on which basis, further on, Garcin de Tassy, George Grierson and other western literary critics built a Hindi canon. An example for this canonization can be drawn from the list of subjects to be taught at the College. The list included:

> Arabic, Persian, Sanskrit, Hindustani, Bengali, *Telang* [Telugu], *Maharashtri* [Marathi], Tamil, Kannada; other subjects such as Mohammadan law, Indian

religious codes, *nitishastra*, *nyayashastra*, international law, laws of the British raj in India (including political economy and especially the commercial establishments of the English East Indian Company and their rights), geography, mathematics, modern European languages, Greek, Latin and medieval English literature (the classics), ancient and modern general history, the history of north and south India and their archeology, natural science, botany, chemistry and astrology.[18]

'The rights of the East India Company' appears in this list among other subjects. At a college where colonial officers were trained in the tasks of exploitation and conquest, nothing was possible other than the division of the Indian people in order to make them fight against each other.

Critical Canons of Early Western Critics: Garcin de Tassy, George Grierson, Frank Keay

Writing about the history of Indian literary criticism, Sadanand Shahi asserts:

> The study and evaluation of literatures in the Indian languages in the modern style was developed by the European Orientalists. Now that the political intentions of Orientalism have become evident, it is superfluous to say that this whole field of study was conducted not solely for the love and charms of the Orient, but had other, baser motives.[19]

The strong emphasis on 'Oriental' in this quotation requires one crucial clarification. To characterize the critical practice of British or western scholars as 'Orientalist' clearly does not paper over either our own social contradictions or their 'Orientalist' practice. The point here is the tools of analysis for this phenomenon of Orientalism. Rather than viewing the cruelties committed by the colonizers within the frame of 'self' and 'other', the attempt should be to employ the category of 'colonialism' as establishing the rule of capital. This has been one of the limits of Edward Said's 'Orientalism'.[20] Since the nascent canons of Hindi criticism were fashioned by these western scholars, their written texts were accepted as foundational. The intellectual foundation of such canons is produced by colonialism, and not simply by 'Orientalism'.

This section discusses the goals of canonization that took shape in the early historiography of Hindi literature. The main source for this discussion is *Hindui sahitya ka itihas* [The History of Hindui Literature], which is a Hindi translation of Garcin de Tassy's work in French, *Histoire de la littérature hindoui et hindoustani*. De Tassy's book was an anthology of poets from both the Hindi and Urdu streams of north Indian poetry. Lakshmisagar Varshney published the Hindi section of this book from the Hindustani Akademi, Allahabad, in 1953. The publication includes a translation of the Hindavi section of de Tassy's original text, but not the Urdu section. Rather than dwelling on the rule of selection in this translation, it would be more useful here to arrive at the book's basic aims. The second source for the discussion in this section will be George Grierson's *The Modern Vernacular Literature of Hindustan*,[21] translated into Hindi by Kishorilal Gupt as *Hindi sahitya ka pratham itihas* [The First History of Hindi Literature]. The third key text for this discussion is *A History of Hindi Literature* by Frank Keay, translated into Hindi by Sadanand Shahi.

In the preface to his book *Histoire de la littérature hindoui et hindoustani*, written on 15 April 1839 in Paris, the ulterior motive of the first historian of Hindi literature, the French scholar Garcin de Tassy, becomes apparent. Through this book we can gauge the weight of colonialist compulsions acting on contemporary literary historiography and miscellaneous literary critical writing. In it we can also see the cultural reflection of contemporary modes of colonial power. De Tassy begins his literary history with this dedication:

> It is only natural that I pray to gain the honour of dedicating to your majesty a work which deals with a part of the literature of India, of that vast and beautiful country, which is under submission to your sceptre, and which has never been happier than in its dependence on England. It cannot be gainsaid that under a British administration where there is no fear of looting nor the tyranny of indigenous governments, on apprehending the news of the accession of the Princess, the people of the country were forced to recall their dear Queen Razia. In truth they have recovered in Queen Victoria the vigour and rare qualities of Razia and this consideration can only bind them more strongly still to the country to which divine Providence wanted them to be subject.[22]

The final words of this dedication are also worth quoting: 'I am, with the deepest respect, Madam, of your majesty, the humblest and most obedient servant, Garcin de Tassy.'[23] Thus wrote the first historian of Hindi literature.

From de Tassy's dedication we learn of the writer's location from where he is discussing the modern form of 'Hindustani' literature and its literary history. This reading of the subjection of India based on a view from the west divides the west and east into active and passive roles respectively, in line with the Orientalist readings prevalent in historians' circles, and utilizes culturalist weaponry for the sake of colonial domination. Their implication is that Indians cannot look after their beautiful (i.e. rich in natural resources) country themselves. Thus it becomes the responsibility of the west that in order to end this barbarism, they should rule the country. This country which was never as happy, i.e. in the period of the Indian kingdoms, which included Hindus, Muslims and other religious groups, was always laid waste. It is remarkable that since the 1857 war of independence had not yet been fought by the Indians, no strict lines differentiating religious communities can be observed in de Tassy's work, as emerged in subsequent editions of the same book. In this regard, de Tassy's comparing Queen Victoria with Queen Razia in the 1839 edition is noteworthy. It is expressive of the British colonizers' view of Muslim rule. While the author designates British rule as the deliverer of India from the rapine and oppression of all previous governments, at the same time, due to moral and historicist necessity, the British relationship with India's history is made through Queen Razia. De Tassy's view glosses the cultural project that was institutionalized with the establishment of Fort William College in 1800. Similarly, in the next century, in the chapter on 'The Mughal Durbar' in his literary history, George Grierson writes: 'It may be noted that the reign of the emperor Akbar nearly coincided with that of the English queen Elizabeth, and that the reigns of both these monarchs were signalized by an extraordinary outburst of literary vigour.'[24] We notice here that the association of governance with the cultural sphere and proving the former's retardation in the political sphere were two sides of the same coin of British policy, whose clear aim was control over a colonized land.

Towards the end of his dedication, de Tassy aligns the British with the Indian people on the basis of a religious world view. Ascribing divine providence to the enslavement of India should be understood as a part of the logic of the colonialist cultural project. The background to the fissures of Partition prepared in the political–cultural domain by British colonialism in the twentieth century can be seen in relief here. It also follows from de Tassy's formulations that in the nascent canons of Hindi literary history and criticism, traces of a religious world view are clearly visible. After the beginning of the systematic writing of modern Indian criticism, the Bhakti or devotionalist period remained a point of constant reference in the critical canon, albeit with changing bases of evaluation. Religiosity as a point of reference belongs to the modern political use of religion by colonialist thinkers. Rather than alienation between religion and state, this 'modern' point of view puts religion to explicit use. In this matter, if we characterize the push towards religion as one of the bases of canon formation, then we notice a continuum between colonialist thought and nascent modern Indian cultural thought. This view comes into being at the moment when 'religion' is disengaged from the fundamental tone of the poetry of the Bhakti period, and the discussion moves to the latter's social dimensions as a movement.

By comparing the introductions to the later editions of de Tassy's literary history, the religious framework becomes clearer still. Here we can note the appearance of the inchoate forms of that huge language controversy which remains unresolved even today. In 1839, searching for the heredity of contemporary speech in the first volume of his work, de Tassy writes:

> That which developed in the ancient realm of India was known generally as *Bhasha* or *Bhakha*, and specifically as *Hindavi* or *Hindui* [i.e. the language of the Hindus]. At the time of the establishment of the Pathan dynasty in Delhi, due to the reciprocal relations between Hindus and Iranians, the languages of the victor and the vanquished came together in a mixture in the cities conquered by the Muslims. By the time of the famous conqueror Taimur's victory over Delhi, this mixture had become stabilized. The mixed language of Hindus and Muslims was spoken specifically in the army bazaars. . . . With this the language came to be commonly known as 'Urdu', albeit the poets preferred to call it *Rekhta* [i.e. mixed]. . . . To the south of the Narmada [river] . . . the mixed language of the Hindus and Muslims took on the name *Deccani*. . . . Although in terms of their word choice these languages are different, it is right to consider them to be the same language and congruent spoken languages on the basis of their sentence formation rules, and that they have been always addressed by the ambiguous terminology of 'Hindi' or 'Hind' and by the Europeans as 'Hindustani'.[25]

In this passage, de Tassy refers to two sub-divisions: old and new Hindustani. He gives two sub-classifications of modern Hindustani on the assumption that Hindustani is the successor language of Sanskrit: northern and southern; the northern he further sub-divides into Urdu [the language of the Muslims] and Braj [used by the Hindus]. Further, he praises the expressive powers of Hindustani and proclaims it to be enriched with the qualities of Arabic, Persian and Turkish. Even if we ignore the later historical insights on this issue, British administrators would have only seen this account of language as intended to produce a history of language and nothing else. While the colonialist interests are reflected in this intention, the communalist bases are not that deep or clear. Whatever de Tassy added in the introduction to the subsequent editions of his work must be studied in relation to the changing political landscape of the times.

The introduction to the second edition (1870) also begins with the knotty question of the Hindavi–Hindui–Hindustani language controversy. But this time a preface is inserted before the introduction. At the beginning, the preface announces the discovery of some new source material, and then answers the article by Munshi Jamaluddin carried in the *Awadh akhbar* of 24 November 1868, regarding the origins of Hindustani. In the preface, de Tassy also mentions Sayyid Abdullah's edition of the *Sinhasan battisi* in relation to the language controversy. The introduction to the second edition refers to the languages of the bazaar. In contrast to the introduction to the first edition, this introduction clearly reflects the politics of language. The shift in de Tassy's views can be seen in passing in the following quotation:

> As long as Muslim rule continued, the official language of government was Persian. For a long time the British followed this policy but experiencing the difficulties arising from the use of this foreign language in India they gave room to the common languages of the different regions by 1831 for the good of the people. Naturally, Urdu was adopted for the northern and northwestern regions. This clean task was appreciated by all and in the next thirty years this arrangement has been successful and there have been no complaints. But in the last few years the same undulations related to ancient races have arisen in India which have disturbed Europe too. No longer being under Muslim rule a reaction has set in amongst the Hindus. After having failed to wield power, they want to remove at the very least unappetizing things from the time of their enslavement by Muslims and want to obstruct Urdu itself, or to remove the Persian script, while retaining the appropriate forms, which they consider to be the stamp of the Muslims.
>
> Their arguments in defence of their strange reactionary position are indefensible. Without facing the fact that while Hindi, inspired by the narrow feeling of nationalism which they want to revive, at this time was no longer used in writing in the literary sense, which in every village, as in fact like the people of the province, keeps changing, while Urdu has stabilized in its forms through its beautiful poetic corpus, they assert that the language of the land (i.e. of the villages) is Hindi and not Urdu. Hindus take exception to the Persian script and they prefer the Nagari script. But the reality is the obverse of this. In comparison with the Persian script, and Shikasta as well, it is more difficult to read the unappealing scribble of Nagari. The Muslims have withstood this attack courageously and, to my mind, have successfully rebutted their opponents with force. Clearly this is a racial and religious opposition, albeit neither is willing to accept this fact. This is a struggle between polytheism and monotheism, between the Vedas and the Bible [under which the Muslims are subsumed]. I cannot say if the British government would yield ground to the Hindus, or whether they would protect the dialect of the Muslims of whose government they are the successors.[26]

A few pages before this, de Tassy writes:

> Taimur, of the Mughal race, arrived in India, became the ruler of Delhi and
> conclusively laid the foundations of a powerful empire established in 1505 by
> Babur. It was then that Hindi filled itself with the hoard of Persian, which by
> that time had become mixed with Arabic words brought to currency by the
> Arab conquerors and their faith. The army bazaar was set up in cities, which
> acquired the Tartar name 'Urdu', whose closest meaning is 'army' or 'camp'.[27]

A re-reading of these quotations can lead us to the early history of
Hindi literature and, embedded in it, to the nascent canons of criticism.
The 1870 additions to the 1839 introduction put the categories of Hindu
and Muslim to a more intensive political use. De Tassy's polemic on the
language question affirms the pre-existing colonialist conceptions. The
history of our language, caught in the web of names such as Hindavi–Hindi–
Dehlavi–Gujri–Dakani–Rekhta–Urdu–Hindustani, is deeply embroiled
in the political events of colonialism and the cultural renaissance. Calling
the language that de Tassy discusses 'Urdu', and placing its origins in the
military bazaars and encampments, is a view negated by modern research.

Disagreeing with views expressed about Urdu (which are reminiscent
of de Tassy's) in Henry Yule and Arthur Burnell's *Hobson Jobson: Being a
Glossary of Anglo–Indian Colloquial Words and Phrases, and of Kindred Terms;
Etymological, Historical, Geographical and Discursive* (1886), Shamsur
Rahman Faruqi writes:

> First of all, before Babur there was no dearth of Turks in India. Therefore,
> it is not necessary to connect the entry of the word 'Urdu' with the coming
> of Babur. Secondly, Babur never stayed long in Delhi. Thirdly, the language
> known as Hindi/Hindavi/Dehlavi was spoken in Delhi and its environs much
> before Babur's time. No new language was born in north India as a result of
> the coming of the Mughals.[28]

In the introduction to the second edition of his book, de Tassy speaks
of the naming of all north Indian languages as 'Hindustani' (Hindui and
Hindi; Urdu and Dakani) by the British, and the rejection of the term
by the speakers of that language. According to him, the people of India
prefer to call the 'Hindu' speech written in Nagari 'Hindi'; and the 'Muslim'
speech written in the Persian script 'Urdu'. Now that we know that 'as
late as 1795–96 *zuban-e-urdu-e-mualla* was being generally referred to as
"Hindi" rather than "Persian"',[29] and 'the name of our language [i.e. the
language now known as Urdu] for Shah Alam was "Hindi"', the colonial
language policy stands clarified in that light.[30] Faruqi observes: 'In the

British writing and policy, the chief reason for favouring "Hindustani" over "Hindi/Hindavi" was to declare this language's affinity with the Muslims. They were insistent on declaring "Hindi" as the language of the Hindus and thus as a separate language.'[31] This language policy created the confusion of Hindi–Hindu and Urdu–Muslim, which affected the Hindi reawakening [navjagaran] movement in its entirety.

De Tassy records the nationalist upsurge in the introduction to the second edition, written in the aftermath of the independence struggle of 1857, but he views the whole phenomenon from a distinctive angle and translates it into colonial terms. He calls the nationalist upsurge 'narrow', and in the matter of language, he underscores the Hindu articulation and foists upon the Hindu and Muslim communities the relation between Hindi and Urdu, using the metaphor of war. This metaphor comes into operation as well in the form of the growing struggle between polytheism and monotheism. The next step in this thread of argument is the assimilation of Muslims within the Christian Biblical world, which is the colonialist move to pit them against the Hindus on religious grounds. In 1857, the year of the birth-pangs of a new nation, when Hindus and Muslims were in search of a national identity of their own, when Azimullah Khan wrote the national song, and all these efforts were against the common enemy of British colonialism, the policy of the British rulers faced by these forces was to embroil the two communities with each other and to favour by turn one against the other. Under such conditions, we can observe the policy of abridging the cultural nationalist aspiration of anti-colonialism into communalist tendencies in the matter of monotheism–polytheism, as raised by de Tassy. Colonial policy reduced the nascent nationalism, for its anti-imperialist character, as an 'other', and posited Hindus and Muslims as 'others' to each other, and this greatly impacted the initial dynamic of the Hindi reawakening.

This is the place for investigating the outlook of early western literary critics and literary historians on the Bhakti period (historically coincident with the turn of the second millennium and well into the medieval period) in the context of their distinctive thought process and the establishment of various canons of literature. Leaving aside the Krishnaite poets (such as Sur) and Ramaite poets (such as Tulsi), their views on other poets of the Bhakti period are adequate for understanding the processes of canon formation for this period. The colonial ideology interfered in the cultural field through language, and then used religion in order to lay down the canons of literature. De Tassy compares the religious reform movements in Europe and India in the context of Hindustani thus: 'It is the language of religious reform in India. Just as the Christian reformers of Europe adopted the living languages in order to support their beliefs and religious teachings, for propagating their doctrines the preceptors of the Hindu and Muslim faiths have also extensively used Hindustani.'[32] Here the common basis for commending the preceptors of both faiths is the composition of literature in the demotic language. But this point of comparison using Christian saints is developed only later in the work of Grierson.

The reasons for Grierson's favouring the Bhakti poet Tulsi and placing him above all in the canon will become clear from the following quotations. Commenting on Tulsi's *Ramayana/Ramcharitmanas*, he writes: 'It has saved the country from the tantric obscenities of Shaivism.'[33] He gives Ramanand, the legendary purveyor of Bhakti in north India, credit for protecting Bengal from the 'evil influence' of Shaivism, and writes about Tulsi:

> Tulsidas was the great apostle who carried his [Ramanand's] doctrine east and west and made it an abiding faith. The religion he preached was a simple and sublime one. . . . But what is most remarkable in it, in an age of immorality, when the bonds of Hindu society were loosened and the Mughal empire was being consolidated, was its stern morality in every sense of the word.[34]

In the same work, Grierson writes at another place: 'The worship of the deified prince of Audh [*sic*], and the loving adoration of Sita, the perfect wife and the perfect mother, have developed naturally into a doctrine of eclecticism in its best form'.[35] Thus, here is a reading of Tulsi's devotion[*bhakti*] that sets the poet apart from his poem's core meanings.

Grierson pits Tulsi in opposition to Tulsi's society, i.e. the imaginary excesses, pleasure-seeking and immorality prevalent during the time of the Muslim rulers, but above all against their misrule. Undoubtedly, the point of comparison is the 'great' British rule in the realm of government and Christianity in the realm of culture. Without equating Tulsi with Christianity, this goal could not be met. Grierson does recognize Tulsi's power to express the joys and sorrows of the Indian people, but in interpreting this power, he twists it around. He is unable to appreciate Tulsi as the representative poet of popular feeling among the peasants of Avadh and the Hindi-speaking region at large, because his critical judgement is determined by colonial thought. In the poetry of the Bhakti period, faith is used as an everyday idiom. The colonizers combined the religious element with political intentions and thereby secured several objectives simultaneously. We should note here that in the critical canons to come, not only did Tulsi retain his prominence, but he also continued to be a necessary part in the establishment of a theologically sound canon. In the process of including

Tulsi in the canon, Ramchandr Shukl deploys various arguments along with a heavy dose of arguments from religion. Here too religion in its modern meanings is rediscovered, just like the nation, its eternality praised, and a religious identity is secured by assuming other faiths to be the other.

The politics of religion-based hierarchization is clearly reflected not just in the case of Tulsi, but also in western writing about the entire Bhakti period. If Bhakti thought was addressing the human itself, then its basis was freedom from, in Tulsi's words, the 'service of mortals'. If we take the progressive critic and poet Gajanan Madhav Muktibodh's view, the Bhakti period was an expression of the political aspirations of new social energies by demolishing older social formations. As they saw the poets and the character of the movement from their dominant viewpoint of colonial power, the early western literary critics shaped a new kind of canon. Grierson's words in praise of Ramanand and Tulsi, and in criticism of Sur and Krishnaite poetry, are as follows:

> Here we first touch upon that marvellous catholicity[36] of sentiment . . . a doctrine which, while teaching the infinite vileness of mankind before the Infinitely Good, yet sees good in everything that He has created, and condemns no religion and no system of philosophy as utterly bad that inculcates, Thou shalt love the Lord thy God with all thy heart, and with all thy soul, and with all thy strength, and with all thy mind; and thy neighbor as thyself. . . . But at its best the Krishn element is wanting in the nobler elements of the teaching of Ramanand. Its essence is almost selfish – a soul absorbing, nay all-absorbing, individual love cast at the feet of Him who is Love itself. It teaches the first and great commandment of the Christian law, but the second, which is like unto it – Thou shalt love thy neighbour as thyself – it omits.[37]

After this statement, Grierson further clarifies his view with regard to Tulsidas: 'There are hymns in our Church hymnals which might be literal translations of passages written by this great poet.'[38] The use of translation to characterize the relation between Christian and Hindu catholicities reveals the nature of cultural and literary comparison at the heart of the colonial enterprise.

Frank E. Keay's reading of Kabir is comparable here. Keay is a literary historian from a later period than Grierson. His literary history was published in 1920. He writes in *Kabir and His Followers*:

> It is quite possible that a desire to assimilate the life of Kabir to that of Christ has helped the growth of such legends; but while these would show that Kabirpanthis have come under Christian influence, they have no bearing

on the connection between Kabir himself and Christianity. The Bhakti movement, of which Kabir was an outstanding leader, was almost certainly influenced by Christian ideas.[39]

If we use Hazari Prasad Dwivedi's language here, if not straightforwardly then ham-fistedly, a common apocryphal authorship is established between the Bhakti movement and Christianity. We do not need to venture far to find a reason for such apocryphal thinking. Thus the cultural weaponry of religious superiority appended to politics was used to sustain colonial interests.

By 1910, in the first edition of *Hindi navratn* [The Nine/New Hindi Jewels], one of the key texts of canon-making in Hindi in the colonial period, Kabir was not considered a part of the canon proposed by the Mishr Brothers. In the second edition of the same work, he was counted among the jewels of Hindi, and was promoted to third position by the time of the third edition. In this situation, the work done by Keay on Kabir was aimed precisely to bring him into the canon using a different set of religious arguments. In his literary history, Keay announces his 'secular' vision in a chapter on the 'Present Position and Prospects of Hindi Literature':

> Indian people themselves are often largely unaware how much of the new movements for political freedom, social emancipation, and religious reform are really inspired by Christian ideals. India has seen the vision of a future glory for herself and her children greater even than her past achievements, excellent as these have been. New ideals of righteousness and of duty, of brotherhood and of service have come before her, and inspiration for these has been very largely due to the life and teaching of Christ, who in this as in so many other ways is the fulfilment of all that is noble and excellent in Indian life.[40]

The suspicion cast by the book's Hindi translator, Sadanand Shahi, upon this 'secularism' and power talk is justified in the main: 'It would not be amiss to conclude that ascribing the real aim of a majority of Hindi promoters to praising the excellence of Christianity, English and the English race was to provide an intellectual basis to the colonial enslavement of India.'[41] While it is natural to recall from this triangle of religion, race and language the other triangle of 'Hindu, Hindi, Hindustan', instead of locating the British promoters of Hindi within this nationalist slogan's apparently similar intellectual frame, it would be more appropriate to see them as colonialists, as their emphasis was more on political gains than on excellence. Consequently, we can appreciate how, parallel to their successful efforts to deepen the language conflict, the British promoted Hindi at one time and Urdu at another.

Scrutinizing the idea of the nation, the Subaltern Studies historians reveal the fundamental contradiction in that concept. In their Preface to the Hindi translation of selected essays from the Subaltern Studies collective, Shahid Amin and Gyanendra Pandey write:

> We are the citizens of a nation, India, which in its geographical, political, social and foundational representations has not always existed. Nation formation is a historical process. No nation in the world is found readymade since antiquity – no nation was formed outside the limits of history, although each nation strains to present itself in the form of an always fully formed, self-knowing, ancient form. Like in other nations, in the process of nation formation in India too, different impulses, thought processes, desires and efforts clashed with each other. Some emerged victorious for a particular time while others were defeated for a long or short period of time. But the stamp of this contest remained on the process of our national formation and continues till today, as it has in the formation of each nation.[42]

In the matter of language, too, this policy became more pronounced because language is not merely a medium of expression, but also the medium of employment, expressing rank and status, and well-being and influence for communities. These communities provided the material basis to the Hindi–Urdu conflict as generated by the British. The cultural strategy of affiliating Hindi with Hindus and Urdu with Muslims took the forerunners of the 'reawakening' movement in the direction of turning Hindi into a symbol of communal identity, where, along with the 'lament for Madame Urdu' [*Urdu begam ka syapa*], the search began for a golden past for Hindi, which was never a unified language in history. This search emerged concomitantly with that other search for the nation's golden past. Vasudha Dalmia highlights its political connotations as below:

> The nationalist supporters of Hindi in the sixties and seventies of the [nineteenth] century, implicated deeply in the creation of the myths and genealogies concerning the origin of Hindi, would have treated any suggestion that their language was an artificial creation as a preposterous proposition. The notion that Hindi had never been the mother tongue of any native-born Indian stood in direct opposition to their own insistence that Hindi was spoken in homes across the breadth of North India and that this had been the case even before the Muslim invasion. . . . As so often, there was consensus at least on this one point amongst the imperialists and the nationalists: that the Hindus possessed a language of their own, which set them off not only from contemporary Muslims, but also from Muslims in the past.[43]

In this context, we can notice the reflection of the same mindset not just among Bhartendu and his contemporaries, but later on as well in the critical canons proposed after Ramchandr Shukl.

This partisan attempt to politicize culture by the colonizers consolidated the attempt to drive to the margins of culture the anti-imperialist and anti-communalist unity of Hindus and Muslims of 1857. History is witness to the success of this effort and the long shadow it cast across Indian nationalist thought. Later, Ramvilas Sharma gave a new direction to this discussion by reopening and re-reading this chapter of history in the field of literary culture. The effect of this twentieth-century effort on discussions about the interrelations between language and community in Hindi criticism in the early nineteenth century will be taken up in a later chapter.

'Modern religiosity' aside, Victorian morality is also one of the standards proposed by de Tassy through which he selects his chronological list of works. If we discuss the meaning of canon in de Tassy's first edition via Namvar Singh's pithy remark that canons create a 'hierarchy of values', we can conclude that in writing about Hindi/Hindui, de Tassy and his co-religionist early western critics gave pre-eminence to values of Victorian morality. Thus, one standard for selecting works for his literary history was the division between the felicitous and the obscene. Among the poetic faults recognized by Sanskrit and Urdu poetics, standards of morality are not so strict or important. In relation to the *riti* period, i.e. late medieval poetry of erotic themes and verbal ornamentation, this was not even a topic of discussion. If we leave aside the discussion on sensuality as the particular mentality of feudal licentiousness, we will observe in the discussion on the canon a 'modern' definition of 'obscenity'. The extent to which the attempt to study *riti* poetry from the viewpoint of a 'progressive sensuality' is appropriate, or whether it is influenced by the politics of canon-making, or whether such an attempt would yield a feminist reading, are matters for separate discussion; suffice it to say here that it was the first time that the values of morality were imposed on the Hindi/Hindavi poetry of previous times. In the second volume of the first edition of his literary history, de Tassy announces:

> But from the selections before me, or the ones that I had myself prepared, I had to excise a very large part because either they were contrary to our way of thinking, or they treated immoral matters, or they were polluted with obscenity, or, in the final instance, they are filled with such rhetorical embellishments that will be impossible for European readers to understand.[44]

In the first place, if de Tassy produces a canon for Indian literature meant to be read by European readers, then obviously only that Hindi literature is desirable which is stretched across critical standards based on his personal understanding of it alone. Consequently, elements of poetic conventions and of ancient Indic poetics that elaborate and rejuvenate traditional forms are cast out of the canon. In this situation, the greatest harm is done to those poetic genres which, working on the same ground and through the same thread of feeling, take the tradition forward by drawing deeply from it. On this basis, too, an internal principle of exclusion comes to be applied to the work of master poets from past centuries. Whether it be Jayasi, Tulsi, Sur or Ghanananda (from the Avadhi and Braj traditions), or Mir, Sauda, Ghalib or Zafar (from the Urdu tradition), the knowledge of an extensive poetic tradition is part and parcel of their work – in particular, in their similes and imagery, in their use of poetic conventions and really, in their entire poetic syntax. In de Tassy's system of reasoning, many important sections from the work of these major poets stand rejected.

Secondly, de Tassy manages also to find a religious point for his argumentation: in his mention of 'obscenity in the Muslim poets'. He remarks: 'one point to consider is that among the most famous Muslim authors of Persia and India, who are known as saintly personages, such as Hafiz, Sa'di, Jur'at, Kamal and others, almost all such poets wrote obscene verse'.[45] The same argument canonizes the poets of the Hindavi tradition. In his monograph, while praising British writers with particular reference to F.S. Growse, Ramadhar Sharma notes a similar logic of selection: 'These writers openly praise Tulsi and do not think much of Sur in comparison with the former. In Sur's imagination they notice a hint of sensuality, and they consider the unrestrained sentimentalism of Krishnaite poetry to be the cause for the subsequent decline of literature.'[46] In his literary history, Grierson too does not give Sur the same status in the canon as Tulsi, despite praising the former's ability to write in different styles. He declares: 'Natives of India give him the very highest niche of fame, but I believe the European reader will prefer the nobility of character of all that Tulsidas wrote to the often too cloying sweetness of the blind bard of Agra.'[47] Elsewhere he adds, 'But at its best the Krishn cult is wanting in the nobler elements of the teaching of Ramanand.'[48] De Tassy pushed out Sauda's satires from his canon-based literary history despite their commendation by Mir himself. The accusation against Sauda was the old one of immorality.[49]

The Hindavi/Hindustani controversy has shown that language was an insuperable wall erected by British and other western scholars, against which the house of a colonial cultural programme was constructed. While de Tassy's book also includes the unified history of Hindi–Hindustani (i.e. Urdu), in his literary history Grierson separates the section on 'Hindustani/

Urdu'. In de Tassy's case, it is clear from the arguments made at the beginning
of the text that his voice changes from the first edition (1839–47) to the
second edition (1870–71). Separating Hindi from Urdu, Grierson makes
the case that Urdu was the language of the urban Muslims of India and
of Hindus influenced by Persianate culture. Sadanand Shahi summarizes
Grierson's view: 'In Maulana Karimuddin's *Tazkira-e-shuara-e-hindustan*
[Anthology of the poets of India] the litterateurs of Hindi and Urdu are
present together. The work of dividing Hindi and Urdu was accomplished
by George Abraham Grierson. He did not consider Urdu to be a language
of the people.'[50] As a result of this colonialist intervention, we lost our
intermixed language. Later the intellectual foundation of this view was
constructed by the national movement launched in the name of Hindi.

Ramchandr Shukl made sense of this language riddle in his own way and
expressed it in his influential writings. He knew western scholars were stoking
the Hindi–Urdu controversy. Because of his nationalistic reasoning he does
solve the colonial riddle, but precisely by deploying the same standards of
cultural value proposed by the colonialists themselves. He accuses the British
of partisanship towards Muslims. He does not focus his critical attentions on
the promotion of communal hostilities in India which was a part of Britain's
colonial political programme. In this matter he sides with the British view
that Hindus/Hindi and Muslims/Urdu are distinct linguistic communities,
and that Hindi is the older traditional language. Describing the development
of prose in the first section on the modern period in his literary history of
Hindi, he writes: 'as we have just mentioned, the quarrel of Hindi and Urdu
continued till the time of Raja Shivprasad and Bhartendu. Sitting in France,
Garcin de Tassy too contributed to this quarrel. . . . When the quarrel arose,
he [de Tassy] assumed the position of Urdu due to a religious affinity.'[51]
While Shukl signposts de Tassy's 'religious affinity', he is unable to go further
and investigate its political underpinnings, otherwise he would not have
taken the view on Urdu that he did. In order to prove the unpopularity of
the Persian–Arabic-intermixed language, he took recourse to quoting the
language of Christian translators in favour of his argument:

> These translators [Christian missionaries] took the purified language of
> Sadasukh and Lallulal to be the ideal; they kept Urdu-ness at a clear distance;
> this indicates that the common folk had no affection for the Persian–Arabic-
> intermixed language through which the faith had to be preached. . . . The
> Sanskrit-infused language, which has become a fashion for some to criticize,
> the common population has been and still is more acquainted with than with
> Urdu.[52]

Shamsur Rahman Faruqi also writes about the language of Lallulal that Shukl is expounding above; he quotes the linguist Tarachand on Jules Bloch on this issue: 'Bloch also accepts that Lalluji Lal, "under the inspiration of Gilchrist", changed everything by writing the famous *Prem sagar* [Ocean of Love]. According to Bloch, "its prose portions are more or less in Urdu, but instead of Persian words Hindi–Aryan words have been used."'[53]

Shukl's argument, based on the popularity and unpopularity of Sanskritized Hindi and Urdu, respectively, should be examined in the light of W.B. Bailey's 1802 thesis. Bailey writes in his thesis, which was read out at Fort William College on 6 February 1802:

> For administrative purposes in India the need is far greater for Hindi than other languages; the Hindustani language which is mentioned in my argument is also known as Hindi–Urdu or *Rekhta* and it is a compound of Arabic, Persian and Sanskrit or *Bhasha* and it has been prevalent in all times throughout India.[54]

Further discussion on Shukl, and the critics and intellectuals preceding him, will be taken up in subsequent chapters. Here it should suffice to say that the colonialist logic – both in opposition to it and under its influence – that gave rise to the 'modern man' in colonial India was fraught with deep contradictions. While one element of culture was sought to be rejected, a new one was not available readymade for the canon to be based on. A large-scale vision of comparison with the west was the underlying ground for canon-thinking in the nineteenth century. This vision was not simply based on cultural or aesthetic principles but had a deep connection with the ideology of colonialism. For this reason precisely, even while manifestly opposing the British, the canons proposed by western colonial scholars had a far-reaching influence on the canon of literature formed by nationalist critics and intellectuals.

NOTES

[1] Varshney (2004 vikrami), p. 25.
[2] Ahmad (1994), p. 225.
[3] Ibid., p. 224.
[4] Sharma (2009), p. 11.
[5] Marquess Wellesley, 'The Governor-General's Notes with respect to foundation of a College at Fort William', No. LXXXVI, in Martin, ed. (1836), pp. 326–30.
[6] Varshney (2004 vikrami), p. 25.
[7] Shukl (1997), p. 227.
[8] Ibid., p. 228.

[9] Varshney (2004 vikrami), p. 162.

[10] Ibid., p. 10.

[11] Ahmad (1994), p. 114.

[12] Gilchrist (1802), p. i.

[13] Faruqi (2007), p. 20.

[14] Varshney (2004 vikrami), p. 48.

[15] Faruqi (2007), p. 12.

[16] Chandpuri (1965), p. 215.

[17] See section on the development of Khari Boli prose in Shukl (1997), pp. 224–38.

[18] Varshney (2004 vikrami), p. 14.

[19] Sadanand Shahi, in Keay (1988), p. 6.

[20] For a Marxist critique of Edward Said's *Orientalism*, see Aijaz Ahmad, '*Orientalism and After: Ambivalence and Metropolitan Location in the Work of Edward Said*', in Ahmad (1994), pp. 159–218. Ahmad highlights the contradictions contained within Said's idea of Orientalism and its definitions, and argues for viewing the 'east' and the 'west' not as absolute categories but through the political economy of capital.

[21] This book is sometimes also referred to as *The Modern Vernacular Literature of Northern Hindustan*. Shukl uses this name to refer to the book in his literary history, although all later historians drop the word 'northern'. Varshney also omits 'northern' in the title of his Hindi translation.

[22] de Tassy (1953), p. 1.

[23] Ibid.

[24] Grierson (1889), p. 34.

[25] de Tassy (1953), introduction to vol. 1 of 1839 edition, pp. 1–2.

[26] Ibid., introduction to vol. 1 of 1870 edition, pp. 57–58.

[27] Ibid., p. 5.

[28] Faruqi (2007), pp. 14–15.

[29] Ibid., p. 16.

[30] Ibid., p. 17.

[31] Ibid.

[32] de Tassy (1953), introduction to vol. 1 of 1870 edition, pp. 60–61.

[33] Grierson (1889), p. 43.

[34] Ibid.

[35] Ibid., p. xvii.

[36] Kishorilal Gupt translates Grierson's 'catholicity' as 'great liberality' (*mahan udarta*). While this is a correct translation, a more culturalist translation would yield the particular meaning of denominational superiority in Grierson's usage. Another example will be apposite here: Grierson's translates a line from Tulsi ('*man mati rank manorath rau*') as 'My intellect is beggarly while my ambition is imperial.' In particular, '*rau*' is translated as 'imperial'. In various Indian contexts, *rau* can be raja, king, or the ruler of any large or small principality. But it does not carry the ring of an imperial sovereign. Grierson casts this word in the mould of imperialism. This elaboration of the meaning of *rau* glosses his imperialist position. This example shows the workings of politics in translation or how the translator's political position can influence the text.

[37] Grierson (1889), pp. xvii–xviii.

[38] Ibid., p. xvii.

[39] Keay (1931), p. 172.

[40] Keay (1920), p. 107.

[41] Shahi, ed. and trans. (1988), p. 11.

[42] Amin and Pandey (1995), Preface, pp. 7–8.

[43] Dalmia (1997), pp. 149–50.

[44] de Tassy (1953), introduction to vol. 2 of 1847 edition, p. 18.

[45] Ibid.

[46] Sharma (1962), p. 8. The comment draws on the introduction to *The Ramayana of Tulsi Das* (1891) by F.S. Growse.

[47] Grierson (1889), p. 25.

[48] Ibid., p. xvii.

[49] de Tassy (1953), introduction to vol. 1 of 1870 edition, p. 78.

[50] Shahi, ed. and trans. (1988), p. 8.

[51] Shukl (1997), pp. 237–38.

[52] Ibid., p. 232.

[53] Faruqi (2007), p. 35.

[54] Varshney (2004 vikrami), p. 206.

CHAPTER TWO

The Nationalist Project and the Canons of Hindi Criticism

THE MISHR BROTHERS: CONTAGION IN MODERNITY

Literature is organized according to time. People of that time [the *riti* period] required no more than the works produced at the time. The taste of the majority, especially the lordlings and the nobles who were bothered only with Eros [*shringar*], was developing. It [Eros] was their mother; it was present abundantly in poetry. Today is another time. The sad state of the country has reduced everyone's flab. We are back to our senses. Old talk is out of place today. Therefore, today's need should be fulfilled by the belletrists and litterateurs of today. They alone are answerable to it; they must fill the void in their literature. People are beginning to make efforts towards this.[1]

We have seen in the last chapter how the British colonizers increased their intervention in Indian social life after the people's revolt of 1857. On the other hand, A.O. Hume had already helped establish the Indian National Congress in 1885. A third important event was the rise of nationalism. It was under such circumstances that modern prose in Hindi was born. The previous chapter looked at the form of the kernel of this 'modernity' and its permeation in early literary histories in the configuration of critical canonical standards. It was within this milieu of India's social formation that the language of criticism in Hindi was born.

As much as for establishing new rules and the modern literary age, Bhartendu Harishchandr and his circle deserve the credit for inaugurating criticism in Hindi. In this series of developments, the first work is *Shivsingh saroj* [Shivsingh's Lotus], which outwardly mentions some principles of criticism within the framework of a literary history and lives of the poets.

But the first bona fide critical work in Hindi is Bhartendu's essay, '*Natak*' [Drama], written in 1883. It is significant that even this early critical writing undertakes to trace the development of the local dramatic tradition of the time by discussing Sanskrit drama and other theatrical traditions. But the rise of criticism in a practical form is believed to be really effected through book reviews. In this light, the review of Lala Shrinivas Das's *Sanyogita svayamvar* [Sanyogita's choice of groom] by Balkrishn Bhatt in *Hindi pradip* and the review of Premghan in *Anand kadambini* are noteworthy. These book reviews examine finer points of poetic practice but from the point of view of canon formation they are not very important.

Subsequently, Mahavir Prasad Dwivedi picked up the gauntlet of codifying literary rules. It is universally acknowledged that he consecrated the journal *Saraswati* as the only platform for literary discussion. Although Dwivedi did not write a systematic book of criticism, his miscellaneous essays and several topical books, such as *Sampatti shastra* [The Book of Wealth], did provide a systematic basis for critical language. He opposed writing that relied on poetic conventions [*riti*], and advocated interpreting poetry without reference to poetic treatises. He stressed that the languages of poetry and prose should be one and the same. Most importantly, he argued for the correlation of social conditions with literature. In view of the newly arising middle class and the 'reawakening', Dwivedi not only proposed criteria for idealism, but also subjected the literary tradition to a thorough evaluation. He took on this task in essays written on the Sanskrit poets, particularly his essay on Kalidas which addresses the latter's carefree quality. Articles commissioned for *Saraswati* on economics, sociology, art and other new subjects not only increased the store of knowledge in Hindi, but also improved the vigour of the language. From this perspective, Dwivedi is without peer for his role in establishing a canon for Hindi. As for the question of criticism, I have chosen the Mishr Brothers' *Hindi navratn* [The Nine Hindi Jewels] from this period of its development as exemplary for this study.

For the pre-Dwivedi canon, the Mishr Brothers' *Hindi navratn* is an important book which has been credited as the first book of modern criticism in Hindi. It was first published in 1910. After this, along with the abridged and other editions published during their lifetime, a total of ten editions were brought out. Each edition included additions and omissions of previously included poets. The basic text went through six editions in 1910, 1924, 1928, 1937 and 1941 (the abridged edition was brought out in 1934). After the abridged edition, too, newer editions came out in 1940, 1943 and 1944. The changes in these latter editions are not devoid of interest. The Mishr Brothers divided the 'nine jewels' into three triads. The major triad of the first edition comprised Tulsi, Sur and Dev. In the middle triad they included Bihari, Bhushan and Keshav. In the minor triad, Matiram, Chand (Chandbardayi) and Bhartendu Harishchandr were included. The order of excellence was approximately similar in each triad for the Mishr Brothers. Kabir was allowed entry into the basic text of the 1924 edition of *Hindi navratn*. The count remained at nine; to preserve this after the inclusion of Kabir, among the ten jewels, Bhushan and Matiram were counted as one under the appellation of the 'Tripathi Brothers'. The process of Kabir's canonization in the Mishr Brothers' book will be discussed below.

For the canons of Dwivedi-era criticism, *Hindi navratn* may be taken as an exemplary book not because it represents the literary views of Mahavir Prasad Dwivedi, but because it exhibits the opposition between the traditional understanding of poetics and the values of 'modernity'. While the book includes new and modern values, at the same time, at the level of taste, the *riti*-period-inflected views of the writers permeate their critical canons. The tradition of criticism from Bhartendu's time had a modernist hue, but Braj Bhasha continued to be the language of poetry. The meaning of comprehensive criticism [*samalochna*] for the Mishr Brothers was the same as that inscribed by Lala Bhagwandin on the title page of his book, *Bihari aur Dev* [Bihari and Dev]:

> The poet Din utters truth; some shiver to hear it, some fume.
> True comprehensive criticism is only that which stays away from taking sides.

The demand for 'truth' and not taking sides points to the value system of early Hindi literature. This value, discovered in the Dev–Bihari controversy (both poets of the mannered *riti* style of poetry), can be found in the Mishr Brothers too. It is noteworthy here that western modes of analysis proved to be formative in modern Indian criticism.

We may note a strong influence of the western *theoria* in this period. Jagannath Das Ratnakar translated Alexander Pope's *An Essay on Criticism* for the *Nagari pracharini patrika* as 'Samalochan adarsh' [Ideals of Comprehensive Criticism]. Journals of the time began carrying 'book review' columns. Concepts in English such as 'essence', 'spirit of the times', 'classic' and 'poet of general vision' came into use. This trend continued from this time onwards. In praise of Sur, for example, the Mishr Brothers addressed him as a 'poet of general vision'.[2]

In their analysis of Tulsi, the Mishr Brothers took the help of western philosophy. We have already seen in Chapter One above, the bases on which Grierson and others evaluated Tulsi. In the words of the Mishr Brothers:

Goswami *ji* [Tulsi] gave his teaching in a simple Hindi for all the common peoples' understanding. . . . He described Ramachandra vividly and with absolute propriety [*maryada*], which made for a heavy impact of his teachings, and because of his simple language, he became the greatest teacher and improver of character in north India.[3]

The first issue that stands out in the above statement is the comment about the identity of Tulsi's language. In Hindi, ironically, the literature of the popular languages (*bolis*) is viewed as its own, and in the quotation above, the Mishr Brothers do not even mention Avadhi by name (the language of the *Ramcharitmanas*). This is not merely a question of the script of the language since even Marathi used the Nagari script. It follows that the cultural roots of this aggrandizing view of the popular languages of north India lie in the Hindi reawakening, during which various communities tried to consolidate by assimilating other miscellaneous identities within themselves. This was true of Shukl too, in relation to the language question.

In the passage quoted above, the word 'propriety' [*maryada*] also calls for attention. This word was dear to both Indian thought and to western scholars at the time. The superiority of the Bhakti age over the *riti* age was built in the shadow of this concept/word. We have already seen how Grierson's canonization of Tulsi is based on the same concept of 'propriety'. What are the coordinates of this propriety? Can it be proposed that this propriety is the anxiety of intellectuals in the colony to achieve self-identity? But even if this were possible, it would not account for Grierson's usage. Is it not possible, then, to conclude that it was Grierson's usage that entered this history in camouflage? This is the way the history of canons built on religious grounds begins, i.e. with a notion of purity, and arrives at the idea of national identity centred on propriety.

We can thus see the influence of English ideas on the formation and development of Indian canons of criticism. As an exemplary case, the remarks of Badri Narayan Chaudhari 'Premghan', who was a Sanskritophile in his language use and, on that basis, a great man of the Indian tradition, draw our attention here: 'Review [*rivyu*] or comprehensive criticism means to analyse without taking sides, and with clear discernment, the objective merits and demerits of any book and to give an account of its author.'[4] Here, analysis of 'merits and demerits' is installed as the principle of criticism. This was something new in Hindi criticism. While Shukl denigrates the analysis of merits and demerits approach as compared to the 'investigation of inner tendencies' of poetry (which is his distinctive contribution to Hindi criticism), his indignation is more against the enumerating logic of the

Mishr Brothers than with their method of establishing the shortcomings of a writer. This is because despite their heterogeneous methods, many of the analyses of the Mishr Brothers are found in Shukl's work too. For example, the search for the roots of the Bhakti movement is common to both sets of critics. The Mishr Brothers write: 'Due to the use of force against religion [*dharm*] the Hindus considered it important to preserve society, which in turn led religious thinking towards *bhakti*.'[5] This echoes the reasoning offered by Shukl: 'when the Muslim community was established widely . . . the Hindu community was enveloped in dejection. Other than focusing its attention on God's power and compassion, what other path was open to a community [*jati*] despairing of its masculinity [*paurush*]?'[6]

An investigation into the interrelationships between 'review' and comprehensive criticism shows that the need for criticism arose along with the growth of new prose genres that had occurred during the reawakening. British colonialism had a role to play in the making of the reawakening; or, one could say, British colonialism was an unwitting tool for the reawakening. It was in the battle against the former that the modern imagination of the 'nation' took shape. But, as we have seen in the previous chapter, the idea of nation that formed around 1857 was interrupted and Hindi criticism took another route on which there were clear influences of colonialism. The fashion of 'reviews' led to the development of 'comprehensive criticism' in Hindi, as pointed out by Premghan above. The second issue is 'truth' [*sachchayi*]. Several critics of the time argue for conducting criticism on this principle. So much so that Mahavir Prasad Dwivedi's ideas on this issue appear similar to that of the Mishr Brothers, although in the following he is writing about the ancient poets: 'it is not wrong to make a comprehensive criticism of the ancient poets and in good faith to show their manifest demerits. Such criticism, rather than causing harm, has its benefits.'[7] The Mishr Brothers too joined in with the music of the times: 'those who can afford to spend time on this matter; it is their duty to describe accurately the merits–demerits of literary works so that human interests are also developed.'[8]

The three related keywords, 'analysis of merits–demerits', 'refinement of interests' and 'duty', help us comprehend the self-understanding of criticism during this period. In the context of criticism, Shukl takes note only of the 'analysis of merits–demerits' and applies the other two to other literary genres. The foundations of the canon, for the Mishr Brothers, were the following in their own words:

> Whether the poet wanted to say something or not, how does he say it? In
> simpler terms, the first question can be rephrased thus: what is his message? .

. . If the message is a strong one, literature will become secondary and lose its flavour, and if literature is kept strong, then the message will be lost.[9]

It was the Mishr Brothers' goal to select eminence from the total fund of Hindi literature. Although they established standards for this, the problem was the lack of coincidence between *what* the poet says and *how* the poet says it. They managed to settle the correspondence between the 'what' of the content and the 'how' of style only in parts. The interrelations between discourse and craft, or form and content, are inexplicable in the framework of the Mishr Brothers. This unresolved opposition plays a prominent role in their project of canon formation, and this can be seen in the entire *Navratn*.

The Mishr Brothers included Kabir in the second edition of their book. And the reason given for this was more Kabir's 'saintliness' than his poetry. The same standard was not applied in the case of Tulsi. Here, poetic quality too played a part in establishing the standard. The question before them was how Kabir is not a great poet despite being a great religious preceptor. The answer is best read in their own words:

> Does Brahmanand attain the status of a poet or not? . . . Brahmanand's outpourings are good for verse because that is his medium. . . . There is no doubt from the theological standpoint that he is the best of men. It is possible that some other gentleman announces Goswami Tulsidas and Surdas to be higher than or equal to him. In our view, though, these great souls did not reach the godly, religious heights of Kabirdas.[10]

Kabir was removed from the 1910 edition of *Hindi navratn*. The Mishr Brothers argued that Kabir is more a *bhakt* [devotee] than a poet, and since *Navratn* is a canon-making text, he is not included despite his saintliness. Later it was his saintliness that justified Kabir's entry into the canon. It is important to note here that while *Navratn* was criticized from different perspectives, no one took exception to the exclusion of Kabir. He came to be included in the Mishr Brothers' canon thanks to their own critical conundrum. In this regard, Vishvanath Tripathi's comment on Tulsi and Sur in *Navratn* applies less to those two poets than to Kabir: 'Here [in the *Navratn*] Tulsi and Sur are protected by their "saintliness", rather than their poetry.'[11]

This trend in Hindi canon formation may be visualized through a scene from a proverb-like, popular *doha* [couplet] in Braj Bhasha. This couplet, which is repeated equally in literary works and popular culture, presents a sample of the process of early canon formation in Hindi:

> Sur is the sun, Tulsi the moon, Keshavdas the stars.
> Today's poets are like fireflies, shining fitfully.

The writer of the couplet must be considered anonymous as no authorship has been mentioned. But we can date it with some precision to the time of Keshavdas (1555–1617) or some time after that, since the couplet mentions his name. In the canon announced in this couplet, established in truth by the oral tradition of criticism, Sur occupies the first position, i.e. he is the best of poets. Tulsi comes second and Keshav, a *riti* poet, comes last. Surprisingly, from the very beginning, we find Hindi criticism at odds with the canon suggested in this couplet. Whether for Grierson, de Tassy or the Mishr Brothers, or even Ramchandr Shukl, among the poets in the couplet's canon, Tulsi is the sun and Sur is the moon. Early on, Grierson was making efforts to place Tulsi at the top of the canon. Why did this happen? Reasons may be found for why Tulsi is positioned first in the canon, but the reason for the dismissal of Sur from the first place is not so straightforward. For this, we will have to study the criticism that declares Tulsi supreme and the critics' Sur-related views. It is, however, clear already that the canon of the *riti* period (suggested in the couplet above) was built on different standards from those of the modern canons.

If we now return to the *Navratn* canon and attend to the new thought emerging from the Hindi reawakening, Shukl's comment that this is the age of prose seems fitting. Doubtless, the significance of calling the period the age of prose was not to raise the status of prose over poetry; rather, it points to a specific turn in culture. This was the moment when standards and the canon based on poetry were remade by the development of prose-based criticism. This was also the time when literary forms were overhauled. The extent of this change can be marked by the change in poetic language, from the expansiveness of Braj to the albeit unsteady and ungainly tread of Khari Boli (i.e. the lexical base of modern Hindi and Urdu). Not just prose, but also the criteria of understanding poetry changed. The Mishr Brothers stand at the cusp of this turn.

On the one hand, the Mishr Brothers preferred the narcissistic quality [*mugdha*] of the poem's heroine, i.e. the qualities of softness, savouriness and attractiveness. They swore by allegory (*anyokti*), proverb (*lokokti*) and natural description (*svabhavokti*). Therefore, the primacy given to Dev, the *riti* poet, is due to the long-continuing tradition of poetics through which the Mishr Brothers, using a formalist approach, analysed the work of poets such as Dev and gave them a high station. On the other hand, the highest example of their dualistic conundrum is Kabir, who is included in their canon for his saintliness rather than his verse. But despite his inclusion, Kabir only makes it to the seventh rank in the canon. Mahavir Prasad Dwivedi took note of this and asked in a review of *Navratn*, published in

Saraswati: 'through what kind and height of excellence did you consider Matiram a jewel as you did [Bhartendu] Harishchandr?'[12] An answer to this question was implicitly given by Ramvilas Sharma in his book *Mahavir Prasad Dwivedi aur Hindi navjagran* [Mahavir Prasad Dwivedi and the Hindi Reawakening]. Expressing his anti-*riti* agenda in this book, Sharma praised Dwivedi and wrote apropos the Mishr Brothers:

> Not only did they [Mishr Brothers] mark out Tulsi, but they distinguished Sur from the *riti* poets; and in comparison with Dev, Bihari, Matiram *et al.* not only did they consider Tulsi and Sur superior but also placed Bhartendu Harishchandr, the pioneer of the reawakening in the Hindi provinces, at a higher position than the former two. Modern Hindi literature could develop only in opposition to and by devaluing the literary value of the *riti* tradition. . . . It was natural for those who opposed the *riti* way in the twentieth century to affiliate themselves with the saint [*sant*] poets and with Bhartendu Harishchandr.[13]

Sharma brought the Mishr Brothers and Dwivedi face to face in order to implicitly reject the intervening term, *riti*. This quotation recalls another famous pronouncement by Sharma in his 1943 book, *Viram chihn* [Punctuation Marks], in the chapter titled 'The Mishr Brothers and the Heroine's Properties [*Nayika bhed*]'. Here, too, the agenda is the same but the mood is different. The Mishr Brothers are quoted here but in support of *riti* poetry:

> Prior to writing the introduction to *Pallav*, the Mishr Brothers attacked wholeheartedly the fortress of the poets who wrote about the heroine's properties [*Nayika bhed*]. The first among these were the ones who wrote poetic treatises. There was an abundance of such poets in the *riti* period who did teach versification, but could not write good verse themselves. The Mishr Brothers quip, 'they were blind in both eyes, but possessed nine types of eye liner'. One can find thousands of teachers of poetic conventions but poets are hard to come by.[14]

In the above two instances, we may note the ways in which Ramvilas Sharma deploys the Mishr Brothers' views: first, to burnish the image of Mahavir Prasad Dwivedi as the pioneer of the Hindi reawakening; second, to mount an attack on the erotic description of the heroine's attributes in the poetry. Juxtaposing both instances reveals that what moves Sharma most is not the 'investigation of inner states of poetry' (*à la* Shukl) but opposing the *riti* manner of poetry.

If we now return to the moment when Mahavir Prasad Dwivedi

questions the Mishr Brothers for placing Harishchandr and Matiram in the same class, it gives rise to another question: can there be a Hindi canon by excluding the *riti* period from it? Can a whole historical period be excised from the category of great poetry? Does this moment in thought not remind us of the debate on 'outcasting' which expelled the whole of the medieval period by calling it the dark ages? One can argue that this question arose from a transformation in consciousness in the wake of the Hindi reawakening, but was the self-understanding of this consciousness developed enough for it to create the canon of *Indian* literature? This may look like an exorbitant question, but we have already seen that colonial knowledge had made inroads into thought through structures of power. On the other hand, the *riti* period itself is not a one-dimensional phenomenon. If there exists in this period, the 'breast she touched against the hero' kind of poetry, then so does the 'witnessing the high-summer afternoon' kind of poetry (i.e. nature poetry) exist in the *riti* tradition. How could it be possible that suddenly a whole literary tradition is pronounced dead and 'modernity' is said to be inaugurated as a consequence of foreign invasion? Following this line of reasoning, Ramchandr Shukl's argument about the rise of the Bhakti period – that invasions have deeper effects than tradition on literature – is more sound. It is ironic that despite the delegitimation of Shukl's view today, Mahavir Prasad Dwivedi's fierce attack on *riti* poetry is treated as the touchstone for modernity.

In *Navratn*, Bhartendu and Bhushan are included for wholly different reasons: for predominantly 'modern' reasons, i.e. for their 'depiction of the honour of the religious community'. Consequently, the struggle between the content of the poem's discourse and how it is delivered becomes the basis for deciding the canon. Here we can also identify the struggle between the position of *riti* poetics and the Hindi reawakening. We have already seen the three bases on which the Mishr Brothers established their canon: (i) what is said? (ii) how is it said? (iii) when is it said? Only those poets who remain true to each of these bases find a prominent place in *Navratn*. The third basis is a wholly new one. In view of the new canons formed during the reawakening, it is the primacy of content that was being carried in new forms. Content became prominent in canon criticism thanks to nationalist thought and the independence movement. Undoubtedly, this content was determined by the historical time due to which values such as 'nationality' or caste [*jati*] became prominent.

It would be pertinent here, considering the historic crossroads at which the Mishr Brothers are located, to consider their views on Muslims and Muslim rule. On the topic of Tulsi, the Mishr Brothers wrote: 'what luckless person would he be who despite knowing the Hindi alphabet, or being related to Hindi, Hindu and Hind [northern India], does not have even a little familiarity with the name, fame and the milk-raining poetry of that great brahmin soul, Tulsidas?'[15] We come to realize that caste consciousness was working silently behind the act of reading poetry, as its basis. Bhartendu's formulations, strewn about in his speech '*Bharatvarshonnati kaise ho sakti hai*' [How is Indian Progress to Happen?], delivered in Ballia (present-day Uttar Pradesh), and in which anti-colonialism was articulated as a programme, were elaborated by the Mishr Brothers into the trinity of religion, language and nation. We have already seen the deployment of this trinity in the work of cultural nationalists. My aim here is not to characterize the development of the old cultural tradition as 'cultural nationalism', but to investigate into the essential character of the Hindi reawakening, which would clarify the bases of the emergent canons based on literary criticism.

The religious element too influenced the phenomenon of national awakening or 'nation' formation. Undoubtedly this 'religion' was different from the conception of religion in the medieval period. To a certain extent, in the medieval period, the separation of religion and state was visible; but after the formation of the 'nation', when the process of this separation should have been strengthened, the reverse happened. The capitalism that developed in colonial India emerged out of colonialism. To expect this capital to radically change the relations and means of production was unrealistic. Instead, capital compromised with old economic relations, rather than struggling against them. Consequently, the cultural undertones of this compromise also came to light. This was the reconstitution of religion, which, in contrast to medieval religion, was positing and organizing itself. From this foundational perspective, we can revisit the ideas of the authors of the first book of modern Hindi criticism, in the context of their discussion of the emergence of Tulsi in *Hindi navratn*:

> At that time, the state of Indian religious creeds was unenviable. By manifesting their complete faith in monotheism, the Muslims introduced a somewhat new element into Indian philosophical thought. In the ancient period, monotheism was certainly prevalent, but along the lines of the three Buddhist jewels. The ideas of our very own Brahma, Vishnu and Mahesh caused a subtle disruption in it. Due to this conjuncture, we forgot the monotheistic path and began to believe in these three as three different deities and the primal divinity too came to be seen as a separate goddess. Thus emerged the religious turmoil between Hindus and Muslims. . . . For its removal the great soul Kabirdas was born, who preached the true sermon of monotheism and made possible

the unity of Hindus and Muslims. Although the great soul Kabirdas did not
fully preach the idea of an attributeless spirit but rather of God as the vessel
of love and the hearer of laments, in his God there remained a peculiar aspect
of attributelessness, while almost none of the devotion towards a God with
attributes remained. Therefore, despite being most excellent and most useful,
the teachings of the great soul Kabirdas did not prove to be profitable for the
people. The great soul Tulsi lived almost fifty years after Kabirdas. The former
gave up the thought of unifying the Hindu and Muslim faiths and tried to
make one all the branches among the Hindus.[16]

The contorted ideas of the Mishr Brothers are clearly evident in this
long quotation. We also note here their attempt to define their cultural
roots in terms of contemporary pressures. Their thought process proceeds
in this way: we began as monotheists; the Buddhists disrupted this, i.e.
they misled the people. Later, it was through the same monotheism that
Muslims gained acceptance in India. They too harmed Hindu-ness through
monotheism. Previously we have seen that de Tassy uses this point about
monotheism to present the formula for friendship between Muslims and
Christians of the west against Hindus. Monotheism is a riddle for the Mishr
Brothers who try to solve it through Kabir, but the latter is not a part of
their canon. That place is occupied by Tulsi. So, what are the qualities for
which Kabir is singled out? He is present in the canon for fighting the new
monotheistic challenge to the Hindu faith. In this he is unsuccessful. In
giving the reasons for his failure, the Mishr Brothers confuse different forms
of reasoning. According to them, Kabir 'did not prove to be profitable
for the people' because 'in his God there remained the crucial aspect of
attributelessness'. Contrarily, while recounting the sequence of the glories
of ancient India, they had earlier described monotheism as indigenous to
the land and excoriated the Buddhists for the destruction of this glorious
monotheism. That their monotheism was better than Muslim monotheism,
is the illogical consequence of this argument. Thus, according to the
Mishr Brothers, the worship of a deity with attributes, for which reason
Tulsi becomes a cherished poet, comes from the Buddhists – and so, how
could the latter be denigrated? The Mishr Brothers over all believe that the
continuity of Indian tradition was disrupted by the Muslims, and that it
was Tulsi who corrected social behaviour and organization.

In the same chapter, the Mishr Brothers write: 'In the Muslim age
the period is considered good and peaceful but for the same period Tulsidas
calls the king an "unbenevolent heart" as well as "land stealer", which
suggests that the Hindu populace was not living in peace even then.'[17] The

power and limits of the reawakening are evident in this stance of the Mishr Brothers. How are we to read their calling the ruler an 'unbenevolent heart' and 'land stealer'? The writers understand Tulsi's anguish on a new social basis: that of the emergent bourgeois heart in which identity is the metaphor for recognizing oneself, and not from the viewpoint of the oppressed people, on questions of agriculture and land. While the Mishr Brothers empathize with the pain visible in the writings of a great poet about the situation of the peasantry in the Mughal empire, they restrict their understanding to their contemporary conception of religion. In this manner, the anguish of the peasant, as expressed in Tulsi's verse, remains only as the anguish of *Hindu* subjects. This reading echoes Ramchandr Shukl's reading of Malik Muhammad Jayasi's work. In his reading of the *Padmavat*, for example, Shukl too presents Jayasi as a poet of the 'general life'. While interpreting the verse, 'I am without husband, who will repair my hut's roof?' [*haun bin nah, mandir ko chhava*], he calls attention to Nagmati's abandonment of queenly airs and concludes from this that Jayasi expresses here the pain of the generalized Hindu woman. This 'Hindu woman' is no ordinary woman, though; she is given a religious specification. In this regard, the Mishr Brothers seem to have influenced Shukl. This was the period when, amid anti-colonialism and deep thinking on the national question, identities were also being cast and formed. The receptacle of identities was the very same bourgeois 'heart' which lay at the heart of the Hindi reawakening.

The quest for religious community-based identity in its most comprehensive form was the new project of the age of the Mishr Brothers. Almost all contemporary writers were concerned with caste in their investigation of literary matters. An exemplary find of this investigation is Bhushan. Bhushan's poetry was popular, but he entered the canon thanks to this particular quest for religious identity. In the words of the Mishr Brothers:

> In Bhushan there exists the fulsome quality of religious collectivity [*jatiyata*]. The degree of concern and pride that Bhushan had in the Hindu race cannot be found in any other great Hindi poet, with the exception of Bhartendu. . . . In truth, the hero of his poetry in one sense is neither Shivaji nor Rao Buddh, nor Avadhutsingh, nor Shambhaji, nor Shahuji: his true heroes are the Hindus. . . . During that period there was a concerted effort in India to establish self-rule. He [Bhushan] gave priceless assistance to that task through joyous exhortation. . . . Despite being restrained in speech he became the energizer of the religious collectivity [*jatiyata*].[18]

The Mishr Brothers do not notice in Bhushan's case the characteristics of

Tulsi's land-stealing king with an unbenevolent heart, because, for Bhushan, the king is not a ruler but a religious leader fighting against the foreign might of Muslim rule. It was the same religious collectivity [*jatiyata*] that established Bhartendu as its leader.

In this light, we can see that the Mishr Brothers stand in the middle of a process of canon formation whose essence is anti-colonial. Simultaneously, they are adept in aspects of Hindi criticism and poetics dealing especially with poetic conventions [*riti*] and poetic–erotic attributes. That is why they include the *riti* poets in their canon. On the other hand, since criticism developed with the coming of modernity and the reawakening, concerns about the latter, the nationalist concern in particular, became an undifferentiated part of their critical vision. We will see below that this anti-colonialism itself is divided across various streams; thus the Mishr Brothers too are anti-colonial from a delimited class position. During their time it was the reformist politics of the Indian National Congress that formed the main stream of anti-colonialism. Nation-building appears to have been the basis of canon-building in this early period of Hindi criticism.

Ramchandr Shukl: Reawakening and the Nation

Namvar Singh discusses Shukl's critical standards in his introduction to the latter's selected works. Although his observations are not fully pertinent to our discussion on canon formation, they help us in deducing Shukl's criteria for canonization. Singh writes:

> The specialty of this yardstick is that it measures what may be included and excluded from literature as well as decide the greatness of a particular literature; both these issues are decidable with the same yardstick. Another great quality of Shukl's yardstick is that it is available in both its theoretical and practical aspects. . . . In short, Shukl established a principle of literature based on the triad of materialism, totality and generality, which, for lack of a better term, may be given the name of 'realism'.[19]

Does this mean that both the theoretical and practical aspects of criticism form the bases of Shukl's views on the canon? If that is so, how are these two aspects related to each other? I begin this section with this question, and attempt to describe the process of canon formation in Shukl's critical project and assess the new knowledge produced by his canon-thinking within the existing languages of criticism and thus also his relations with his predecessors.

The debate on the critical endeavours of Shukl and other critics of his time has centred on which aspect of criticism is primary and more important: whether it is the theoretical or the practical. A chronological account of Shukl's critical project can help contextualize this question. After the publication of his essay on 'Sahitya' [Literature] in Saraswati in 1904, and the 1909 essay, 'Kavita kya hai?' [What is Poetry?], he inclined more towards translation. Almost thirteen years later, in 1922, his essay titled 'Kavya mein prakritik drishya' [Natural Scenes from Poetry] was published in Madhuri. Apart from these three theoretical essays, Shukl was busy translating Ernst Haeckel's Riddle of the Universe (1899) and Edwin Arnold's The Light of Asia (1879); his introduction to these two works also deserve our attention. Only after this period, while he was working on the critical editions of classical Hindi poets, did his critical acumen take root, and in 1923–24, it was from his essay-length introductions to critical editions of Tulsi, Sur and Jayasi that most of the formulas of his critical project emerged. Soon after this the theoretical concept of the 'state of popular consciousness' [janta ki chittvritti], which he devised while writing on the Bhakti poets, was elaborated, and this was continued in his magnum opus, Hindi sahitya ka itihas [The History of Hindi Literature] in 1929, originally meant to be an introduction to the Hindi Shabd Sagar [Hindi Dictionary]. Only after the completion of these works were all his other important essays, on theoretical reflection and on affect, written. It is important to note in this chronology that his early essays and his introductions to the critical editions underwent constant rewriting. In summary of his career, we can say that Shukl's critical principles developed mostly from the practical, moving towards theoretical reflection, even if in the later works, practical criticism was supported on clearly enunciated theoretical bases.

Shukl includes Jayasi, Sur and Tulsi in his canon. Among the later poets, he includes Bhushan and Babu Bhartendu Harishchandr. What were the criteria for this selection? First, we should ascertain the bases of inclusion of these poets. Shukl does not consider pre-Bhakti poetry in his canon. Jayasi is dear to Shukl because, according to him, the former tried to reduce social fragmentation through the path of devotion-based love prevalent among the masses. Jayasi appears in Shukl's conception as a Muslim Sufi poet who uses earthly love to express the transcendental, even as the poetic articulation of that love remained earthly. Shukl also honours Jayasi as a saint–poet who used love to end the acrimony between Hindus and Muslims. Characterizing the post-Kabir age as the foundation for Hindu–Muslim oneness, Shukl writes:

A century earlier Kabirdas had rebuked the extremism of both Hindus and

Muslims. . . . The common people had acknowledged the unity of 'Ram and Rahim'. . . . Having coexisted for long, Hindus and Muslims had begun to open their hearts to each other, which brought to pass a time of getting immersed and immersing others in the everyday feelings of humanity. The people's inclination shifted from fragmentation to unity. Muslims were ready to hear the Ram story of the Hindus and the Hindus, the Muslims' tales of Hamza.[20]

In the same vein, Shukl writes in *Hindi sahitya ka itihas*:

In our estimate, the tales used by the Sufis were prevalent for a long time in Hindu households, which, according to their own convenience, they manipulated. The emotional core of these tales is Hindu. Along with humans, showing flora and fauna too as bound with the string of empathy in order to create a sense of collective existence was a characteristic of Hindu romances.[21]

Apart from the theme of Hindu–Muslim oneness, what else drew Shukl to Jayasi? First, the poet's execution of the epic style. At least in the latter cantos of *Padmavat*, Shukl asserts, the epic quality has been fulsomely executed. The other quality is Jayasi's contact with the popular. The canto recounting 'Nagmati's separation' is beloved to Shukl as the poet situates Nagmati on a universal ground of affect. In his own words:

He has seen both humans and animals bound by the same life-thread through the world-pervading feeling of the heart-substance. . . . The horizon of Nagmati's state of separation in love stops not just with the human species but extends to the flora and fauna. . . . In her anguished state of separation Nagmati forgets her queenliness completely and sees herself as woman *tout court*. . . . But Jayasi shows within womankind, or at least within the generalized situation of only the Hindu wife, the development of a brilliantly scintillating form of the erotic motif of separation. . . . This is far from the shameless chatter of lovers and beloveds and is the exalted voice of separation of the Hindu wife.[22]

In contrast with the indigeneity (i.e. Hindu-ness) of *Padmavat's* poetic femininity, Shukl considers the mysticism in Jayasi of foreign provenance. He faults the poet for attempting to join the sensible with the supra-sensible; nevertheless, he considers Jayasi the poet to be close to the Indian sensibility.

In *Acharya Ramchandr Shukl aur Hindi alochna* [The Great Teacher Ramchandr Shukl and Hindi Criticism], despite disagreeing with many of Shukl's opinions on Jayasi – for example, on the anti-progressive role of those who believe in an attributeless God [*nirgun*] and the foreign origins of mysticism – Ramvilas Sharma characterizes Shukl's position on Jayasi as leaning towards a contiguity with popular elements. He writes:

> He considers Jayasi, like Kabir, to be the poet of Hindu–Muslim unity and of a comprehensive humanism. He disagrees with those who evaluate Jayasi and others through the prejudices of a community. He argues on behalf of the poets of amorous devotion saying that they are superior to the *riti*-age poets. Evaluating Jayasi on grounds of realism, he exposes the unnaturalness of the courtly poetry of both Urdu and Hindi and proclaims Jayasi to be the poet of a humanly accessible eros.[23]

The picture that emerges on comparing Shukl's views and those of Ramvilas Sharma, his prominent commentator, is that Jayasi is canonized because of his contiguity with the popular and his vision of Hindu–Muslim oneness. Shukl designates the latter half of *Padmavat* as being on the side of 'exertion towards bliss'. So why is Jayasi less dear to him than Tulsi? Or, in other words, why is Shukl unable to grant the highest place in his canon to Jayasi? Jayasi's verse does not completely fulfil the principles of epic-writing, identifying emotionally resonant locales and 'preserving the popular' [*lokrakshan*]. A Sufi allegorist, to his mind, does not represent the popular consciousness as Tulsi does. Furthermore, there is the crucial issue of propriety [*maryada*]. The 'propriety' of *Padmavat* cannot equal the propriety of the *Ramcharitmanas*. And if we argue from the other end, since poetry is a vehicle for affective communication, good poetry is that which impels us to action or endeavour, or at least radiates earthly love and beauty. The whole framework of Jayasi's poetic creation hardly keeps the realm of human endeavour in its midst, and, Shukl complains, the fundamental appearance of love in it is un-Indian and transcendental. We can conclude from this that Shukl reads Jayasi very closely using these fierce presuppositions. This is an aspect of Shukl's realist critical project. The paradox is that while he highlights the queen's forgetting of her queenliness, he does not forget to note, at the same time, that these Sufi saints borrowed from Hindu household stories and not the shameless chatter of lovers and beloveds in Persianate poetry, all in order to loftily express the anguished separation of the Hindu wife from her husband. What would happen if we were to excise the word 'Hindu' from these quotations? Would it lead to a better understanding of Jayasi? The version of Hindu–Muslim oneness that emerges from Shukl's critical project is one of equality on the basis of *Hindu* superiority. Nanddulare Vajpeyi recognizes the inherent problem of this project: 'In Shukl's ideas the prime importance is of the Hindu social system and of idealism. He gives both the appearance of a nation-wide set up.'[24] Therefore, we should not ignore this paradox that is inherent to this critical project, nor should we treat it as so synthesized that Ramchandr Shukl becomes a dialectical materialist *avant la lettre*. Just as we keep in mind, while reading Bhakti poetry, that the social crises of the time entered poetry through the idiom of Bhakti, we cannot ignore the fact that in the arguments of the Hindi reawakening, apart from progressivism, a Hinduist basis was always active too. Negating this basis will not resolve the paradox. From this paradoxicality, we can better understand the nature of Shukl's critical project.

Ramvilas Sharma points to the several drawbacks in Shukl's analysis of Jayasi: for example, the issue of mysticism and its purportedly foreign roots, its alienation from Indianness, the influence of the Nath *panthi*s on Jayasi, blaming the Sufis for Jayasi's emotive sweetness, the poet's attempt to join the sensible with the supra-sensible, etc. Despite these drawbacks, when Sharma characterizes Shukl's Jayasi as produced from the ground of realism,[25] the corollary is a disjointed picture of Jayasi in Sharma's own critique. Sharma does not clarify the underlying ground between the drawbacks and achievements of Shukl's Jayasi criticism. Thus, Sharma questions the extreme criticism of the poets of the attributeless [*nirgun*] divine and objects to Jayasi's exclusion from their category. He even reminds us how Shukl considers this set of poets to be saviours of people from subaltern groups, but rather than critique this cross-section of Shukl's thought, he simply describes it and moves on, with the result that Shukl's opposition to the attributeless divine thereby becomes weaker. Sharma attenuates the intellectual substance of the debates in Shukl's time without which we cannot comprehensively understand his critical project.

It is significant that Shukl establishes Jayasi's poetry in his canon on the idea of collectivizing the popular and the intermixing of Muslims in the vast Hindu populace. Jayasi narrates the true story of Hindu households, we are told, and instead of kings and queens, as Shukl insists, the poet speaks of the common people. In addition, Shukl insists that non-Indian Islamic poets and devotional practices accepted the superiority of the Hindus. Unsurprisingly, Shukl does not name any Hindu poet who wrote the stories of Muslim households.

Further down the canonical order, Surdas is Shukl's second most beloved poet. Shukl considers Sur to be a great poet because he preserved the survival instinct of the hopeless population of his society. Associating Sur with the older tradition of Krishn-devotion writers of erotic poetry, such as Jayadev and Vidyapati, Shukl anoints Sur as the peerless poet of Krishn worship. He writes:

The beloved milk-flow of Jayadev's divine speech, which had been subdued by the harshness of time, changed into easy popular speech and appeared in *koel* song from the mellifluous throat of Vidyapati in the mango orchards of Mithila, and further onwards flowed through the bamboo-shoot groves of Braj, irrigating desiccated hearts there. Then arose the eight lutes [*veenas*] with the seal of the maestros in musical praise of the love-sport of Lord Krishn, of which the highest pitched, the most tuneful and melodious reverberation belonged to the lute of the blind poet Surdas. . . . After showing the ungraspability of worshipping the attributeless divine, he involved himself in showing the heart-grasping aspect of devotion. He accepted only the form of God-as-love. . . . Had he wanted it, the colourful forms of the other conditions of the heart [enthusiasm etc.] could have been absorbed in Krishn, but he turned away from them. Although this enunciated identity of God is unidimensional – only as love – it proved useful in ending the listlessness due to hopelessness about life in the hearts of the people of the time. Showing the domains of beauty and music, these Krishn-worshipping Vaishnav poets instilled passion for living, or at least preserved the instinct to live.[26]

Shukl underlines the people's dejection and hopelessness due to changes in the social circumstances with the beginning of Mughal rule as he explains the advent of the Bhakti period. Here too he covers the same foundational ground in his ideas. For it is this very ground of the popular on the basis of which he includes Surdas in the canon. While Sur's verse, inspired by the principles of 'fostering' the soul [Vallabh's system of devotion], appears useful to Shukl for disseminating emotions in the popular consciousness through the path of a fusion-based devotion, it does not belong on the side of ethical exertion based in the common good. Sur appears to be 'establishing the path towards the solitary contemplation of devotion'. Sur's love is 'best in the world and lies beyond it'. The occasions of life in Sur's description of love and separation are enticing to Shukl, the pastoral scenes of a cow-herding culture are dear to him, Sur's deep understanding of the psychology of boys appeals to him, and the business of love in subtlety attracts him. Overall, Sur's contiguity with the popular endears him to Shukl.

The other principle of Shukl's canon criticism is his opposition to mysticism and devotion to the attributeless divine. Shukl opposes the former because it cuts people off from life. Later critics, however, criticize Shukl for evicting mysticism from the poetic realm altogether. One instance of this charge appears in Nanddulare Vajpeyi's book, *Surdas*:

But a time has never come to pass that a literary authority can proclaim that only a religion- and philosophy-free poetry is the best kind of poetry. . . . A

great characteristic of our literature is that it can connect the lowest of the
lowest earthly object with the highest of the highest spiritual elements.[27]

It is a matter of debate that whatever comes within Shukl's category of
mysticism, would it all be considered to be outside of his critical realism?

In his commentary on Shukl, Ramvilas Sharma also notes in Surdas
a sensibility for preserving the social, apart from having a diverting effect
on the social. Shukl does not place Sur above Tulsi in his canon precisely
because of Sur's limited philosophical vision and lack of any passion for
what Shukl calls social preservation. Disagreeing with this view, Sharma
identifies anti-feudal values in Sur's poetry:

> That Sur was indifferent to the problems of his time and lacked the feel for
> social improvement, cannot be defended. Sur has given an artistic description
> of Krishn's yellow trailing cloth and his arm raised high as he leaves his chariot
> and runs with a discus in his hand. . . . The love for the milk-maids challenges
> popular creed and clan honour. . . . [All these] surfaced after breaking the
> bonds of race, caste and property in feudal society. This love tramples on the
> proprieties of clan honour, popular creed, and the polarity of sin–virtue and
> its victory call is a challenge to feudal society itself.[28]

For Shukl, in contrast, it is not this love which preserves the people, but
propriety or the popular ethic. If Sur's anti-feudalism, for Sharma, is reflected
in the poet's opposition to notions of social honour and the popular creed,
does he apply the same parameters to judge Shukl's celebration of Tulsi? On
his part, Sharma sees in Tulsi the same anti-feudalism. But if both poets are
anti-feudal in outlook, what becomes of the vaunted notions of honour and
propriety identified especially with Tulsi? In any case, Shukl gives precedence
to Tulsi over Sur on the question of preserving the social. There are several
levels to Tulsi's presupposition and role as social protector. Despite the
element of anti-feudalism in his poetic outlook, his social protectionism
cannot be accommodated completely within that anti-feudalism.

Tulsidas is the first poet of choice in Shukl's canon. Among his reasons
for considering Tulsi a great poet, the first is his sensitivity towards social
preservation. In his critical project, Shukl always insists on the view that
the best poetry connects the reader with the realm of endeavour. In his
famous essay 'Kavita kya hai?' [What is Poetry?] (1909; 1929), he considers
poetry to be that which drives man's heart from the narrow circle of selfish
interests towards the emotional ground of common life. According to him,
the transmission of emotion in poetry leads to an expansion of the realm of
action. In such a situation, the poet finds sorrow in the sorrows of the social

and happiness in the happiness of the social.[29] But in this too, Shukl considers worthy that domain of action that is aroused by poetry which stands in for resistance against injustice, notwithstanding failure or success. In two important essays, titled '*Kavya mein lokmangal ki sadhanavastha*' [The State of Amenities for Social Bliss in Poetry] and '*Anand ki siddhavastha*' [The State of Perfection of Happiness], on the topic of the emergence of poetry, Shukl raises an argument against Leo Tolstoy and Rabindranath Tagore, attributing their compassion to aestheticism, mysticism and Christianity. He writes that

the emergence of poetry cannot be thought of solely in terms of the soft evocation of feelings of love as held by the followers of Tolstoy or some other aesthetes. If the feeling of compassion lies unarticulated in the folds of the structure of ire and other fierce and terrible feelings, it is the manifestation of absolute beauty.[30]

With reference to Tagore, he writes:

By reading together the above quotes by the honourable Rabindranth, it becomes clear that he aims at a poetic ground that vocalizes the perfected state of happiness, i.e. the realm of enjoyment. It has already been noted that it is on this ground, through auspiciousness, radiance, profusion, brightness, softness, etc., that emotional diversion is planned. Choosing auspiciousness and radiance on the emotional side and, through their unusual employment, preparing a stock of wondrous emotion, and, on the side of emotions, presenting the wondrousness of sensitivity and suggestion – these have been the aim of the old and new adherents of art-for-art's-sake.[31]

Shukl finds the ideal of social preservation in his favourite poet, Tulsi, and among the latter's works, in the most beloved of books, *Ramcharitmanas*. Now, with Tulsi as the context, we must look at the range of the notion of social preservation in Shukl's artefactual criticism. From our earlier discussion on social preservation in the context of Surdas, we can extend that context here, and quote at length Shukl's meditation on social preservation in praise of the Chitrakut episode from the *Ramcharitmanas*:

1. Let us take the relation between the ruler and the ruled. The entire populace of Ayodhya leaves all worldly cares aside and walks behind Bharat single-mindedly, like him, for the love of Ram, and then on witnessing Ram in Chitrakut, it wants to remain there for fourteen years out of sheer joy.
2. Bharat's other-worldly love and feeling of devotion towards his eldest brother is reflected everywhere and is the basis of everything.

3. For fear of appearing arrogant before the holy men and teachers, Bharat and Ram shy away from even expressing their views.

4. Ram's affectionate greeting of each of the mothers conveys not just his politesse, but also manifests the softness and purity of his inner state.

5. On seeing the married daughter walking behind her husband, when Janak expresses his joy – 'The daughter brings purity to both the families. Everyone says: her pleasing fame dazzles the world' – he is arrested by a pious feeling.

6. Both Bharat and Ram, declaring Janak as being in the place of the father, leave all responsibility on his shoulders.

7. Sita*ji* is sitting with her mother at her father's dwelling. In the meanwhile night falls and she faces a dilemma – 'Sita doesn't say anything, hesitance in her heart – to spend the night here is not good' – her husband sleeps on the ground in an ascetic's garb while the wife is away from him in royal comfort, that is the conundrum.

8. Since Kaushalya and others have arrived, Sita has been engrossed in their hospitality.

9. The heart-stealing image of the honour given to the Brahmin class by the ruling class is matched by the reflection of the Brahmin class's eagerness to work for the interests of the state and the world.

10. The boatman's paying obeisance to the holy man from afar and the holy man's embracing him, both illuminate the excellence of etiquette.

11. How tender and good is everyone's behaviour towards the tribals of the forests, such as the Kols and Kirats.[32]

The instances of social preservation mentioned by Shukl are worth examining to understand his procedure of argument. For him, that society is ideal which has love between the ruler and the governed rather than opposition between them. *Pace* Ramvilas Sharma, how is Ram's realm, as described in the *Ramcharitmanas*, not feudal in nature? And if it is so, why is Shukl so given over to this ideal? Second, the kind of family Shukl supports is the joint family. In it, the relations between teacher, mother, father, brother, husband, wife, in-laws and natal family are all pre-determined and incontestable. In this imagination of the joint family, oppression is tucked under hollow ideals, personhood is taken away, and patriarchy and dominance are entrenched within the family. What kind of a social structure is it that Shukl proposes? Is it not precisely the result of feudal social relations?

Alongside this, the friendship between the Brahmin class and the ruling class, and the slotting of Shudras and sages according to their caste rank, testify to Shukl's support for the caste system. Both groups behave according to their pre-set propriety: this is a situation that pleases Shukl. Today we know how the caste system enslaves people already at the margins. Does Shukl, then, see the path to social preservation leading to the improvement of the lives of these people on the margins through the beauty of action? In an essay on Goswami Tulsidas, Ramvilas Sharma, writing against Shukl's views, is forced to concede: 'The one work of Shukl's which has the highest number of inconsistencies and contradictions is his book on Tulsidas.'[33]

Despite these shortcomings, it is necessary to situate his preference for the caste system and the ethics of propriety in the totality of his intellectual project. The decades between the 1920s and 1940s, in which the greater part of his thought, from politics and society to Hindi literature, emerges, the main talk is about 'propriety'. M.K. Gandhi's entry into Indian politics ushered in a particular kind of ethics. His politics had the undertones of propriety, exemplarity and struggle. In this milieu, along with its anti-colonialist essence, the goal of eradicating social ills also became central to the pioneers of the Hindi reawakening during these decades. The contradiction is that in their fight against social ills in order to resist the British, these intellectuals had to turn backwards and seek to adopt its values and systems in the shadow of the ancient village society.

Tulsi is included in the canons proposed by both Ramchandr Shukl and Ramvilas Sharma, but their reasons for including him differ. Here we may recall the version of Tulsi included in the canons proposed by western scholars, mentioned in the previous chapter. Tulsi appears there as a proponent of Christian mercy, ethics, propriety and social harmony. Shukl excised many of the elements of this view. He focused attention on 'social bliss' in Tulsi's poetry in place of the colonialist understanding of Christianity and Christian mercy. He notices in Tulsi's poetry the night-wandering demons burning in Ram's death-kindling anger, and the belief in war, loss and sacrifice for establishing justice against all injustices. This belief is born out of the anti-colonialism of the nationalist movement. In this regard, Ramvilas Sharma's view is more than correct where he associates Shukl with the armed revolutionaries, and, referencing Baikunth Shukl's book, he describes the intellectual affinity between Shukl and Chandrashekhar Azad. Bhagat Singh too belonged to the extremist stream during the same phase of the nationalist struggle, and was the author of such articles as 'Why I Am an Atheist' and 'Communal Riots and Their Solutions'. Shukl concurs with the revolutionary stream only on select matters: for example, the peasants' struggle. The totalizing theories developed by the revolutionary stream in opposition to Brahminism, communalism and feudalism come close to Marxist ideas. Shukl, however, does not arrive at this point of concurrence. In this inability, we find him only voicing the dominant current of nationalism of the time, which prioritized anti-imperialism at all cost. This is similar to Ramvilas Sharma's stubborn attempt to keep 'anti-colonialism' topmost in his critical project, at the cost of consistency in argument.

As for the internal contradictions in Shukl, Shivkumar Mishr articulates them in the form of a contemporary binary between Shukl's ritual beliefs and his critical judgement:

> In effect, this view of society which he found in the form of traditional descent and rituals, he found both assimilated in his blood. Although his intellect sometimes releases him from ritual bondage, he is unable to completely sever himself from it. The rituals are so powerful that they keep flaring out. At such moments he not only ends up strongly condemning arguments for human equality and social equity, but also appears to joke about them.[34]

The central basis of Shukl's canon-thinking is opposition to poetry of the *riti* period. In his history-writing, psychological essays, practical and theoretical criticisms, in short in his entire oeuvre, Shukl cites the *riti*-period poetry only in negative terms. Later critics such as Ramvilas Sharma and Manager Pandey view his anti-*riti* position as a form of anti-aestheticism based on his notion of 'social bliss' [*lokmangal*]. According to them, since it ordains the happiness of the people at large and is this-worldly in its opposition to mysticism, Shukl's theory of social bliss becomes a counter to aestheticism/*riti* poetry. On the same issue, in his book *Alochna ki samajikta* [The Sociality of Criticism], Manager Pandey situates Shukl's opposition to the *riti* period as a part of his nationalist position. In Pandey's words:

> His [Shukl's] struggle to oppose the *riti* period is part of the nationalist struggle. This is a result of the desire to see the concurrent development of Hindi literature and the nationalist movement. On the one hand, he derives the energy for the struggle against the *riti* period from the popular awakening of the Bhakti period, and on the other, from the new literary consciousness of the Bhartendu period. He considered the movement of literature on the *riti* path to be a sign of barbarity.[35]

At different places in his writings, Ramchandr Shukl opposes embroidered and ornamental art, and considers only that feeling worthy of poetry which leads to the highest ground of action. In his remarks on Bihari, for example, the very thing that rankles Shukl is that the former's poetic feeling does not reach the highest ground. In his *Hindi sahitya ka itihas* [History of Hindi Literature], while referring to the *riti* period in the general introduction chapter, he clarifies his position:

The poet's vision did not turn to the heterogeneity of nature, the various ponderables of life and the many secrets of the world. It was bounded in one way and became reduced somewhat. Its domain narrowed, its voice stream began to flow only in manufactured drains, due to which various perceptible and imperceptible contents of experience became saturated with sentiment [ras] and remained unmanifested. The other result was that few occasions remained for the expression of the poet's individuality.[36]

Ramvilas Sharma identifies Shukl's positions against riti poetry with the ideology of anti-feudalism. He believes that since, in this period, poetry had taken refuge in the feudal courts and was being written for the pleasure of the feudatories, its relationship with society was broken. According to him, Shukl was cognizant of the changes in the class character of poetry: 'He [Shukl] clarifies time and again the narrow class basis of the poetry of the riti period; rather than sympathizing with this poetry, he makes a stringent critique of it.'[37] In this way, Sharma defines aestheticism or art for art's sake in terms of its feudal values by pitting aestheticism against 'social bliss'.

As we have reached thus far, we must investigate the nature of Shukl's so-called anti-feudal thinking. If we assume for a while that Shukl was opposed to poetry patronized by the court for its class basis, can we use the same argument in relation to the primeval and heroic periods of Hindi literature? We do notice that despite assessing it as courtly poetry, Shukl does not consider poetry of the primeval period as unappetizing as the poetry of the riti period. Describing the background of the ancient period in his History, Shukl praises the heroism and valour of the battles between contemporary rulers. In this regard, he redeploys the same notion of cultural struggle, i.e. between Hindus and Muslims, in order to assess the traditional heroic tales:

> Bisaldev moved northwards in order to evict the Muslims from the land of the Aryans. . . . Similarly, after the killing of Maharaj Prithviraj and the conquest of Delhi and Ajmer by the Muslims, for a long time many independent Hindu rulers in Rajputana battled against the Muslims. . . . The era of poets appearing in the court of King Bhoj and praising his generosity in lengthy verse and earning lakhs of rupees therefrom was long over. . . . In those times the bard or balladeer who wrote with intricate tropes of the valour, victory, and capture of enemy-women by some ruler, or went to the battlefields to instil the passion of courage in the hearts of the warriors, was honoured.[38]

It turns out that Shukl's standard of judgement is the same here as the one he uses in analysing the riti-period poetry. In the quotation above, he does not devalue the poetry of bards and balladeers who wrote about war and duty since it predisposes the reader towards the domain of action. One ruler's war against another and the struggles of Hindu rulers against Muslim rulers are characteristic of that age. This poetry fulfils one of the criteria proposed by Shukl, that poetry inspire man to fight injustice and connect him with the realm of action, but he acknowledges that the scope of this poetry is narrow. Since his understanding of the social [*lok*] is much vaster than this poetry, while giving importance to it Shukl does not deploy it in his discussion of the fundamentals of his canon. Following the same basis and criteria, Shukl finds the fullest development of this tendency in the work of the *riti*-period poet, Bhushan. Bhushan also wrote poems about his royal patrons, Shivaji and Chhatrasal, but Shukl values his work for another reason:

> But the exploits of the two protagonists which Bhushan turned into subjects of his heroic verse were of two historically famous warriors ever prepared to crush injustice and who were thus defenders of the Hindu faith. The devotion and honour for them established in the hearts of Hindus existed at that time and continued, only increasing, in subsequent ages. This was how Bhushan's words became the property of the people's hearts. . . . The enthusiasm with which the Hindu people remember these two warriors can be found in the poetry of Bhushan. He is the representative poet of the Hindu collectivity.[39]

If we compare now the ways in which the poets of ancient heroic poetry and of *riti*-period heroic verse are both similar and different in their work, we may begin to recognize the bases of Shukl's canons of criticism and literature. His conception of feudalism and imperialism pre-dates that of Ramvilas Sharma, and therefore the extent of his anti-feudalism is markedly different. Otherwise we cannot view Shivaji and Chhatrasal as anti-feudal figures. Are they protectors of the Hindu people or the feudal class? It is possible that a better explanation was available with Sharma on this question.

As for the anti-*riti* viewpoint, Manager Pandey is right in arguing that it should be contextualized in Shukl's relationship to the nationalist struggle. We may better understand Shukl's opposition to the *riti* period in view of the kind of nation imagined by the Hindi reawakening and the manner in which the medieval period was conceived in this imagination. The composition of Shukl's view of the post-medieval period also includes the search for past glory according to which Mughal conquerors damaged Indian cultural glory. It may be more instructive to turn to Muktibodh in order to understand this debate.

The *riti*-period poetry should be conceived in the same way as Muktibodh conceived of the rise of the Bhakti period, i.e. based on social classes and class-based turmoil among them, if we are not to support the blanket dismissal by the anti-*riti* canonical thesis. If ever a literary history is written of Hindi and Urdu together, both of which developed alongside historically, would the *riti* period emerge in the same light in which it has been treated by critics? What would be the critical assessment of a poet such as Mir Taqi 'Mir' from Urdu, who combined serious style with unabashed erotic address?

Now we turn to a discussion of two canonical essays by Shukl, acknowledged for their directly political content and intense arguments over them by later critics. The first essay is titled '*Bharat ko kya karna chahiye*' (What India Should Do), and it was published in the February issue of *Hindustan Review* in 1905. In this essay woven around concern for political reform, Shukl expresses his view of how to improve contemporary conditions in India. He considers social reform to be the key issue and the first step towards political advancement. He writes: 'In fact, we have the simultaneous need for a social reformer, politician, activist, poet and pedagogue. . . . In view of utility, the first thing we must attend to is the task of removing social ills.'[40] Shukl considers child marriage and illiteracy to be the major social ills in the society of colonial India. What is illiteracy, and what is the usefulness of education in an India that is enslaved? These are questions Shukl poses as part of his argument. He refuses to confine learning to the domains of education and employment, and connects it with the project of national liberation:

> By education I mean the communication of our leaders' views about ordinary matters to illiterate people, so that when the time comes their [the illiterate people's] support [for the leadership] is not missing. Every villager must know why he is paid less when labour demand increases, and, in effect, every Indian must know clearly why his country is getting more and more impoverished.[41]

Further on in this short essay, Shukl takes aim at the British conspiracy to destroy indigenous Indian industry, and exposes the bases of the systems of justice and equality under imperialism. He exposes the false claim of equality made by the British and the exploitation of the Indian people that lies behind it:

> India's economic situation demands that before anything else its industry should be transformed and refined, and this is most dependent on what we call technical education. . . . Imperialism has been the motivating force of British rule in India. . . . They [the British] have created a situation wherein not a shred of their own British imagination can be seen in the system of Indian administration. There is no doubt that they preserve the form but

annihilate its essence. . . . The *swadeshi* movement . . . has been launched to save lakhs of people from starvation and to provide employment to lakhs of people wandering about due to lack of regular employment.[42]

In order to clarify the background of this essay, we may turn to two other writings by Shukl. We have already seen above that the foundation of the Indian reawakening and of Indian nationalism was laid in opposition to British colonialism. Alongside, it should be remembered that within the emerging middle class, there was a contradiction between devotion to the regime and devotion to the nation. Also, the energies of anti-feudalism were largely hidden under the religious garb of various social reform movements. Before Shukl's essay, the most important voice of anti-imperialism in Indian intellectual thought was Bhartendu's essay, 'How would Indian progress happen?' Even in the confusions of a transitional period in modern Indian history, Bhartendu pointed towards some fundamental issues.

This essay by Bhartendu was first presented as a speech at the Dadri fair in Ballia (present-day Uttar Pradesh), in 1884. In the speech, he praises the justice-dispensing British administration, exhorts people to take advantage of the system, harks back to ancient glories, excoriates Indians for their laziness, worries about population growth, propagates ideas of religious and social reform, asks Muslims to coexist peacefully with Hindus, speaks about the need for employment, and, in the end, announces that the entire population of India is Hindu. This is not the occasion for an independent analysis of the essay, but an allegory catches our attention here in which, using a folktale, Bhartendu tries to understand the gradations of exploitation: 'Three frogs were sitting piled one on top of the other. The topmost frog says, "fancy schmancy". The middle frog utters, "boo hoo". The bottommost frog cries out, "we're goners". Thus, the condition of the common folk of India is this: "we're goners".'[43] Bhartendu's allegory describing the various layers of exploitation of imperialism is reminiscent of Mao Tse-tung's famous allegory in which Mao refers to the mountains that sit atop the Chinese people. In this allegory, atop the common people are the exploiters of the feudal classes who in turn are exploited by the British imperialists, and the people are ground down under this double weight. Although Bhartendu does not clearly designate the middle section, the tone of the essay suggests that the princely states and the feudal class are the ones in the middle. The issue of how the middle section would contribute to national liberation became controversial in later years. The controversy also pertained to who belonged to this middle section. Below we will see the extent to which Ramchandr Shukl agrees with this allegory.

Several key writings by nationalist thinkers come to our notice if we trace backwards the tradition in which Shukl wrote his major socio-political works. Bhartendu had already written the maxim, 'Under British rule happiness is well arranged / But it is extremely humiliating that all the wealth goes abroad.' Around the same time, in 1886, Dadabhai Naoroji wrote *Poverty and Un-British Rule in India*, which was the first work to propose the theory of 'drain of wealth'. It calculated the value of wealth that was looted from India and sent to Britain. But it is also the case that Naoroji had already written *The Benefits of British Rule for India* (1871), in which he petitioned the British for wholesale social reform. In the transition spell from regime worship to nation worship, Sakharam Ganesh Deuskar elaborated on Naoroji's work in his *Desher katha* (The State of the Country; translated into Hindi by Padarkar). The book powerfully delineates the economic exploitation under imperial rule. It speaks of the devastation of the peasantry, economic loot in the name of development, the destruction of local industry and the value of the wealth looted from India. In this work of 1904, the ideology of the Swadeshi movement is the same as in Shukl's last-mentioned essay:

> No one can deny that these days Indians are thinking deeply about the development of the indigenous [*swadeshi*] craftsman. People in Bengal have vowed, within all possible limits, not to touch foreign-made goods. People in the provinces of Bombay, Madras, middle India and Punjab, following the Bengalis, have joined in this vow to boycott foreign goods.[44]

Both these exemplary writings from the early years of the twentieth century signpost the anti-imperialism of the Indian intellectual tradition. Shukl's critical acumen was aimed in the same direction. But what was this stream of anti-imperialism doing on the front of anti-feudalism? It did not pay considerable attention to the lives and struggles of the workers, dispossessed sharecroppers, peasants, women, minority groups, the aboriginals and other groups at the margins. Under these circumstances, many questions were posed both from within and without the nationalist movement, which refused to see the panorama of anti-imperialism as one of unity, and issues of religion and caste were often raised in disagreement with the orientation of the anti-imperialist movement. For example, Jotiba Phule (1827–1880) directed questions of caste, women, peasants and Brahminism at the anti-imperialists. These questions strongly interrupted and negated the project of the reawakening for the quest of past glory. In later decades, B.R. Ambedkar sharpened this stream of thought. By the time of the Poona Pact of 1932 between Gandhi and Ambedkar, these questions had taken on a radical urgency and sharpness which shaped the nature of the polity that emerged after independence.

With this founding statement of Shukl's project, we can move on to his other important essay, which he wrote for the *Express* and which was published from Bankipore, Patna in 1922. This essay, titled 'Non-Cooperation and Non-Mercantile Classes' (written in English), is the reason why both Ramvilas Sharma and Veer Bharat Talwar have connected Shukl with the nationalist struggle and given an engaging analysis of his intellectual project. In the essay, Shukl divides India's social structure into two classes: mercantile and non-mercantile. In the mercantile class are included the new and old merchants, the imperialists and their Indian agents. In the non-mercantile class are included political activists and the peasantry. In his own words: 'The division of the mass of people and their interests into commercial and non-commercial classes is as true today as it was two thousand years ago.'[45] Shukl unapologetically proves his view by reference to a lineage-determined human psychology and tradition, that for centuries Indian society has been divided between these two classes alone, and, he declares, this division was not inherently repressive in nature. He identifies disruptions in the system with the coming of the British:

> Before the arrival of the British, both these groups were content with themselves. One class was devoted to private schemes of wealth accumulation, while the other played a primary role in its everyday affairs in providing soldiers and public service to the state. . . . The ruler could never be the merchant. The merchant could never be the ruler. . . . In the form of the East India Company, the odious mercantilism of Europe entered India and the harmony that was prevailing in society thanks to its binary division was thrown into disarray.[46]

Shukl prefers the old, self-enclosed society where there is a minimum of social upheaval, where one group cannot trade places with another and where 'harmony' prevails. This vision of harmony evokes the caste system, in which the labour of each person is determined in advance of their birth. Shukl argues that before the coming of the British, capital had no effect on political rule; in his own words, the positions of ruler and merchant could not be exchanged. This is the founding premise of his essay. On this basis, Shukl goes on to analyse the effects of the arrival of the East India Company on Indian society. He argues that

> the permanence of the relationship between land and the agricultural classes[47] vanished and they were left in a state of gradually increasing immiseration. . . . Because of legal complexities, litigation around land-related matters

became such an unavoidable feature that after meeting the demands of the government nothing much remained with the middle landholder/zamindar.[48]

If, as Shukl narrates, the economic policies of the East India Company led to the dispersal of the harmony that prevailed in India before its arrival, and generated profits for the mercantile class and destroyed the non-mercantile class, what were the changes that followed in the social structure? The government still levied a huge amount of revenue according to the old custom among the zamindars. This led to destruction of the peasantry. On the other hand, the moneylender and the businessman did not give any revenue to the government and enjoyed life as usual. According to Shukl, the Company was bent upon destroying the non-mercantile classes even as it was benevolent towards the mercantile classes. He signposts the destruction of indigenous industry. Taking aim at the practice of buying up landholdings by the newly formed banker class under the auspices of the East India Company, he pleads for reservations in employment for the non-mercantile classes. In the previous essay, he had narrated that faced by a total rout, the non-mercantile social strata jumped at employment opportunities and thus formed the 'educated middle class'. The petition for reservations was made particularly for people associated with the 'warrior' (*kshatriya*) profession:

> For those who don't partake in political power, or those who do not belong to ruling families, to be awarded royal titles is, for the majority of Hindus, a matter of immense humiliation to their national glory. . . . In Uttar Pradesh and Avadh, it is not clear when and how the *kshatriya* families, whose ancestors were actual rulers, lost their power. . . . Generally speaking, they are the representatives of good ancient families and their princely states were a result of grants from some medieval sovereign or of victory over somebody else's domain [*Report on the Constitutional Reform*]. Along with an investigation into their conditions, it is necessary to keep the doors of the martial profession open to them. . . . It is a necessary duty of the government to provide reservations in the armed forces for such princely states.[49]

Shukl is clearly worried about the interests of the old zamindars and the rulers of princely states. While he demands reservations in employment for this class, he does not ask anything for other groups, such as peasants and workers, among the non-mercantile classes. Although he mentions the deprivation of these two groups, his generous wish for reservations is expressed only for the warriors or '*kshatriya*'. On this count, Shukl goes on to clarify his views on the condition of workers and peasants. He writes:

There is no insuperable wall between peasant and zamindar. A peasant can become a zamindar and vice versa. They themselves can sense that the real purpose behind these actions is the weakening of the whole rural population and turn them into impoverished peasants in such a way that no opportunity remains with them to acquire social prestige and dignity. . . . Agitators are busy rousing a large majority of the gullible workers to maximum turmoil by their passionate speeches. In effect, their terroristic and uncouth activities exploit similarly both peasant and zamindar. In a situation where scarcity of work already causes great worry amongst the farmers and obstructs agricultural production to a great degree, how humane is it to go there and exacerbate their difficulties? We use the word 'zamindar' to approximately mean landowner but we never consider small-scale farmers who, despite being conscious of their nobility, are conducting their life with great difficulty on the most minimal income. . . . They are those who have become the victims of our agitators' largesse. The bankers' establishments in cities have sucked in a large part of the worker population, which is why peasants and zamindars are at a loss to continue agricultural work. . . . The attempt to completely disrupt the supply of work for peasants is very destructive! . . . May we not consider such agitators agents of the more powerful city folks?[50]

This picture is reminiscent of Bhartendu's allegory of the three frogs that suggests double exploitation of the common people of India. In his view, the topmost rung in the circle of exploitation is occupied by the imperialists, who exploit both the Indian feudatories and princelings and the common people. The feudatories, despite being themselves exploited under imperialism, exploit the Indian people. Shukl makes this difference two-tiered. His zamindars are middle peasants who are as exploited under imperialism as the common people. This is the non-mercantile class. The other class is mercantile, in which the imperialists and their agents and brokers, who are Indian moneylenders and bankers, do not experience the exploitation of imperialism but, rather, flourish under it.

Ramvilas Sharma debates Veer Bharat Talwar on precisely this aspect of Shukl's class politics in his book *Acharya Ramchandr Shukl aur Hindi alochna* (The Great Teacher Ramchandr Shukl and Hindi Criticism). His argument is set up to conclude that Shukl wants to prepare a united front of peasants and middle zamindars against imperialism and its local agents. Veer Bharat Talwar pronounces Shukl to be a partisan of the zamindars, in opposition to which Sharma paints a picture of the latter in a reduced state, turning into peasants, after the arrival of the English East India Company. Based on Rajani Palme Dutt's *India Today* and Marx's articles on India in the *New York Daily Tribune*, he argues that old feudalism was less pernicious than the new kinds of exploitation. In this connection, he discusses the devastation of zamindars and peasants, and the birth and flourishing of a new class of zamindars and usurers.

We need not engage here in a discussion about society before the British arrival in which Ramvilas Sharma notes the development of mercantile capitalism. Manager Pandey takes issue with this theory of Sharma's.[51] This discussion will emerge later when we assess Sharma's standards of canonization. In the present context, Shukl successfully signposts both imperialist exploitation and the exploitativeness of the business class of the country. He is correct to conclude that the new class of bankers and moneylenders were gaining landowning rights and marginalizing the agricultural class, but the real issue, according to him, lay elsewhere. There is some difficulty in his analysis of the internal class differentiations of the non-mercantile class and the determination of their situation. In other words, if we were to assume that Shukl's project is to create a frontline of zamindars, peasants and workers against imperialism and the Indian compradors, then the next question that confronts him is: who is going to be the leader among the three? In the long quotation above we encountered Shukl's opinion about the workers who demand more benefits for themselves, and abandon agriculture and migrate to the city for higher income, under incitement from agitators. (Here we may recall from Premchand's novel *Godan*, the middle zamindar Rai Sahib, Hori who is not a zamindar-turned-peasant but a peasant on the way to becoming a worker, and Hori who is on his way to the city from the village.) Thus, the working class cannot provide leadership to the frontline because they are themselves misled and are causing harm to the social movement. The second class is that of the peasants. Shukl removes the distinction between peasants and zamindars; he maintains that it is their combined class which will lead the movement while its association with workers will strengthen it. Although he is able to remove the class barrier between peasants and zamindars, the same does not happen between peasants and workers. In this way the composite picture of the anti-imperialist frontline appears thus: at the helm are the zamindars who are turning into peasants but whose 'nobility' remains, then come the peasants, followed by the workers. In the same context, Ramvilas Sharma invokes Mao's formulation of an anti-imperialist front. But wasn't that front formed based on the combined interests of the peasants and the workers? Did Mao too consider the workers, as Shukl does, to be the propagators of 'terroristic and uncouth activities' and being misled by agitators? The sum of this view is that although the united front proposed by Shukl included peasants and workers, his sympathies lay with the zamindars and the middle zamindars-turning-into peasants.

Apart from its exposition of class politics, this essay written in the 1930s also proposes new ways of thinking about the relations between literature and politics. We have witnessed how, prior to Shukl, Indian nationalism in literary criticism developed through the ideological goals of anti-imperialism, reform and glorification of the past. Shukl consecrated the viewpoint of the foundational classes of this nation within literature. These are the classes he called the 'non-mercantile class'. According to him, within the contemporary political scenario, the nationalist movement under the leadership of M.K. Gandhi was moving in the direction of the interests of the mercantile class, which only highlights the importance of the non-mercantile class to the movement. In this manner he identifies the masses living in India's villages as the moving force of the independence movement.

At the beginning of this chapter we noted, in the context of Shukl's thinking on canon-building, that a deep attraction to a peasant-centric, familial rural structure and a passion for the protection of 'propriety' were embedded features of his analysis. These positions led him towards a theoretical investigation of the non-mercantile class. In Shukl's investigations, there is room for the revival of ancient things as well as a critical desire for the new. He is able to pierce the veil of imperialist exploitation because of his intellectual curiosity regarding both western and eastern knowledges, and his affinity with villages (which is an aspect of his nationalistic presuppositions). From this vantage point, we can further gloss his project for 'social bliss'.

In summary, Shukl's analysis completes the imagination of the nation and throws into relief its inter-struggling classes. It was necessary for a nation sculpting its identity in opposition to imperialism to sharpen its self-definition. It is this concern that is embedded in Shukl's canon-building project. From his point of departure in canon-thinking, we arrive at his one-time disciple, Nanddulare Vajpeyi, and Hazari Prasad Dwivedi who argued for the inclusion of hitherto excluded authors, subjectivities and classes in the Hindi canon.

NANDDULARE VAJPEYI: CANONICAL TRANSFORMATION

The Hindi canon undergoes a sea change when Nanddulare Vajpeyi arrives on the scene of criticism. As we have seen earlier, the task of measuring Shukl's canon with the yardstick of contemporariness was accomplished by his disciple, Vajpeyi. Although Nanddulare Vajpeyi worked on the poetry of Sur and wrote a book on it, and edited the Gita Press edition of Tulsi's *Ramcharitmanas* from Gorakhpur,[52] his true energy (and newness) lay in debating with his contemporary writers and literary criticism from the past. Therefore, his book *Hindi alochna: bisvin sadi* [Hindi Criticism: The Twentieth Century] is a milestone.

In Vajpeyi's work, the concept of canon is clarified. He includes sixteen writers in his Hindi canon among who are all the major poets of the Dwivedi age, *Chhayavad* (romanticism; lit. 'chiaroscuro') and the later progressivist–experimentalist poets. Apart from these, the introduction of the book mentions several other writers. But at heart he is the critic who marks the transition from the Dwivedi age to *Chhayavad*. Accordingly, it is appropriate to consider him as the vanguard critic of *Chhayavad*. In constructing his canon, he falls upon the standards of the Dwivedi age, establishes the credentials of *Chhayavad* and maintains a somewhat 'agonistic' attitude towards progressivism. In the field of canon criticism, his significant works are on Ramchandr Shukl and Jaishankar Prasad.

When Vajpeyi began writing in the field of criticism, Shukl was a towering presence. It was not only difficult to propose a new canon without grappling with Shukl's canon theorization, but also without it the canon's viability could be questioned. In short, Vajpeyi accepted these challenges and wrote three essays on Shukl (in 1931, 1940 and 1941). These essays are proof of his critical acumen and attest to his prominent role in the process of Hindi canon formation.

The backbone of Shukl's critical discrimination is 'social bliss', which he derives by manipulating the *ras* theory of Indian aesthetics and adjusting it to his own sense of historical reality. In his very first essay on Shukl (written in 1931), Vajpeyi questions the idea of *ras* and the more idiosyncratic 'social bliss'. Referring to the tradition of *ras*-based thinking, Vajpeyi follows other schools of criticism in associating it with the *riti* period. Just as other schools in the past pushed poetry on to the *riti* way, so did the *ras* school.

Shukl had refitted the *ras* principle and raised it to the highest ground of 'social bliss'. Vajpeyi is not convinced by this move. He holds a new view of criticism for the sake of creativity in the modern age in opposition to his teacher, and finds Shukl's theory to be inadequate. He writes:

> In the modern age, the attempt is to understand the ordered development of the poet's intellect and art, to acquaint ourselves with his personality and circumstances, and to draw a synthetic picture of his oeuvre. Firm principles of poetic commentary have been established and the science of commentary is also coming into being. . . . As psychology matures, it is becoming more

useful to poetic interpretation. The modern commentator cannot benefit much from the analytic process of the *ras* system. . . . Coordinating the social ethic [*lokdharm*] with the ancient principle, Shukl definitely gives it a refined form, but he is unable to establish it on the ground of art, psychology and progress. He ignores the crucial devices of poetry, the mental faculties and social consciousness in favour of the one principle. The popular ethic too turns out to be a static exposition of the concept.[53]

Thus Vajpeyi puts on trial Shukl's *ras* principle signalling the values of modernity and progress on grounds of artistic practice.

We know by now that according to Shukl, it is through generalization of the effects of the triggers of poetic feeling [*alamban*] that man is inspired away from the field of moods towards the field of action. This is the foundation of his concept of 'social bliss'. Vajpeyi's contention against this view is that the edifice of 'social bliss' can only be stood on the basis of epic verse. This vast concept cannot be operationalized through songs and short lyric verse as it can be in epic verse, he argues. Identifying the reason for this, Vajpeyi notes that Shukl's critical moves are a reply primarily to the epic-verse writers of the Bhakti period, and thus his principle of 'social bliss' works very well there, but when he evaluates modern creative writing through the same principle, it leads to problems. The importance given to D.L. Roy against Rabindranath Tagore, for example, is an anomaly precisely of such a critical move by Shukl. For the same reason, his evaluation of romantic *Chhayavad* poetry too appears to miss the mark.

Further in his critique of Shukl, Vajpeyi makes the second point that in his formulation of it, he reduces 'expressionism' (*abhivyanjanavad*) to a single dimension. Highlighting the importance of stressing the mindscape of poetry, Vajpeyi writes:

Shukl's notion of the social ethic cannot encompass the range of progressive works. Because of its convention-boundedness it is unable to recognize good poetry. The reason for this is that in praise of this principle Shukl completely neglects the determinate and intellectual devices of poetry. In addition, he ignores time and historical development.[54]

His third point of contention against Shukl is that when the conceptual terminology of 'sensible perception' [*gochar*] and 'manifest reality' [*pratyaksh*] enters practice, it is transformed into a kind of miniaturist art. In this situation, there is no possibility of the transmission of feelings. The implication is that in Shukl's interpretation, there is very little room for the expansive feelings of the psyche. On this point of disagreement, Vajpeyi uses the notion of imagination in place of expression, and using examples from Jaishankar Prasad's poetry, establishes that the modern age is the age of expansive feelings. Therefore, in order to voice the sentiment of world brotherhood and world unity, it is necessary to go beyond the categories of the perceptible and the manifest. But do these categories have any relationship with realism? In his analysis of Prasad's *Kankal* [Skeleton], for example, Vajpeyi himself uncovers the realism contained in the poem. Does a connection then emerge between Shukl's categories of the perceived and the manifest, and the same categories used in Prasad's poem? Here, the first problem facing Vajpeyi is one that subjects Prasad the poet and Prasad the storyteller to different standards of evaluation. We can take a generous view by noting that Vajpeyi tries to elaborate Shukl's perceived and manifest. It is equally true, though, that in making this elaboration he relies all too heavily on psychologisms. Secondly, the contradiction remains unformulated: on the one hand, Shukl is a pioneer of the ideals of the Dwivedi age, and on the other, he gives enormous importance to the perceived–manifest binary in poetry. Finally, Vajpeyi leaves unaddressed the opposition between the ideal and the perceived.

In summary, Vajpeyi argues that Shukl's expressionism based on sensible perception and manifest reality, in which the logic of social bliss is derived from ethical elements within the system, in effect reduces poetry to philosophical and individualistic theses. Are we to conclude therefore that ethical tendencies should not be used in the analysis of poetry? If such be the case, how should we understand the seventh principle of the statement in *Hindi alochna: bisvin sadi* which calls upon criticism to study poetry's harmonizing of existence and the message it carries?

At another place in his oeuvre Vajpeyi discusses *ras*, and this time his emphasis falls on Shukl's individualism and pointed idealism in the interpretation of that concept. In this instance, he locates the foundational form of Shukl's socio-political consciousness in the theory of caste. Relating Shukl's creativity to his social and historical circumstances, he writes: 'The whole of Shukl's intellectualism is based on the individualistic, emotionalist and idealist ethicality of the Dwivedi age. He does not carry out a materialist analysis of society, culture or the psyche.'[55] Vajpeyi comes clean about his opposition to personalized ethics. But when he addresses the philosophical bases of Prasad's creations, he changes his tune; he sees Prasad as an individualist like John Stuart Mill and situates him within classical liberalism. In the same discussion, he also invokes the slogan of liberty, equality and fraternity, which is contemporaneous with the beginnings of the industrial revolution. Vajpeyi considers this slogan to be a kind of

materialism; therefore, he considers the individualism of Prasad's poetry to
be superior to Dwivedi-age individualism.

As far as idealism is concerned, Vajpeyi's debate with Premchand after
the publication of the *Hans* issue on autobiography is relevant here. In
that debate, how is Vajpeyi's tone less idealistic than what he condemns?
He writes, for example: 'Literature is really ethical life. . . . Where no
independent substance remains in the personhood of a person, that is the
emotional ground of supreme poetry. That is the realm of non-covetousness
and is not portrait photography.'[56] If this were indeed the case, it would be
next to impossible for the critic to reach the deep effects of personhood in
analysing a poem such as '*Aansu*' [Tears, by Jaishankar Prasad]. Similarly, an
interpretation of Suryakant Tripathi Nirala's '*Main ne main shaili apnayi*' [I
adopted the I-style] cannot be made coherent if we follow Vajpeyi's credo.
Won't establishing the individuality of the individual on the higher ground
of the ideal obtain the same didacticism of the age of Mahavir Prasad
Dwivedi to which Vajpeyi is in opposition?

In his second essay on Shukl, the topics of deliberation include *ras* and
the issue of Tulsidas. Vajpeyi signals the three markers based on which Shukl
includes Tulsi in his canon:

    a. The world is the expression of the unexpressed and poetry is the expression
       of that expression;
    b. The complete unfolding of art in life's elaborate activities; and
    c. The principles of 'turning towards' and 'turning away'.[57]

He criticizes each of these points in order. He holds that the expression of
the unexpressed can also be the productive ground of great poetry; in other
words, mystery and otherworldliness can also bring forth beautiful verse.
Second, elaborate emotional states of living can be expressed only in long
epics and it is not necessary that in other smaller poetic forms, grand poetry
cannot be written. This is the same as the change in the definition of the
hero according to which the hero must exhibit force, goodness and beauty.
Third, he considers the tussle between 'turning towards' and 'turning away'
to be an over-elaboration by Shukl.

The sharpness of his criticism of Shukl is a product of Vajpeyi's milieu
which comprised the 'romantic'/*Chhayavad* and post-'romantic' creative
energies. Vajpeyi was conscious that *Chhayavad* poetry had developed
new foundations for poetry, while the basis of criticism was still mostly
the Bhakti period in its formulations. He tried to span this contradiction
through his critical endeavours. In the introduction to his book on criticism,
he proposes seven pointers in criticism:

a. The poet's interior vision in the composition
b. Artistic effectiveness
c. Study of the composition's external parts
d. The stimuli of time and world
e. The poet's analysis of the psyche
f. The poet's views on philosophy, society and politics
g. Study of poetry's life-related harmonies and messages.[58]

Among the above, what is missing from Shukl's critical project? Analysis of the psyche and the interior vision of the poet are the only two points that can be said to be of some interest in relation to his critical project. It is undeniable that Shukl emphasizes some of these points at the expense of others, but that can be found in Vajpeyi too. Vajpeyi appears to emphasize some of the points precisely in order to criticize Shukl. In other words, in his turn towards Shukl's criticism, Vajpeyi tries to separate himself from the tradition-derived critical sense and questions it, but when faced by the challenge of explicating the principles and consolidating the criticism, he is unable to elaborate this separation.

Just as Vajpeyi holds Shukl's critical principles to be a product of the Dwivedi age, his own principles of criticism develop from the ground of romanticist/ *Chhayavad* creativity. He proceeds to question the central point of Shukl's analysis of *Chhayavad*, i.e. its mystical quality, and concludes that mystical themes do not harm poetry. According to Vajpeyi, what the *Chhayavad* poets have created through their imaginative power is a microscopic world. There is no point in looking there for the unsubtle, gross tendencies of the Dwivedi age. He does not consider mysticism to be against existence but, rather, a revelation of the deep inner world of man. To make this point, he returns to the Bhakti-period poets and praises the diffusion of mysticism in their poetry. In his view, Shukl's anti-mysticism is of the same nature as Raja Ravi Varma's painting.

However, on one matter, Vajpeyi and Shukl concur. The spiritualist understanding of mysticism is the same in both the writers. On the basis of his notion of 'social bliss' Shukl makes a case against *Chhayavad*, while Vajpeyi supports *Chhayavad* in light of the reflections of the mindscape. But Vajpeyi does not attempt to uncover this 'mystic' quality and the *Chhayavad* critics who succeeded him followed suit. In his study of *Chhayavad*, Namvar Singh brings out the monotony of *Chhayavad*-related critics in these words: 'The lack of clarity in Sushil Kumar, the spiritualism of Mukutdhar Pandey, the mysteries of [Mahavir Prasad] Dwivedi, Shukl's shadowy spiritualism, Vajpeyi's "consciousness of the spirit's shadow", and Nagendr's "rebellion of

the subtle against the gross" – all belong to the same order of thought.'[59]
Thus Namvar Singh situates this mysticism within social dimensions and
considers it to be born out of the elaboration of the self in *Chhayavad*, thus
relating it to individualism.[60]

This requires us to assess the influence of Vajpeyi's *Chhayavad* criticism
on later Hindi critics. He develops a new argument about the contradiction
between the epic [*prabandh kavya*] and the lyric while gesturing towards the
lyricality of *Chhayavad* poetry. He declares that lyrical poetry is not confined
to internal impressions. While praising Prasad's lyric poetry, he points to
the poet's uncovering of deep psychological truths in these poems. Should
we not consider these to be the principles for identifying individualism in
Chhayavad poetry? Again, while writing about Prasad, Vajpeyi notes: 'In
terms of his social thought, like [John Stuart] Mill, he is an individualist,
and finds inspiration from those ideals of collective progress which emerged
from the intellectual and commercial rise of the middle class.'[61] Secondly,
while highlighting the characteristic nature-descriptions of *Chhayavad*
poetry, Vajpeyi relates these to an inquisitiveness. Later, Namvar Singh too
identifies this inquisitiveness as one of the basic principles of *Chhayavad*
poetry.

In comparing *Chhayavad* poetry with the 'nationalist' poetry of the
Dwivedi age and uncovering the 'humanist' characteristic of the former,
Vajpeyi writes:

> Maithilisharan Gupt's beautiful poem '*Nilambar paridhan harit pat par sundar
> hai*' [The sky-blue dress is pretty on the green plain] establishes a four-cornered,
> concrete picture of the nation and goes on to praise its characteristics with
> increased enthusiasm. At some places in Prasad we find this four-cornered-ness
> but descriptions such as the following are more usual –'towards the direction
> the flying birds face, finding a dear nest there, this sweet nation of ours, in the
> dawn' – which any patriot can sing with reference to their nation. . . . If we turn
> to Nirala's song '*Bharati jai vijai kare*' [May India be victorious], we will note
> in it an increased absence of country-ness. The lines communicate a natural
> and enlightening humanism and reach beyond gross patriotism. Although it
> is based on nationalistic and humanistic ideals, Gupt's entire oeuvre remains
> devotionalist, while his subsequent compositions entered within the actual
> limits of real life.[62]

Now we can compare the above with Namvar Singh's characterization of
Chhayavad:

The *Chhayavad* poet was against all kinds of caste and nationalist discrimination. Therefore when he heard that the British king Edward VIII had abdicated the throne for the love of an ordinary widowed woman from America, he sang praises of the king for the sole reason that he fell upon the decrepit dams of wealth and honour and delivered the message of humanity.[63]

It requires little skill in comparison to note that Namvar Singh is only elaborating Nanddulare Vajpeyi's position. When Vajpeyi declares mysticism to be the backbone of *Chhayavad* poetry and compares Mahadevi Varma with Mirabai, it is his attempt, by other means, to arrive at the same poetic formalization of the social world that Namvar Singh also attempts in his very important and authoritative exposition in the essay 'Devi, Ma, Sahchari, Pran' [Divinity, Mother, Wife, Soul].

Indeed, there are several contradictions in Vajpeyi's own principles of criticism. For example, as noted before, the question of realism remains unresolved in his work. His principles of criticism go awry when he applies them to distinguish between the realisms of Prasad's *Kankal* and *Kamayani* [The daughter of eros]. Second, Vajpeyi's view of Premchand is not consistent. Although he considers Premchand an important writer, he cannot get over the 'propaganda' in his work. He considers *Kankal* to be a better creation than *Godan* [Gift of a Cow]. Drawing attention to this, Nirmala Jain writes:

> Vajpeyi uses double standards because of the coexistence of several beliefs in his mind which he deploys in his analysis of poetry. He considers Shukl's criticism erudite but characterized by a personalist hobby, and accuses it of not being 'objective' and 'scientific'. The question really is whether Vajpeyi himself is innocent of these accusations. Is Vajpeyi, who admires Prasad's novel *Kankal* for its realism, unable to see the excellence of Premchand's literary writing precisely because of this one quality?[64]

In summary, the views of Vajpeyi that are applicable to *Chhayavad* poets are also applicable to his own critical endeavours. The task of expanding the base of the nation's four-sidedness and opening it up to new horizons, which was performed by the *Chhayavad* poets, is also Vajpeyi's mission. This is the core of his critical project. His arguments with the later poets of experimentalism draw upon the same foundational ground. In opposing Shukl and taking the side of the *Chhayavad* poets, Vajpeyi's thought shows itself to be in the process of expressing the effects of bourgeois interests in Hindi criticism.

Hazari Prasad Dwivedi: The Will to an Assimilated Nation

Almost all the important works by Hazari Prasad Dwivedi on criticism and history were published around 1940. In his book *Dusri parampara ki khoj* [In Search of Another Tradition], Namvar Singh has characterized the innately riotous and maverick quality of the 1940s and the subsequent decade as a characteristic of Dwivedi's entire oeuvre as well as one of its foundations. Dwivedi's Kabir is also endowed with this maverick quality. His '*Kutaj*' [The Kutaj Tree] and '*Ashok ke phul*' [Ashok Flowers] are both companions of this pervasive maverick quality. If we set aside the discussion of the 'rollicking poets' and focus on Dwivedi, then the exploration of the intellectual grounding of this maverick nature becomes important.

In the final section of this chapter, I will investigate the political dimensions of Dwivedi's 'maverick' quality. Towards this end, the argument below focuses on his historiographic vision, his populism, and his understanding of Indian culture as reflected in the placing of Kabir at the foundation of Dwivedi's canon. But before we begin this investigation, it is necessary to present a retrospective of the milieu of the 1940s.

In order to characterize Dwivedi's maverick, Namvar Singh writes the following in his *Dusri parampara ki khoj*:

> In fact in the fourth decade of the twentieth century, revolt took on one or the other maverick shapes in its manifestations. If one of its shapes appears in Nirala's '*Kukurmutta*' [Mushroom] (1940) as loudmouthed-ness, then the second can be seen in Rahul Sankrityayan's story collection, *Volga se Ganga* [From the Volga to the Ganga] (1942).[65] . . . According to historians, this period was a time of terrible topsy-turviness and churning. The structure of idealism of the Gandhian age was breaking down in all areas of life. Several political and ethical ideals had come to appear dubious. In the same period, the ideas of Marx and Freud were together influencing and stirring the Indian middle class. The effects wrought by the second world war on the economic aspects of common life had only increased the sense of insecurity. The problem of Hindu–Muslim unity had only become sharper in the context of the independence movement.[66]

The above exposition by Namvar Singh based on a historical reading needs further elaboration if we are to assess the career of Hazari Prasad Dwivedi against the background of the 1940s. Among the key questions of this period is the Hindu–Muslim question which had developed greatly in political potency. It was brewing throughout the decade of the 1930s, especially at the Round Table Conferences in the form of demands for separate electorates. With the advent of the 1940s, the Hindu Mahasabha and the Muslim League emerged as autonomous forces. A blood-drenched manifestation of this process came to pass just seven years later in the form of the Partition of the nation, riots and an unprecedented human disaster. Thus, in the same period when Dwivedi was emphasizing the miscegenation of Indian culture, the crop of 'cultural purity' was standing high on the political field of colonial India. In his own way, Hazari Prasad Dwivedi was struggling against this purity. By the 1940s the intellectual heat of the Hindi reawakening had cooled down and the Arya Samaj was no longer the reformist body of earlier times. It was therefore necessary for the nation that was struggling for independence to find a solution to this question.

A remarkable fictional representation of this decade is available in the Pakistani (then British-Indian) writer Mumtaz Shah Nawaz's English novel, *The Heart Divided*, written between 1943 and 1948. The writer acutely presents here the culturalist divisions that had begun appearing in contemporary urban relations between Hindus and Muslims. The conversations among her characters throw into relief the contradictions of the milieu of these decades, more than any historical account:

'Life under the Congress regime is becoming impossible,' said one young man. 'We cannot go on like this. Something drastic will have to be done.'

'Things are getting worse each day,' said another. . . . If we accept this, we shall lose for ever our language and our culture, and in time our children will even forget their own faith. . . .

Our children are forced to discard the token of their own religion and culture, just imagine, they have to give up even their traditional greeting – Aslam-o-Alaikum [sic], but are made to sing the *Bande Mataram* every day. . . .

Urdu has been replaced by Hindi which is sometimes called Hindustani to mislead people, even from this, words of Persian and Arabic are being weeded out. Perhaps the worst thing is the way history books have been changed. There is gross abuse of Muslim kings and emperors, and our national heroes are derided.[67]

The context of this conversation is M.K. Gandhi's Wardha scheme, in which the former had made a proposal for elementary education in the country.[68] But by that time the divide between the Hindu and Muslim communities had become so wide that no possibility of mutual trust remained. Mumtaz Shah Nawaz's novel gives a fictional representation of this historical situation. It is the same situation that Namvar Singh alludes to in the form of the Hindu–Muslim question of the 1940s.

From the historical perspective, by the beginning of the decade of the

40s, the politics of cultural purity had become popular among the middle class. The ongoing debates within the Hindu and Muslim communities concerning partisanship on questions of employment, language use and English education were being expressed more and more in terms of political power. This was approximately the time when Gandhi took a bow from Indian politics despite giving the ringing cry of 'Quit India'. The political centre of the Indian National Congress shifted to Jawaharlal Nehru. This was the end of a whole generation in the independence movement. Now the national bourgeoisie was poised to stake its claim over political power. The curtain of idealism was parted and even the Hindu–Muslim question articulated itself in starkly modern terms, i.e. as a question of participation in political power.

Against this backdrop, Dwivedi chooses Kabir as the basis of his canon. Till that time Kabir had not become established as the central poet in the world of literature. Before this some critical work had been written on him, but Dwivedi's work was key to establishing Kabir firmly within the Hindi canon.[69] The Kabir we read today in school textbooks emerges from Dwivedi's canon-building.

We have previously seen that the Mishr Brothers did not include Kabir in their first iteration of the *Navratn*. Kabir's personality and creativity posed a constant challenge to critics and aficionados of literature. However, this was the time when Kabir was being fashioned with another persona through the efforts of Rabindranath Tagore and Kshitimohan Sen. Ramchandr Shukl conceded, in the 1940 edition of *Hindi sahitya ka itihas*, that Kabir had proved to be a timely support to a people for whom the love of sentiment and devotion had become void, and 'additionally foregrounded the commonplace feeling of humanity thereby awakening a sense of pride among the people of the lower class'.[70] Despite this, Kabir was not granted a place in the canon. The Mishr Brothers did include him in subsequent editions of their book, but that did not substantially change the process of canon formation.

In Hazari Prasad Dwivedi's work, Kabir links us with the second stream of the tradition. His credo of 'Neither Hindu nor Muslim' became topical once more in the 1940s when, inspired by the example of Tagore's Santiniketan, Dwivedi began articulating 'cultural miscegenation' against the idea of 'cultural purity'. In his essay '*Ashok ke phul*', Dwivedi writes:

> Man's life-force is very ruthless; it has been trampling on the useless attractions of civilization and culture. This life stream has flowed on, bathing and uprooting countless ethical comportments, beliefs, feasts and holy observances. Struggle

has given new force to man. The social form that confronts us today takes shape through who knows how many assimilations and exceptions. The purity of the nation and the race is merely talk. Everything is adulterated, everything is miscegenated.[71]

Namvar Singh draws attention to *this* cultural quest, and points to the dissociation of writers such as Ramdhari Singh Dinkar, Govind Chand Pandey and Agyey from it. The implication here is that against the stream of Indian cultural nationalism proposed by V.D. Savarkar and extended by M.S. Golwalkar and others, which bases itself on a distinction between 'fatherland' and 'holy land', and considers Muslims of India to be secondary citizens, Hazari Prasad Dwivedi was searching for those necessary elements of assimilation and humanity in the formation of culture.

We now need to situate this theoretical argument in the context of the political dynamics of the 1940s. If we think of the prehistory of the increasing political acrimony between the Hindu and Muslim communities, we would notice that despite all the reasonable tendencies in the Hindi reawakening, the question of faith holds its intellectuals in a particularly vicious grip. If we leave some exceptions aside, such as Premchand and Bhagat Singh, the question of religion in the Hindi domain was almost never reasonable. Hazari Prasad Dwivedi chose another path for himself which elaborates the nation's basic structure without changing it. This is a process of extensive elaboration.

In the modern period, there have been several debates around the relationship between political power and religion. Most scholars consider the religious interception of modern power or its admixture with the latter as a remnant of the medieval period, i.e. religion is a thing of human individuality and not a medium for political power. This may be taken to be one of the points of emergence of modern Indian secularism. The definition of 'secularism', however, remains contested. One stream of thought relates secularism to the idea of '*sarvadharm sambhaav*' (all religions are the same in existence). The implication of this common 'existence' is that political power recognizes every religion and looks upon them equally. For another stream of thought, '*sarvadharm varjayate*' (all religions are prohibited) is the most adequate form of secularism for political power. Between the two streams, a fundamental difference is implied. While in the first there is a situation where political power is in a position to recognize religion, in the second political power does not accept religion or, at the very least, political power is against the recognition of religion as such.

The ruling class in India decided to opt for the first stream of 'secularism' in view of the religious composition of Indian society. Both Nehru and Ambedkar, in their thought and political practice, displayed this choice. They supported the constitutional acceptance of this definition. Ambedkar too left one *religion*, i.e. Hinduism, to adopt another, i.e. Buddhism. It would be clear by now that Dwivedi too adopts the first definition of religion. Following his practice, he extensively elaborates 'religion' [*dharm*] and brings it to its core etymological root of 'carrying' or 'preserving' [*dhaaran*].

Dwivedi also elaborates the term 'culture' beyond its commonplace reference. In his definition of culture, nothing is left out. Dwivedi includes that which is still not a part of the mainstream of the Indian nation after the nation's consolidation in his discussion of culture. Whether it is the ascetic cultures, Dravidians, Buddhists, Gandharvs, Kinnars or non-Aryans, all cultures joined the stream of Indian culture with full vigour and force. In this light, Dwivedi's essay '*Thakurji ki bator*' [God's Assembly] demands to be read with attention. It is his view in this essay that even ancient Indian culture contained heterogeneous influences. After the advent of Islam, it found itself challenged. Dwivedi enthusiastically endorses the equalitarian society of Islam, as well as highlights its aspects of force and strength. Apart from the issue of Hindu and Muslim cultures, the essay's culture criticism is also worth discussing. In his own words:

> Some non-Aryan hero who attained demigod status in the Indus valley or some child god with divinity in the northern provinces came to occupy the place of the highest god in the age-old established Holy Faith [*Bhaagvat dharm*]. Since then millions of non-Aryan races settled to a similar quiet life chastened by His blessed name. . . . From the northwestern corner of the region of Bharat [ancient India] armies were entering like ants. Rapine, skirmishes, fighting – nothing was beyond them. . . . All of northern India becomes like a burning ghat for a moment. Then, what do we see – the same races settle down on the land and within fifty years feel honoured to announce themselves to be true devotees [*Bhaagvat*] on their royal coins. . . . That day has now passed. In the west, a *sui generis* enlightened religious sentiment came into existence in whose one hand was a tightly held sword and in the other the ambrosial boon of the assurance of equality. The god of its existence is inward facing. . . . He does not compromise with anyone. . . . Wherever he turned, the wheel of time moved with Him. This was Islam. . . . Today the area of Gandhar has turned Muslim, it has acquired the ambrosial boon of Islam, but so what? . . . The scions of Panini and Yask are roaming in the land of Bharat today selling asafoetida. . . . O Islam, when will you be able to see all this?[72]

The first thing voiced in the above quotation is the absorptive capacity of Indian culture. Secondly, we may notice here the main point of focus of Dwivedi's thought. In his interpretation, Islam is not the opposite of Hinduism. He treats Islam with the same consideration he gives to Hinduism. But it is clear that he views religions to be the agents for developing ordinary humanity. While Namvar Singh acknowledges that Dwivedi never wrote anything on the slogan of cultural unity in post-independence India, it should not be forgotten that the principles of this cultural view emerged from the writings of Dwivedi himself.

The point of cultural unity finds it clearest articulation in *The Discovery of India* by Jawaharlal Nehru. Nehru writes:

> When Islam came to India and attained political victory, a struggle began here. It had a two-sided effect. On one hand, it promoted that tendency in Hindu society to sew itself in its own skin and determinedly close itself off; on the other, it blew such a fresh breeze breathing which had transformative effects on us. Hindu society was shackled by conventional social practices. From the outside, the Muslims too had brought in a closed social system. In this way the great problem that India had to face in the medieval period was to develop healthy relations between the two tightly wrought social systems with tenacious roots.[73]

Nehru was writing this in 1960. Namvar Singh notes: 'Since the promulgation of the policy for syncretic culture after independence, Dwivedi did not write anything about it.'[74] But how can we ignore the fact that after independence the ruling class under the leadership of the Congress party established its dominance precisely on this cultural-assimilationist argument? Nehru's words quoted above are part of the same political argument from the ground of culture.

We can discern the same elaboration of the meaning of culture in the warp and woof of nationalist thought in the following statement by B.R. Ambedkar:

> At a personal level, I would like to say that I do not believe that there is any room in this country for a special kind of culture: whether it be Hindu, Muslim, Kannada or Gujarati. These are things which we cannot overlook, but these should not be considered as divine blessings; rather they are curses which loosen our determination and remove our goal further from us. The goal is this that we develop such a feeling that we are all Indians.[75]

Ambedkar's goal is Indian culture, and that culture is larger than all the enumerated cultures. The production of a modern nation is that point at

which we can uncover the principle of equality in both Ambedkar and
Dwivedi. Although Ambedkar arrives at his notion of equality through
other means, Dwivedi seems approximate to it in his position on achieving
this goal. It is not a coincidence that he too considers it important to
theorize the pluri-cultural society of India. This does not mean that there
are multilayered similarities between Ambedkar and Dwivedi, and yet the
idea of the revaluation of culture as a part of the modernizing process of
the nation is common to both. It comes as no surprise that a large part of
Ambedkar's cultural criticism is focused on Buddhist and post-Buddhist
social formations; Dwivedi too is on the quest for a path towards study
of the same post-Sanskritic society. It cannot be denied that a common
intellectual path draws both thinkers towards Pali, Prakrit and Apabhransh.

In his above-mentioned essay, Dwivedi conducts a dialogue with the
Islamic divinity as well as derives an answer that equality is a great condition,
power an even greater condition, and that those who are beyond this world,
they are as good as absent. It goes without saying that these formulations
are Dwivedi's own. In the same essay, he discusses the effects of the Islamic
invasions. On the controversy regarding the rise of the Bhakti movement,
Shukl and Dwivedi hold comparable positions.[76] In the same vein, he
concludes in his book on Kabir that the latter was a social reformer. He was
a devotee [*bhakt*]. But he reconstructs Kabir's devotionalism and love on
the highest and most virtuous humanistic ground. Thus, in his treatment
of Islam he does not cast it as an enemy but defines it as a religion of the
people. The category of culture is elaborated in a way that makes room
for various cultures, kinds of thought and practices, as well as differences.
Such an elaboration of 'culture' posed a definite challenge to the Indian
intellectual milieu of the 1940s, which Dwivedi himself acknowledges.

Now we can return to the figure of Kabir in Dwivedi's canon. What
were the intellectual conditions that allowed for the introduction of Kabir
– who had been hitherto missing from it – into the canon ? In this period,
we may note that the forces struggling for the Indian nation had come
to believe in the certainty of their inheritance of political power; in other
words, the hope for independence had strengthened and along with it the
question of government had become the central question. This required
a recasting of the Hindu–Muslim dispute. It is to Dwivedi's credit that
he situated this dispute on a broadly conceived humanistic ground. He
underlined the appositeness of Kabir also in the sense that he, Kabir, raised
religion to the highest ground of humanitarianism.

In this light, we can see that Dwivedi's Kabir is neither the hero of a
purified religion nor of a privileged caste. He belongs to the community of

caste-corrupting ascetics. Dwivedi's genealogical analysis of the beginnings of the *julaha* caste reminds us of D.D. Kosambi's method, although the latter's domain is more modernist and is expressed in straightforwardly class-based terms. Dwivedi opposes the view of caste as an ahistorical truth; he argues for a transformable category of caste and enquires into the conditions of these transformations. He manages to show how, before the time of Kabir, some caste groups that had been excluded from society due to the stringency of the caste system were engaged in work like weaving, and it was into such a group that his hero was born:

> Among them, the ascetics, renunciants and the enlightened were not householders, but among their disciples there were several outcaste householders who had taken on the robes of the ascetic group. The Hindu faith had no respect for these outcaste people and actively pursued their exclusion. These outcaste householders were neither Hindu – because they did not favour any of the ideas, beliefs or practices of Hinduism – nor Muslim – because they had not accepted the Islamic credo. After a sustained contact with Islam, these people began to gradually tilt towards the Islamic faith.[77]

Dwivedi searches for the aspects of social relations that led to their decline in social status and arrives at the question of economic relations:

> There is perhaps no other social group which had such a sharp sense of discontent with regard to its current social status as may be found among the weaver caste. It appears that in an earlier period this occupation was considered best and for some unknown reason the people of this group fell from their position of honour to the lowliest, and within them the remnants of their older practices became the cause of their discontent.[78]

Drawn to the idea of equality and in their struggle against the priestly caste order, these caste groups became attracted to Islam.

The reason for the fall in the social position of these caste groups, which Dwivedi considers unknown, is delineated by the historian Irfan Habib, as quoted by Namvar Singh:

> The technological developments of the thirteenth and fourteenth centuries are very significant. These improved the artisanal and agricultural production. Commercial activity also picked up pace. This must have led to changes in class relations. The desire for acquiring artisans who were adept in the new technology must have encouraged the prevalence of individual employment. The dissemination of the use of paper would have helped in the development of markets.[79]

G.M. Muktibodh too explains the causes for the beginning of the Bhakti period along similar lines. The end of this period is also marked by the same processes due to which royal power subsumed under itself the Bhakti movement and because of which it lost its transformative potential.

However hard we try to fit Dwivedi's argument in this explanatory framework, it exceeds its limits. He locates this framework solely in the realm of culture. That is, he does not deploy the terminology of class, even as continuous hints of it appear in his writing. He argues from the position of reinstating to the ground of socio-cultural equality those marginalized groups who were excluded from the common ground of humanity.

Let us return to the milieu of the 1940s. The question that was assuming a complicated significance for Indian intellectuals in the field of culture was the caste question. B.R. Ambedkar made the question of caste urgent in connection with the question of emancipation. Thus he gave a new dimension to the anti-colonial struggle which was being carried out under the leadership of the Congress party. The Poona Pact between Gandhi and Ambedkar took place in 1932 in response to the demands for separate electorates for the minorities at the Round Table Conferences. In 1938, Ambedkar introduced a resolution for the abolition of zamindari in the Bombay Legislative Assembly. He asked the leaders of the independence movement if there was any room for the 'untouchables' in the realm of self-rule. If yes, to what extent? The first condition for the process of national formation, for Ambedkar, was the annihilation of caste. In the text[80] of his undelivered speech to the Lahore-based Jat–Pat Todak Mandal [Forum for Breaking Up Caste] of 1938, he writes:

> There is no doubt, in my opinion, that unless you change your social order you can achieve little by way of progress. You cannot mobilize the community either for defence or for offence. You cannot build anything on the foundations of caste. You cannot build up a nation, you cannot build up a morality. Anything that you will build on the foundations of caste will crack, and will never be a whole.[81]

Ambedkar's words contrast with the drive for the uplift of 'untouchables', by Gandhi and the leadership of the independence movement, through means such as the temple entry movement for 'untouchables'. Like an alarm bell, the question of 'caste' reared its head to challenge nationalism. The nationalists feared that if the struggle heated up on the internal front, it could lead to defeat on the external front against imperialism.

This is not the occasion to go into the deep processes of historical change that were taking place within the nationalist movement in the 1940s. Suffice it to say here that the question of caste influenced intellectuals working in that milieu. It is time now to look at the influence of that period on the work of Hazari Prasad Dwivedi. If we adopt Muktibodh's view on this question, we will note the recurrence of the same circumstances in which the anti-caste Dalit movement emerged out of the nationalist movement. It is well known that the advent of the British and the entry of Marathi-speaking Dalit groups improved the economic condition of the latter. The fundamental power behind the modern Dalit movement came into being with the formation of the Mahar regiment in the colonial British army and with the improvement of the Dalits' economic conditions under British rule. The words of Jotiba Phule who considered British rule to be a godsend for the Dalit people are relevant here. Thus the demand for political representation of the Dalits emerged from these transformed economic circumstances. This prehistory must not be forgotten in our assessment of the critical trends of the 1940s.

Among the points of contention in Dwivedi's argument against Shukl was the important question of identification of the social circumstances of Kabir and other saint-poets. For Shukl, Kabir is rustic, illiterate and arrogant. For Dwivedi, the same qualities signify self-confidence, which is a virtuous characteristic. He keeps returning to this issue in his study, titled *Kabir*, while making a case for the poet.

We have already encountered Dwivedi's statement about Kabir's birth in the weaver caste. On the origins of castes and the interrelations between them, Dwivedi's essay '*Meri janmabhumi*' [My Land of Birth] is significant. In this essay he mentions the various labouring castes in and around his village:

> In my village, the work of grain-parching is done by the *kandu* caste which is derived from the Sanskrit word *kandavik*. The Gupt kings granted them the position of the commercial caste [*vaishya*]. . . . In my village there is a neighbourhood of distillers [*kalvar*] or the ancient '*kalyapal*', who have completely forgotten that at some point their ancestors were Rajput soldiers who stayed at the rear of the army to guard the '*kalyavart*' or the provisions [*kaleyu*]. Who knows in which period these people took up weighing scales and became shopkeepers [*baniya*]. . . . Another caste group lives here – *turha*. . . . In my estimate this caste is one link in the intermixing of the Aryans and the Gonds. . . . In my village there is a low-caste [*antyaj*] group called '*Dusadh*'. Looking at their facial features and skin colour, no one can say that they are a low caste. As the British were able to establish a state in the country, they had to face several recalcitrant caste groups. In northern India the *Ahir*

and *Dusadh*, and in Bengal the *Dom* were very warlike and always resisted the
rule of law. British cunning overcame their resistance by offering them the job
of the watchman.[82]

What Dwivedi considers as the overcoming of resistance by British cunning,
Dalit thinkers consider to be an agent of improvement of the social and
economic conditions of these groups. The various 'backward' and Dalit
castes that were kept at the margins despite their intense participation in the
independence movement, and which, due to Brahminical ritualism and the
caste order, remained victims of social exclusion, were given employment by
the British even if in the latter's own interests, which improved their social
standing unprecedentedly. Whatever the social standing of these castes in
the ancient period, during the national movement they were able to improve
their economic condition and demand their share in political power.

For another view on this social situation and for a better analysis of it,
we can turn to the 1990s, which is the time of the Mandal Commission
and the protest against caste-based reservations in government employment.
The recommendations of the Commission were adopted under the prime
ministership of V.P. Singh. Consequently, 'high'-caste students started a
movement against the reservation policy. The anger against the government on
issues of education and employment reduced these to a question of caste. The
movement was conducted through self-immolations, suicide and violence.
Rather than enter the debate as to which forces appeased the dark storm of
this movement, the background of the movement is more relevant here. The
surprising fact in this situation is that there was no major movement working
behind the decision to implement the caste-based reservation policy. At that
time, there was no major Dalit movement that could mobilize around the
issue of reservations. What, then, were the reasons for implementation of the
recommendation for reservations? The Indian ruling class had sensed that
in the contemporary state of the economy, the Dalits and other 'backward'
castes had been able to improve their lot in society. In such conditions,
in order to quell any rebellion that might be expected, or to make them
partners in power and to harmonize the social transformation, the ruling
class produced for itself a 'safety valve' by accepting the recommendation for
reservations. After securing their participation in its politics, the middle class
within the Dalit movement, which took cognizance of the changed social
circumstances, had to be engaged in continuously improving its bargaining
power with the ruling class.

From an analysis of these two events from before and after the 1940s,
we reach the conclusion that a similar intensity must have been felt by

the Indian National Congress during the 1940s. But in that period, power had still not been acquired, and a movement was already under way under Ambedkar's leadership. Then, moving one step beyond the programmes for uplift of the 'untouchables' and temple entry, Nehru formulated a concept of Indian culture and a maximally flexible structure of the nation. Such discussion, or sensitivity, about caste is visible for the first time in Hindi in the writings of Hazari Prasad Dwivedi. But what is at the root of this sensitivity? Clearly, not a consideration of class difference, because Dwivedi is not working with the sociology of class. Yet throughout his work he draws on the conclusions of sociological and anthropological studies, and leaves suggestive hints for a class analysis. Looking at this analytic method in its entirety, historicism appears prominently. Dwivedi gestures towards the historical development of the various castes at various points, but this historical development arises from the intensity experienced in his own times. In the thickening atmosphere around 1940, Dwivedi casts another glance at history through a fresh perspective and finds that the groups at the margins of society had played an enormous role in the processes of Indian history. This may be termed as a 'rediscovery of India', in which the intention to assimilate was very strong.

Namvar Singh points to the use made of myths and popular mythology by Dwivedi. Through an examination of Dwivedi's intensive research and rich imagination, we come to realize the way in which myth or popular memory reproduces its social bases, the production process of the mythic and its internal values. But can myth be understood in the same way as historical sources? Undoubtedly, the participation of people in the production of myth broadens the universe of its meaning. Myth is the site for manifesting and occluding meanings, and the uncovering of these meanings is what attracts a researcher. But against this, using myth in its autonomous shape is a deviation that has its own attractions. Myths born out of multiple relations of force sometimes deliver the weight of hegemony, but sometimes also create new ideas by countering them. In such cases, it is most effective to study myth in terms of their historicist and other determinate aspects. In the production of new myths, class relations play an important role. Apart from Dwivedi who makes use of myths, another important investigator of myths is D.D. Kosambi. Without going into details, we can surmise that Kosambi's method is more complete since, first, he tests myth against various scholarly principles and, second, deploys class as the basic terminology of analysis. Undoubtedly, the main domain of study for both Kosambi and Dwivedi is culture, and that is why the discussion here revolves around a comparison of the importance of myth in both their projects.

We may better comprehend the historical sense arising from the question of castes and communities marginalized by the nationalist project if we look at Dwivedi's understanding of historical sense. In his *Dusri parampara ki khoj*, Namvar Singh considers the opposition of 'scriptures' and 'the popular' to be at the heart of Dwivedi's historical sense:

> The force of the popular ensured the surrender of the scriptures [*shastra*]. Clearly this force of the popular is that internal force which carried Indian history towards development. In this way, the central opposition of the medieval period of Indian history is that between rules and the popular and not the struggle between Islam and Hinduism.[83]

Basing his arguments on quotations from Dwivedi, Namvar Singh shows that Bhakti in the medieval period is an advanced form of the evolving tradition of the popular. He cites Muktibodh as well in this context, and shows the divergence between conceptions of the popular in the work of Shukl and Dwivedi.

The issue may be further clarified from another perspective. Since the Dalit movement and Ambedkar had transformed the notion of the popular within the independence movement, Dwivedi's expansive notion of the popular also became a social and humanist term. The popular is not a unidimensional phenomenon. Which communities produce the popular? What is its class affinity? Who will count as the people in the realm of the popular: peasants or workers? Tulsi is a popular poet and so is Kabir; but is the popular of Tulsi and of Kabir the same? The question is particularly relevant for a society that has a graded system of classification of castes and sub-castes, where running through the idea of the popular itself there is the problem of untouchability, where the class system prevails, and a singular and indivisible category of the popular cannot be accepted. Women and the minority communities are to be found within the same notion of the popular. The category of the popular as used by Shukl and Dwivedi can be differentiated precisely on this point. Dwivedi's use of the category is more expansive than that of Shukl. Within it, apart from 'the literate', cultured and educated middle class, there exist several social identities existing on the margins.

However, without an understanding of what these identities are in their actuality and what role is played by the category of class among their determining agents, there are clearly pitfalls in the humanistic view of identities. Without opening up the debate about caste and class here, it should suffice to note that without the perspective of class, many issues of caste would be incomprehensible. For example, the reasons for the consolidation of castes, their historicity, transformations within them and their modernization, etc., can be comprehended through a class-inflected analysis. While it is possible to argue on behalf of the suppressed forces using humanist ideas, if the opponent's strongest links are not recognized in the realm of ideas, it becomes impossible to break that chain. Dwivedi succeeds in conducting, on clearly modern bases, a survey of a popular ground down by Brahminical ritualism, but this modernity remains reformist within the logic of the nation. In his intellectual project, the foundational category of the nation is used ahistorically. For this reason, all his humanistic endeavours fall within the definition of the nation. This nation is a product of the 'reawakening' and its theorization. Anti-imperialism is its most dynamic aspect, while the search for honour in history is one of its primary tasks. Dwivedi works towards a broadening of that which changes its coordinates repeatedly on the anti-feudalism front. He pits honour in history against Brahminism. His historical researches are at heart not anti-imperialist but draw their energies from contemporary, identity-based movements. Thus, a new cultural aspect of anti-feudalism is reflected in his entire project. This aspect of Dwivedi's thought has been well highlighted by Namvar Singh in his debate with Ramvilas Sharma.

We can conclude that the effects of communalist thinking and debates around social identities in this period are visible in Dwivedi's writings on canon formation. In the fast-changing and chaotic circumstances of the 1940s, Indian intellectual thought produced a new understanding of culture and, in this way, accepted the challenges of its historical conditions. But then some issues became problematic on the horizon of Hindi criticism – for example, the Bhakti period. From the time of its emergence, Hindi criticism centred itself on the Bhakti period. Through this node, the question of religion was kept alive. Though criticism did not move beyond a liberalist position on this question, new social questions kept coming up. With the advent of the progressive movement, however, the Bhakti period lost its prominence in critical discussion and new canonical moments became central.

It should be noted here that Bhagat Singh in the political field and Premchand in the literary field held completely divergent views on religion from the Hindi public sphere. While Dwivedi was all praise for Premchand, the central position in his canon was occupied by his version of Kabir. He appears to have been aware of the new paths of criticism, and it may be said that he represented the disaggregated form of the development from old to new critical thought.

NOTES

[1] An article by Badri Narayan Chaudhari, quoted from Naval (1981), p. 16.
[2] See Pradhan (2009), pp. 8–11.
[3] Ibid., p. 16.
[4] Naval (1981), p. 26.
[5] Mishr Bandhu (1965), p. 5.
[6] Shukl (1997), p. 34.
[7] Shastri (1977), p. 134.
[8] Mishr Bandhu (1965), pp. 17–18.
[9] Mishr Bandhu (1987), p. 31.
[10] Ibid., p. 420.
[11] Tripathi (2010), p. 33.
[12] *Saraswati* (1912), p. 74.
[13] Sharma (1977), p. 275.
[14] Pradhan (2009), p. 100.
[15] Mishr Bandhu (1987), p. 36.
[16] Ibid., pp. 56–57.
[17] Ibid., pp. 42–43.
[18] Ibid., pp. 287–88.
[19] Namvar Singh, 'Introduction', in Namvar Singh, ed. (1998), pp. 7–8.
[20] Namvar Singh, ed. (1998), p. 120.
[21] Shukl (1997), p. 40.
[22] Namvar Singh, ed. (1998), pp. 122–25.
[23] Sharma (2003), p. 77.
[24] Vajpeyi (2007), p. 52.
[25] See the chapter titled 'Jayasi's Path of Love', in Sharma (2003), pp. 63–77.
[26] Namvar Singh, ed. (1998), p. 126.
[27] Vajpeyi (2003), p. 108.
[28] Sharma (2003), p. 93.
[29] Ramchandr Shukl, '*Kavita kya hai?*', in Namvar Singh, ed. (1998), p. 54.
[30] Ramchandr Shukl, '*Kavya mein lokmangal ki sadhanavastha*', in Namvar Singh, ed. (1998), p. 68.
[31] Ramchandr Shukl, '*Anand ki siddhavastha*', in Namvar Singh, ed. (1998), p. 77.
[32] Ramchandr Shukl, '*Tulsi ki bhavukta*', in Namvar Singh, ed. (1998), pp. 139–40.
[33] Sharma (2003), p. 95.
[34] Mishr (2002), p. 21.
[35] Pandey (2005), p. 38.
[36] Shukl (1997), p. 131.
[37] Sharma (2003), p. 117.
[38] Shukl (1997), p. 18.
[39] Ibid., p. 141.
[40] Omprakash Singh (2007).
[41] Ibid.
[42] Ibid.
[43] Shambhunath, ed. (2004), p. 390.

[44] Pandey (2006), p. 168.

[45] Omprakash Singh (2007).

[46] Ibid.

[47] It should be noted here that Shukl includes all groups connected with land in his category of agricultural classes: ryots, zamindars, small zamindars, peasants and workers.

[48] Omprakash Singh (2007).

[49] Ibid.

[50] Ibid.

[51] For this debate, see the chapter on 'The Discussion of Colonialism in Hindi Criticism', in Krishn (2008).

[52] It is unfortunate that in the Gita Press edition of the *Ramcharitmanas* Nanddulare Vajpeyi's name as editor is not mentioned anywhere, since this was an exemplary project. Before this edition, the *Ramcharitmanas* published by the Vyankatesh Press (Bombay) under the title *Ramayan* was widespread, the text of which is full of mistakes.

[53] Vajpeyi (2007), p. 60.

[54] Ibid., p. 59.

[55] Ibid., p. 73.

[56] Ibid., p. 82.

[57] Ibid., pp. 70–71.

[58] Ibid., p. xxix.

[59] Namvar Singh (1990), p. 15.

[60] Ibid., pp. 24–34.

[61] Vajpeyi (2007), p. 103.

[62] Ibid., p. xix.

[63] Namvar Singh (1990), p. 25.

[64] Jain (1992), p. 53.

[65] Namvar Singh calls the formulation of history in Rahul Sankrityayan's *Volga se Ganga* 'history by fits and starts' (Namvar Singh 1982, p. 53). This is important to note even besides the context we are discussing. Sankrityayan too did not consider it to be history. His interest lay in making history a site of popular sympathy, and the way in which his book was received, it appears that he was successful in his task. It is also the case that Sankrityayan's goal was to visualize the passage of human essence on the terrain of history, which was also Dwivedi's goal, who believed that 'man is the goal of literature', and who in his novels and essays presented a new understanding of history for the sake of the human essence. A powerful example of this is his novel *Banbhatt ki atmakatha* [The Autobiography of Banbhatt].

[66] Namvar Singh (2005), pp. 53–54.

[67] Shah Nawaz (1990), pp. 329–30.

[68] On this debate, see Kumar (2007).

[69] For a review of Kabir criticism, see Namvar Singh (2005), pp. 43–44.

[70] Shukl (1997), p. 36.

[71] Hazari Prasad Dwivedi, '*Ashok ke phul*', in Dwivedi (2007), Part Nine, p. 23.

[72] Hazari Prasad Dwivedi, '*Thakurji ki bator*', in Dwivedi (2007), Part Nine, pp. 163–64.

[73] Jawaharlal Nehru, '*Samvad hi hamari parampara*' [from *India Today and Tomorrow*], in Shambhunath, ed. (2004), p. 598.

[74] See Namvar Singh, '*Sanskriti aur saundarya*', in Namvar Singh (2005).

[75] Quoted in the epigraph to Ambedkar (1993), p. 3.

[76] This quotation is significant. It should be compared with Shukl's definition. Dwivedi writes: 'Suddenly my imagination was face to face with the terrorized Hindu culture of the medieval age. . . . Its strength had withered after the arrival of Islam . . . but it was not ready to accept defeat. Like trampled forest grass, it was withered but alive. It was attempting to grow again and without finding the means it scrambled for refuge wherever it could be found. At that moment, several flaming lights could be seen running with great speed towards the north from the southern skies. All the dimensions were covered in darkness, the sky was filled with dust, and the earth was soaked in blood. The lights from the southern sky brooked no obstacle; they did not pay heed to anyone. They kept advancing. Suddenly a ray of light revealed that this trampled bough of culture had gained a support. That support was the Vaishnav faith, the ideology of Bhakti.' Hazari Prasad Dwivedi, '*Thakurji ki bator*', in Dwivedi (2007), Part Nine, pp. 165–66.

The above can be compared with Ramchandr Shukl's much-discussed statement: 'After the establishment of the state of the Muslims in the country, there was no room left in the heart of the Hindu populace for honour, pride and enthusiasm. In front of it its temples were being pulled down, idols of divinities were smashed, and holy men were made fun of and they were unable to retaliate. . . . What other path remained open for a populace despairing of its virility except to focus its attention on the strength and mercy of the divine? . . . The southern stream of Bhakti that was already on its way towards the north found ample space to permeate the heart-space of a people reduced to nothing due to political change.' Shukl (1997), pp. 34–35.

[77] Hazari Prasad Dwivedi, 'Kabir', in Dwivedi (2007), Part Four, p. 333.

[78] Ibid., p. 203.

[79] Irfan Habib, 'Technological Change and Society', quoted in Namvar Singh (2005), p. 75.

[80] The text was printed but not delivered because of the withdrawal of invitation by members of the welcoming committee.

[81] Ambedkar (2014).

[82] Hazari Prasad Dwivedi, '*Meri janmabhumi*', in Dwivedi (2007), Part Nine, pp. 98–99.

[83] Namvar Singh (2005), p. 77.

CHAPTER THREE

The Canon according to Marxist Criticism

RAMVILAS SHARMA: ANTI-IMPERIALISM AND ANTI-FEUDALISM

By 1930 the Indian independence movement had positioned and consolidated itself anew. The nation-wide wave produced by opposition to the Simon Commission in 1927–28 and the hangings of Bhagat Singh, Rajguru and Sukhdev in 1931 could be considered one of the crests of the movement. This was a time when the revolutionary movement consolidated itself and moved towards a stronger ideological position. This is reflected in the fact that Bhagat Singh and his comrades changed the name of their organization, 'Hindustan Republican Association', to Hindustan Socialist Republican Association.

On 8 April 1929, Bhagat Singh and Batukeshwar Dutt detonated bombs inside the Central Legislative Assembly as protest against the Trade Union Dispute Bill. This proved to be a milestone in the struggle for independence. Just a couple of years later, in 1931, M.K. Gandhi agreed to participate in the Second Round Table Conference as part of an agreement with the British government. At this conference the British agreed to give the nascent Indian middle class a small share in the government, and thus India gained 'dominion status'. This was also a time when global capitalism was facing its worst economic crisis. Indian peasants too were impacted by this crisis: on the one hand, the prices of agricultural commodities fell sharply; on the other, the rate of taxation increased heavily and repression for the collection of revenue became more intense.

Though the forces of production had developed within the capitalist system, the capitalists, acting in their own class interest, held back on any changes in the relations of production. The contradiction between forces of

production and relations of production is what contributes to conditions of
an economic downturn. Although the production process under capitalism
is collective in nature with millions of workers participating in it at the same
time, the workers have no authority over the fruits of their labour which are
appropriated by the capitalists. Under such circumstances, the condition
of the workers deteriorates progressively, while the capitalists increasingly
reap higher profits. As long as the production process remains collective in
nature but the products of labour remain under individual ownership, the
contradiction between the forces of production and relations of production
cannot but persist. In the erstwhile Soviet Union there was no contradiction
between production relations and productive forces, and therefore no
conditions of an economic downturn.[1]

With the emergence of socialism as an alternative social arrangement on
a world scale, the Communist Party of India (CPI) came into being, though
it should not be forgotten that the diffusion of leftist ideas had begun before
the establishment of the Communist Party. The leftist affiliations of Bhagat
Singh and his comrades are well known today. Overall, it can be said that
by the beginning of the 1930s, a new consciousness had emerged in India.
Within Hindi literature too, we note that the voice of the *Chhayavad* poets
was gradually moving towards realism. Suryakant Tripathi Nirala was a
pioneer in this regard. Although Sumitranandan Pant systematically studied
Marxism, announced the 'end of the age' (*Yugant*) of *Chhayavad* and became
a part of the Progressive Writers' Association (PWA), established in 1936,
the pomp with which he declared himself a progressive was the same as the
pomp and great speed with which he left the 'golden ray' (*Svarnkiran*) and
the 'golden dust' (*Svarndhuli*) in the direction of Sri Aurobindo. It can be
stated with certainty that the formation of a progressive consciousness in
Hindi pre-dates the establishment of the Progressive Writers' Association.
The establishment of the Association was the organizational expression of
this consciousness.

We have already seen that before the advent of Ramchandr Shukl,
Hindi literary criticism was focused on the Bhakti and *riti* periods; Shukl
established the Bhakti period as the sole centre of criticism. Using the facade
of the creative works of his contemporary 'romanticist'/*Chhayavad* poets,
Nanddulare Vajpeyi brought the new middle class and the social milieu in
contact with literary criticism. Hazari Prasad Dwivedi gave a central position
to the cultures excluded in Shukl's criticism and, on that basis, established
a different canon through criticism. In his canon we notice the influence
of B.R. Ambedkar's entry into the independence movement, and growing
awareness and consolidation of the Dalit castes. This was an important

factor for the inclusion of Kabir in the canon. In fact the construction of the national idea at the time, the attempt to express its complete picture, could be seen in the field of Hindi criticism. With the consolidation of the 'backward' agricultural castes, the echo of the widespread peasant agitation in Avadh (eastern Uttar Pradesh) in the 1920s became audible in literature. Baba Ramchandr put Tulsi's *Ramcharitmanas* to fresh use in the peasant movement in Avadh. The greeting of 'Hail Sitaram' turned into a slogan of rebellion.[2] It is difficult today to ascertain whether this slogan was religious or not, but it cannot be doubted that Hindi criticism was touched by these movements. The process of canon formation in Dwivedi's criticism should be viewed against this background. Also, the focus of his criticism was the remote past, i.e. the ancient and Bhakti periods. Critics such as Nanddulare Vajpeyi and Shantipriy Dwivedi did attend to contemporary literary trends such as *Chhayavad*, but the tools with which to evaluate and establish its importance in their criticism were underdeveloped.

The challenge facing Marxist criticism was not simply that the critical criteria for progressive literature needed to be laid down and the significance of contemporary literature underlined; it was faced by the question of how to evaluate the *whole* of the Hindi tradition. Marxist criticism considered the latter question to be its special responsibility, and perhaps for that reason, it became the main tendency in Hindi criticism for decades to come. Whereas the main tasks of anti-Marxist criticism were to oppose Marxist literature and to establish the greatness of its own preferred literature, Marxist criticism tended towards an evaluation of the entire tradition of Hindi literature. Another significant point to be noted is that if the internal debates among Marxist critics were ignored, then one would not find any trend in the criticism of Hindi literature that would exhibit a tradition of debate and discussion. That is why any discussion of the canon in Marxist criticism should bear in mind that its development occurred through bitter debates among Marxist critics themselves. Therefore, the claims of universal acceptance made for this canon will always be dubious, and the debates around the canon will always be in motion.

The article '*Bharat mein pragatishil sahitya ki avashyakta*' [The Necessity of Progressive Literature in India] by Shivdan Singh Chauhan, published in the journal *Vishal Bharat* [Greater India] in March 1937, is considered as the beginning of Marxist criticism in Hindi. This article shows that Marxist criticism was tied to the idea of critically evaluating its tradition in Hindi. The author strikes a familiar note:

In the Bhakti period too, the ideas of self-surrender and immersion in devotion,

etc., were found abundantly in our Sur–Tulsi-like literature. After them, in
the *riti* period, let alone thinking, our poets started writing sex manuals in
verse. What else could be expected from them but this degradation. In the
present age too there is not a hint of healthy thought.[3]

It is difficult to reconcile oneself to the wholesale exclusion and denunciation
of the history of the Hindi tradition in Chauhan's article; the author
himself amended several of his views in later years. But this example shows
clearly that Marxist criticism in Hindi began with the view that instead
of the Bhakti or *riti* periods, the focus of criticism should shift to *modern*
literature. Later Marxist criticism enquired after contemporary forms of
literariness and simultaneously developed a more sensitive lens with which
to evaluate the tradition. However much it is alleged that Marxist criticism
is influenced by foreign streams of thought, and that it is cut off from the
country's circumstances and tradition, its trajectory of development can be
understood only through the critical tradition of Ramchandr Shukl and
Hazari Prasad Dwivedi.

Ramvilas Sharma's advent in Hindi criticism occurs through his critical
writings on his beloved poet Nirala, and in his attempt to understand
Nirala within a critical framework. But Sharma does not stop with that. In
his theoretical and practical criticism, he surveys the entire Hindi literary
tradition and identifies the progressive elements in it. He writes extensively
on other aspects of Hindi literature such as linguistics, history, philosophy
and questions of culture. It is not the case that he does not address the
Bhakti period, but by the time he enters Hindi criticism the Bhakti period
is clearly not at the centre of discussions within Hindi criticism. Although
other Marxist critics are not in full agreement with Sharma's positions, he
has been the inspiration for developing Marxist criticism through debate
and polemics. He presents the intellectual bases of 'Hindi nationality' [Hindi
jati], and makes anti-imperialism and anti-feudalism the criteria against
which Hindi literature must be evaluated. In his analytic mode he often
oversteps Marxist thought, and at places in his argument the dialectical
bases seem lacking. In effect, it is only by systematically understanding the
historical circumstances behind the formation of his anti-imperialist–anti-
feudal standard for criticism that we can spot the inconsistencies of his
project.

A novel contribution made by Sharma to the language of Hindi
criticism is the notion of 'Hindi nationality'. One of the early critical
pushes for the importance of national unity was the writings of the Bengali
intellectual Shyamcharan Ganguli on the question of the partition of

Bengal, published in *Modern Review* in 1911. Before Ramvilas Sharma, we have the equation of the Hindi language and nationalism in the writings of Bhartendu Harishchandr, Mahavir Prasad Dwivedi, Ramchandr Shukl and Hazari Prasad Dwivedi. But the establishment of a concurrence between nationality and literature is Ramvilas Sharma's singular contribution. In his several published works, he addresses the question of Hindi nationality, and the development, consolidation and extension of Hindi as the national language. But what does he mean by nationality? How is it different from the nation? Under what circumstances does it arise? What are its core elements? These are some of the questions I will address in this section, in the course of a discussion on the process of nationality formation in Sharma's thought.

Ramvilas Sharma considers *jati* or nationality to be different from *rashtr* or the nation-state. He writes:

> For the term 'nation', as it is used in Marxist criticism, the appropriate term to use is the old and recognizable Hindi and Bengali word '*jati*'. The term *rashtr* [nation-state] gives the sense of land, whereas the word 'nation' gives the sense of only the people resident on a piece of land. If we keep the two words apart – i.e. *jati* and *rashtr* – we may overcome the confusion that arises with the use of the word 'nation'.[4]

Sharma agrees with J.V. Stalin's views on nationality but departs from him on the question of the evolution of nationalities. Stalin defines 'nation' thus: 'The constitution of a stable group of people in a historical form, in one language, within a border, within economic life and a common mental make-up, all of which are constructed in everyday culture, is a nation.'[5] Along with a shared land of habitation, a shared culture, a shared language and a common historical tradition, the other important aspect of nationality is that it is a product of capitalist relations of production; that is, nationality cannot be conceived in pre-capitalist times. Stalin notes that nationalities came into being after the decline of feudalism and with the emergence of capitalism, but Sharma is of the view that nationalities were first formed in the feudal period and not after capitalism as is widely assumed.[6] In his work *Bhasha aur samaj* [Language and Society], Sharma raises the question:

> Is nationality formulated in the feudal period and if so, what are its bases? With the rise of capitalism nationalities are formed in a way. The basis of this new formation is the establishment of a new market based in capitalism. But before the development of capitalism, and after the dissolution of the old tribes, is there an 'intermediate' form of nationality as a social formation or not?[7]

On this knotty question of sociological development, Sharma points to the fact that Stalin too differentiates between 'nationality' and 'nation' in order to argue that the language of the nation emerges from the languages of the various nationalities.

Sharma pays little attention to the role played by market relations in the formation of nationalities, and draws on V.I. Lenin to demonstrate that at the beginning of the seventeenth century Russian merchants merged together the various local markets in Russia to form a large, pan-Russian market, which led to the formation of the Russian nationality. To further buttress his theory of the emergence of nationality in the feudal period, Sharma cites Friedrich Engels' *The Origin of the Family, Private Property and the State* (1884), and argues that Engels too acknowledged the rise and importance of nationalities in the feudal period. On these grounds, Sharma argues that in India, the Mughal period was instrumental in the formation of the Hindi nationality. Amending the Marxist conception of social development, according to which changes in the forces of production necessarily transform the relations of production and society enters a new stage of development, he writes that apart from production, the other force behind the regulation of society is distribution. He argues that the system of distribution affects the mode of production.

> The market on whose basis nationality is constructed, is first established by mercantile capital. To meet the increasing consumption of goods, changes in the mode of production take place only much later. For this reason, in the economic history of all countries we notice that the rise of mercantile capital takes place first, followed by the capitalist mode of production. Mercantile capital can develop under any mode of production [*utpadan-paddhati*].[8]

Prior to the advent of capitalism, mercantile capital develops the market which cannot be sustained through the old mode of production, and the formation of nationalities takes place under the rule of mercantile capital.

Manager Pandey takes issue with Sharma's theory by arguing that the primary motor of social development is the mode of production, and that distribution is merely one factor in the mode of production. Pointing to the weaknesses in Sharma's formulation of mercantile capital, Veer Bharat Talwar notes:

> The fact is that neither is there a special relation between the development of mercantile capital and the capitalist mode of production, nor even a necessary relation with the mode of production as such. Whatever the mode of producing saleable goods, mercantile capital has no necessary relation with this. It is,

rather, related to the goods realized after production is over. Therefore, it is not at all necessary that along with the development of mercantile capital, there must be developments in the mode of production too. Mercantile capital functions only to buy and sell finished goods, its mobility is caught between these two activities. For this reason, sometimes the mode of production remains very backward with no noticeable changes, while trade keeps developing. In this regard, Marx writes that the development of mercantile capital may be in inverse proportion to the magnitude of development of production.[9]

The farther back Sharma posits the question of the birth of nationalities, the stronger becomes the implication that the aim of his entire effort is to counteract European beliefs about pre-colonial India. He does not want to give any credit, positive or negative, to colonial rule, in the light of India's colonial experience. It is significant in this regard that he disagrees with Marx too, in his writings on India. In Pranay Krishn's words:

Although Ramvilas Sharma acknowledges in Marx's remarks on India the latter's denunciation of British rule and his sympathy for the Indian opposition, he is not ready to grant any progressive character to British colonialism. In opposition to Marx's view, he wrote copiously on language, culture and history, in which he used the dialectical materialist method to uncover those elements in pre-colonial Indian history and culture which could have made India modern without the intervention of colonialism.[10]

This is the same ground on which Sharma propounds his reading of modern Hindi literature as an anti-colonial literature of nationalist reawakening. Humanism, rationalism, progress and development, this-worldliness, independence, socio-economic equality and other similar values, according to Sharma, are not of western provenance but are entirely indigenous. In his post-independence writings, Sharma makes 'anti-imperialism' and 'anti-feudalism' the touchstones of critical evaluation. In India, capitalist imperialism formed a compact with feudalism, and thus it became a pillar of exploitation in rural India. After independence too, the national rulers worked in favour of the strong feudal remnants. Thus 'imperialism' and 'feudalism' are interdependent in the Indian case, and a concerted opposition to both is necessary for the growth of a national consciousness. In this manner, anti-colonial nationalism finds expression in the form of the Hindi reawakening.

Based on this understanding, Ramvilas Sharma's literary canon includes Bhartendu Harishchandr, Mahavir Prasad Dwivedi, Nirala, Premchand and Ramchandr Shukl. The touchstones are the same: 'anti-imperialism' and 'anti-feudalism'. Instead of considering Hindi literature as an expression of the reawakening, Sharma views it as a subset of the latter. In his theorization, the Hindi reawakening takes place both inside and outside literature.

Sharma inaugurates his theory of the Hindi reawakening in his book *Mahavir Prasad Dwivedi aur Hindi navjagaran* [Mahavir Prasad Dwivedi and the Hindi Reawakening] (1977) by conceiving the 1857 struggle for freedom as its first stage. He views the 'Bhartendu age' as the second stage and the 'Dwivedi age' as the third stage of this process. He associates the Hindi reawakening with the formation of the Hindi nationality and considers nationality formation, which he believes to have begun in the twelfth century CE, to be contemporaneous with the development of capitalism. Since the creation of a national language and literature takes place in the modern period, he considers the modern period also to have begun in the twelfth century. Sharma considers the second stage of the popular awakening of the Hindi nationality, which is the reawakening proper and whose essence is anti-imperialist, to be from the time of the Battle of Plassey till the period around 1857. He underlines the major characteristics of the Hindi reawakening to be as follows: an anti-feudal and anti-imperial consciousness, a revaluation of history and tradition, opposition to traditional conventionalism, struggle for the freedom of expression, the development of Khari Boli as the language of nationality, the development of a modern intellectual outlook, the spread of scientific consciousness, opposition to the *riti* period in literature, strengthening materialist thinking, expanding free-thinking and realist tendencies in art, etc.

As part of his debate against Ramvilas Sharma's views, Manager Pandey relates the formation of nationalities with mercantile capital, while connecting the rise of the nation to industrial capitalism. Pandey points out that in his writings after 1955, Sharma considers feudalism to have played a key role in the development of nationality and national language, and, along with this, he posits trade and the market instead of the mode of production as determinants of social development. This is in stark opposition to Lenin and Stalin's view that the languages of the nationalities are born with capitalism. Of course, Pandey also questions Sharma's belief that the last nine hundred years of Hindi literature constitute its modern period.

According to Pandey, Sharma's theorization of the culture and literature of Hindi nationality neglects class struggle and the struggle of ideas for the sake of preservation of tradition.

> Capitalism born in the twelfth century in India did not develop successfully; it
> was obstructed later and remained fruitless. The feudal basis of society and the

cultural edifice built on it prevailed despite its weakening. This is the reason for the succession of the *riti* period after the Bhakti period. The Bhakti movement is the cultural expression of mercantile capitalism as it developed in feudal society and of the social relations resulting from the formation of nationality; the literature of the *riti* period is a consequence and proof of the obstruction of anti-feudal social relations and cultural consciousness.[11]

Manager Pandey notes that in Sharma's theory of the Hindi reawakening, the weaknesses located come from outside the Hindi region. For example, Sharma connects neo-romanticism with Rabindranath Tagore and trends in Bengal, and attributes opposition to science and industrialization to Gandhi's thought and influence in Gujarat. Pandey identifies the following weaknesses in Sharma's analysis: he stops short of *Chhayavad* in his analysis of the Hindi reawakening; he emphasizes primarily the nationality characteristics of Hindi literature while discussing the problems of progressive literature; and he ignores class struggle and the struggle of ideas in order to assert the progressivism of the Hindi reawakening and its literature.

Ramvilas Sharma returns the sally in his book *Bhartendu Harishchandr aur Hindi navjagaran ki samasyaen* [Bhartendu Harishchandr and the Problems of the Hindi Reawakening) (1984), written as a response to Manager Pandey's criticism. He repeats his position on the connection between the rise of a greater nationality and its relations with mercantile capital. Downplaying the difficulty of a nine hundred-year-old modernity, he proposes crucial divisions on the basis of historical tendencies. In making the point that since the major contradiction under mercantile capitalism is between the feudatory and the peasants and artisans, Ramvilas Sharma does *not* consider the obstruction posed by *riti* literature to anti-feudal feeling or social consciousness to be of the same order that hinders the development of capitalism in India. He also denies the accusation that for him there is no weakness internal to the Hindi reawakening, and that all such weaknesses came from outside the Hindi region. He takes mercantile capitalism as the base and relates it to the development of nationality, language, literature and culture, reiterating his views in that light.

Sharma's view of the Hindi reawakening led to fierce debates in Hindi criticism that have not ceased even today. Shivkumar Mishr questions his theory as follows:

> What is the reason that the same Bengal which is accused of exporting mysticism [*rahasyavad*] to other regions is also seen to be a weak link in the movement against feudalism? In the same Bengal, the chord of women's awakening was

sounded most strongly and the same Bengal later becomes the ground from which the people's leftist movement arose. . . . From a Gujarat that is thought to be Gandhian and on that account anti-industrialization, the same Gujarat later becomes a great industrial centre in the country. . . . Maharashtra, which is seen to be the cause for Hindu revivalism, is the same state in which huge movements of women and Dalits come up, great Dalit leaders such as Mahatma Phule and Ambedkar are born there, and Dalit literature is born and develops there. *Et cetera, et cetera.* And in the Hindi region, which is identified with the positive aspects of the reawakening, i.e. its intellectualism, its rationalism, its anti-feudal consciousness, its non-communalist outlook, no big socio-cultural movement and corresponding leadership arise in the same period, which, not just in industry but in all dimensions of social practice (such as women's oppression, *harijans*, Hindu–Muslim amity), is the most decrepit and the most feudalist. It has broken all records in the areas of untouchability, *harijan* and women's exploitation, casteism, communalism, medieval practices, religious superstition, ignorance, illiteracy, conventionalism. . . . We may hypnotise ourselves with the disembodied knowledge of our selves and take pride in our writers, but whenever our gaze falls on the huge Hindi region, we will have to repeat after Bhartendu: O people of the north-west region, what has befallen you? When will you arise? *Et cetera, et cetera.* It is a matter of wonderment that this was the land on which the struggle of 1857 took place, and it is the same region which, because of the growth of communalism, played a most important role in the Partition of the country.[12]

Shivkumar Mishr underlines the issues that follow from positing the 1857 struggle as the precursor to the Hindi reawakening, and demands that these issues be revisited. Similarly, Veer Bharat Talwar raises important questions against Ramvilas Sharma's theory of the Hindi reawakening:

1. In comparison with the other regions of India, what were the circumstances of the Hindi reawakening? 2. Which are the areas of expression for the Hindi reawakening? Hindi writers attempted to find the consciousness of the reawakening only within Hindi literature. Dr Bachchan Singh mentions this only in passing in the context of *khayal* singing, which does not throw light on anything. What, for example, was the status of the reawakening in the pictorial arts? 3. In the processes of religio–cultural and social reform, which castes and classes were included and what were the reasons? It is necessary here to analyse the regional effects of the movement too. For example, why did the Arya Samaj movement not influence Calcutta or Bombay, which had already experienced the reawakening? What was the reason for its greatest influence in Punjab? And in the Hindi region, why did it not influence eastern Uttar Pradesh, as it did

the western part which abuts Punjab? Further, what were the results of taking inspiration from ideas of the past, such as the Vedas, Vedanta philosophy and Buddhism? 4. What sort of relations existed between the colonial masters and the leaders of the reawakening? What was the latter's outlook towards peasants, workers, untouchables and women? 5. Was there more than one current in the Hindi rewakening? 6. Was the Hindi reawakening confined to the cities or did it also reach the rural areas and the lowest classes? 7. Are there any tradition(s) of thought in the reawakening that belong to the lower classes and which are different from and independent of the educated middle-class? Finally, there is the question of the theory and structure of the Hindi reawakening. What is meant by the Hindi reawakening? Does it mean the reawakening through the medium of the Hindi language or the reawakening within Hindi literature? Or, does it pertain to the reawakening in the entire Hindi region or the reawakening of the so-called Hindi nationality? On what basis should the structure of this reawakening be determined? What would be its relationship with the theory and study of the European renaissance and the reawakenings in Bengal and Maharashtra?[13]

These are the kinds of questions which negate, in concrete points, the imagination of the Hindi reawakening and the conclusions drawn from it by Ramvilas Sharma. Talwar makes efforts towards answering these in his masterful study of the reawakening, *Rassakashi: unnisvin sadi ka navjagaran aur pashchimottarprant* [A Tug of War: Nineteenth-century Reawakening and the North-Western Provinces], and writes in the conclusion:

> The Indian reawakening began in the decade of the 1820s in Bengal and in the 1830s in Maharashtra. For almost fifty years, the reawakening in both these regions caused unrest in the elite intellectual society. By the end of the 1870s, the first tidal wave of this reawakening, which took the form of social and religious reform, had receded almost completely. By 1880 the forces of Hindu reaction had come up stridently. These reactionary forces developed in Bengal under the leadership of Bankim and Bhudev Mukherji, and in Maharashtra under Tilak along with several Chitpavan Brahmins. The lustre of the reawakening had dimmed. Whatever the extent and nature of the reawakening in the North-Western Provinces, it began unfortunately in this period. . . . In this region, the Arya Samaj was forced to mellow its sharp voice of religious reform and support popular issues that were not so integral to their foundational agenda. These were primarily the issues of using the Nagari script and cow protection, which had been earlier raised by orthodox Hindu [*sanatani*] leaders. For this reason, there was no chance of opposition from their side. These issues were raised to counter the injustices against the Hindu

elite class. These three issues were democratic demands but the Hindu elite articulated them in a communal way. In order to unite people behind these demands, 'Hindu-ness' [*hindutv*] was utilized and anti-Muslim sentiments were stirred among Hindus. . . . 'Hindi reawakening' is a misnomer. . . . It was, in fact, a movement of reaction of the orthodox Hindu [*sanatan*] intellectuals against the reforms proposed by the Brahmo Samaj and, more importantly, the Arya Samaj. . . . The attitude of the Hindi reawakening on the most important issues of social reform, the women's question, was backward-looking and embattled. . . . Unlike the Brahmo Samaj and the Arya Samaj, they had not launched a spirited movement for the education of women. Even when opposing child marriage, they did not spread any effective propaganda against it. On the question of widow remarriage, apart from a few exceptions, either they stood against it or remained embattled. They did not promote any new thinking from the position of women's consciousness. This is why in the so-called Hindi reawakening in the nineteenth century, no significant woman writer came up who could be compared with the women writers from Bengal and Maharashtra. In truth, instead of 'Hindi reawakening', it should be named the Hindi movement. . . . The competing issues between the Hindu and Muslim elites, which were articulated in the so-called Hindi reawakening, made socio-religious reform a secondary matter. . . . A characteristic of the reawakening in the North-Western Provinces was the formation of different caste assemblies to monitor reform. . . . Despite being strongly opposed, the Arya Samaj remained the primary force in the North-Western Provinces. . . . Due to opposition from the traditionalists, it could never gain ground there. . . . In the 1940s, several of its members joined the Rashtriya Swayamsevak Sangh and the temples–offices of the Arya Samaj became venues for Sangh meetings. . . . Such an outcome of the most important and effective ideological strain of the Indian reawakening is a bitter truth. . . . The problems which terrorize us today in such dreadful shapes – religious community-based fundamentalism, Muslim separatism and the Hindi–Urdu controversy – were all born in the time of the reawakening in the nineteenth century. . . . But, along with this negative aspect, there is a counteracting aspect of the reawakening. This is the sharply critical perspective on religion and traditions, which has become so rare these days.[14]

After such an exposition, the idea of the Hindi reawakening does not appear so incontestable or unassailable as it may appear in Ramvilas Sharma's writings. Talwar correlates contemporary realities of the Hindi region with the history of the reawakening on the basis of the latter's middle-class elite bases, its current of orthodoxy, its silence on the women's and caste question, and its receptivity to communalist ideas. In this genealogy, there is no reference to the moment of 1857, that point of departure which Ramvilas Sharma had established with firmness.

We have already discussed the canon proposed by Ramvilas Sharma based on the Hindi nationality and the Hindi reawakening. But when the very bases of the Hindi nationality and Hindi reawakening become objects of debate, the literary canon erected on their bases cannot be taken as universally acceptable. We can argue with the 'anti-feudalist' and 'anti-imperialist' criteria posited by Sharma in two ways. First, that literature cannot be evaluated based on these criteria; they are useful but not adequate. Second, that the writers whom Sharma chooses to evaluate according to these criteria appear to be overvalued and offered as super-paragons of anti-feudalism and anti-imperialism. Both these have become points of debate around Sharma's critical project. His writings on Nirala and Premchand are considered important, and no major disagreements have emerged about them. But just as Bhartendu's 'anti-imperialism' and Shukl's 'anti-feudalism' are regularly treated with suspicion, critics have noted that it is because of his self-posited definition of critical concepts, their insufficiency for the purposes of literary criticism and a mechanistic understanding of Marxism that Sharma presents a defective evaluation of a writer such as Muktibodh.

In his appraisal of Bhartendu, Sharma presents him as the pioneer of the Hindi reawakening, and shows his literary work to be anti-feudal and anti-imperialist in character. Earlier we have discussed how Shivkumar Mishr notes the harmonization of the music of regime devotion [*raj bhakti*] and national devotion [*rashtr bhakti*] in Bhartendu's thought. Veer Bharat Talwar counterposes Raja Shiv Prasad 'Sitara-e-Hind' with Bhartendu in order to highlight the contradictions in the latter's positions from the question of women's education to that of Urdu. Talwar demonstrates how the echo of communalism of the Hindi region can be heard in Bhartendu's play, *Nildevi*.

Similarly, in 1955, explaining the importance of Ramchandr Shukl in the introduction to his book, *Acharya Ramchandr Shukl aur Hindi alochna* [The Great Teacher Ramchandr Shukl and Hindi Criticism], Ramvilas Sharma writes:

> Shukl holds the same importance in Hindi criticism as the novelist Premchand or the poet Nirala. Using criticism, he opposes the same feudal culture that was opposed by Premchand through the novel and Nirala in poetry. Shukl neither accepts the traditionalism of India nor the individualism of the west. He proposes new literary principles on the basis of the external world and

human existence, and on the basis of the former, opposes feudal literature and concurs with the literary tradition of patriotism and democracy.[15]

While Sharma does not consider Shukl to be a true materialist, he does concede that he is more or less part of the materialist viewpoint, and he establishes that in proposing a worldly reading of the *ras* theory, Shukl dismantles the feudalist view that posits pleasure as the end of poetry and substitutes beauty with the founding feeling of empathy, based on the poetic tradition of Valmiki and Bhavbhuti. His ideal heroes are those who struggle against justice inspired by empathy.

Naturally, Shukl's evaluation of Tulsidas became the nub of Sharma's apologia for Shukl's critical project. Not only does Sharma consider this evaluation valid but he rejects the analysis of Kabir as the central poet of the Bhakti period: 'on balance, all the books written on Kabir on one side, Shukl's three sentences on the other'.[16]

Sharma also presents an unprecedented example of 'destructive' criticism. He is considered a critic in the anti-colonial mode; and that, just like African writers who refused to admit they had no history prior to the coming of the colonial yoke and thus questioned the Marxist axiom that 'the history of all hitherto existing society is the history of class struggles' (or if we replace 'history' with 'written history', in Engels' words), Ramvilas Sharma too gestures towards the inadequacy of classical Marxist readings of colonialism and elaborates these for an Indian situation. But his position becomes untenable as he addresses such peculiarities of the Indian situation as the fearsome exploitation of the *shudras*, or defends Shukl as anti-feudal even as the latter defends Tulsi's views on women, or excludes from his canon Kabir, the poet voicing the growing demands of the subaltern classes and whose cultural articulation may be considered to be the Bhakti period itself. In today's context, when Dalit criticism is searching for its own tradition and conducting a thorough revaluation of the canon, it is not without reason that for it the central poet of the Bhakti period is Kabir, which weakens Shukl's critical evaluation of the poet. And how would Sharma situate Phule's critique, which argued that British rule gave the opportunity for education to the Dalits, ground down by centuries of Brahminism? While an anti-imperialist consciousness is visible in Shukl's criticism, it does not follow from this that he was against feudalism too. Despite his contributions to Hindi criticism in the form of intellectualism and realism, the designation of anti-feudalism, to use Shukl's own phrase, seems rather 'far-fetched'.

Sharma limits his conception of feudalism to the total structure of land relations. The difficulty with his conception is that the social relations constituted along with these land relations, their interpenetration and their mutual transformation, are not at all considered in his criticism by Sharma. Instead he quotes Shukl's advice given to Chandrashekhar Azad:

> The British have created the banker–zamindars through their policies. Leave them aside. The middle zamindar after paying taxes is reduced to the status of a peasant. Include them as well in your organization. They too are ready to revolt along with the peasantry. Great violence has happened. Now only the path of force remains.[17]

While it is justifiable to separate Shukl from Gandhianism on this basis, his anti-feudalism cannot be proven for in the social divisions that prevail in the form of the caste system, apart from the economic system, would the 'middle zamindar reduced to the status of the peasant' forego his hierarchical privilege?

The counter-critique of Sharma's Shukl, in Sharma-esque style, is given by Nilkant in his *Acharya Ramchandr Shukl*. Mirroring the extremes of argumentation in Sharma, Nilkant's own extreme conclusions about Shukl are at least successful in raising serious questions about his epistemology.[18]

Another exemplary situation that reveals the limits of Sharma's critical project is his evaluation of Muktibodh. Sharma's main contention is against Muktibodh's inner world, which he reduces, through several arguments, to sentimentalism. Against the backdrop of the politics of the Cold War period, this point of departure in Sharma's thought provides an opposition to modernism and its subset of aestheticism or art for art's sake. In this situation, Sharma deploys his agenda of anti-imperialism–anti-feudalism in such a way that he completely misses the expression of social dynamism in Muktibodh's poetry. The struggle with the self in Muktibodh, which Sharma fits into the Procrustean frame of existentialism, is precisely the historical condition of the middle class – a condition of contradictions which, on the one hand, pulls it in the direction of subaltern struggles fighting for political change, and on the other, tempts it to climb the ladder of its own social expectations. Against the critical picture of Muktibodh in Sharma's criticism, Namvar Singh presents another view of the poet. The last section of this chapter will address the features and limits of Namvar Singh's criticism of Muktibodh.

Based on the discussion thus far, we may derive a few conclusions about Marxist trends in Hindi criticism. First, within Marxist criticism too there is little consensus on the canon, which is a site of fierce debates. These debates have resulted in revaluations of individual writers as well as of the category

of literature itself. Second, behind Ramvilas Sharma's theorization of the
Hindi nationality and Hindi reawakening, there appears to be the argument
that even if the British had not colonized India, the country would have
become modern on its own. Third, the categories of 'anti-imperialism' and
'anti-feudalism' may be applied to literary analysis but they are hardly the
categories required for the task, and their mechanical application only leads
to faulty conclusions.

MUKTIBODH: THE CLASS QUESTION IN CANON FORMATION

In the processes of canon formation we have discussed so far, the standpoint
of class has been a continuous factor, whether it is enunciated as such or
not. It is an insight of Marxist theory that the dominant ideology, i.e. the
perspective of the dominant class, presents itself as free of contradiction and
in a 'universal' form in such a way that it shows its own class interest to be
over and above 'narrow interests'. It is through consent that it maintains its
hegemony over the plurality of society for a long period, but this ideology is
neither free of contradiction nor able to transcend its class interest.

The process of canon formation in Hindi criticism too has undergone
the long duration of history. We have seen earlier that while in the colonial
period, the literary canons proposed by colonial intellectuals were under the
pressure of maintaining consent for colonial power in the long duration, in
the nationalist period, for critics affected by the national movement, their
function shifted to nation formation. It follows that in different historical
periods, canons are proposed and formed in order to maintain or change
the balance of mutually competing political forces.

Arguably, Muktibodh is the first writer in Hindi criticism to signpost
the role played by mutually struggling or competing class forces in the
process of canon formation. He seems to be writing from the viewpoint
of those classes that had not yet achieved expression, that had merely
'dense, unfathomable experiences'. Therefore, the tasks he set himself in
his criticism had a civilizational breadth: highlighting the circumstances
and contributions of different social classes, examining the failures of the
Bhakti movement, investigating the apparently impenetrable writings of
his own time, and identifying the determinant forces of history and their
antinomies. As a part of this process, he addresses the middle class from the
side of the excluded groups, and elaborates the ideology and expressions
of the oppressed to such an extent that they could challenge existing ideas
of the universal. Within the same project, Muktibodh focuses on a review
of civilization itself; he makes a class reading of the rise and fall of Bhakti,

produces distinctive commentaries on Prasad's modern epic *Kamayani* and verse play *Urvashi*, theorizes 'new poetry' [*nayi kavita*], addresses the middle class from the proletarian point of view and expands the scope of Marxism within Hindi criticism on newer grounds.

Identifying Determinant Forces of History

When Ramchandr Shukl sets aside several existing literary histories of Hindi by calling them merely the 'lives of poets', the implication is that these compositions lack a sense of history. Mere chronology is not history-writing. Therefore, before writing literary history he considers it important to elucidate his idea of a sense of history. As we have seen, Shukl associates literature with states of consciousness [*chittvrittiyan*] of the people, and thus views literary history as the history of a special aspect of *social* consciousness. But this does not exhaust the concept of literary history. The question remains: what is the self-understanding of the social consciousness that leads to the growth of literature, and what are the material forces that give rise to it? Additionally, to which part of society does this social consciousness pertain, even if it were to be adopted by everyone else in society?

Now, if we include culture within this notion of history, we can argue that in the discussions of cultural excellence, social truth is neglected all the time. In this regard, D.D. Kosambi writes:

> There is falsity and mystification in India, there is a religious labyrinth, there is ornamental literature, there are halls decorated with icons and there is melodious music. All these are the products of that same historical process in which there are famine-stricken impassive rural people on one hand, and on the other the opportunism of unempathetic people and their termite-like greed. Each is the result of the other.[19]

In his *Hindi sahitya ki bhumika* [Introduction to Hindi Literature], Hazari Prasad Dwivedi replaces Shukl's 'states of popular consciousness' with 'popular thought' [*lok chinta*]: 'I propose this way of thinking. I do not want to measure popular thought by creeds, teachers, sects or philosophical schools; instead I am proposing to view the latter in the light of popular thought.'[20] The concurrence between Kosambi's and Dwivedi's theories of history is not coincidental. According to Dwivedi: 'History is the life-story of the actually existing human being, which exhibits scenes from the victory march of humanity from within newly occurring events and circumstances that are forever being unveiled through the flow of time.'[21] And according to Kosambi: 'The task of making history is accomplished only by the common people who are considered backward and ignorant, and not by the priests, nobility, leaders of the army, capitalists or the leaders who dupe the people.'[22]

The idea of social progress is a necessary part of the process of struggle and transformation. The viewpoints on history mentioned above reject the conception of history as a thing of the past, and instead make a case for studying rises and falls in the progress of human history. It is obvious that this conception of history is people-centric as opposed to the history of great men, and studies the past with a view towards a better future.

The first serious discussion on the orientation of history as a discipline took place during the European renaissance. Values of humanism, the theory of progress, changes in the conception of temporality and secularism – all these made possible new readings of the human past. The second major revolution in the philosophy of history took place in the work of G.W.F. Hegel and matured in the work of Karl Marx. This thought was both an heir of the values of the renaissance and a fresh elaboration. Marx developed a theory of the formation of classes in human history for absorbing surplus value, and reached the conclusion that 'the history of all hitherto existing society is the history of class struggles'.[23] In the 1888 English edition of the *Manifesto of the Communist Party*, Engels added a footnote to the first part of this sentence: 'that is, all *written* history';[24] all hitherto written history is the history of class struggles.

Critics who adopt a Marxist view of literature give more importance to class difference as compared to 'society' or 'the people' [*lok*]. The word *janta* or the masses is more extensive, and expresses the sense of an undivided and disembodied entity. When Ramchandr Shukl uses '*janta*' in his literary history, it is clear that he does not care for the view that in class-differentiated society the ideas of the exploited are generally the ideas of the exploiters. Marx is the thinker who makes available this insight to criticism.

The use of '*lok*' or the people/popular in Hazari Prasad Dwivedi is at a distance from its authorized meaning and is associated with the lower orders of society. It is his belief that from the beginning of the common era, the Indian intellectual tradition was orientated towards the popular. But what were the conditions of its possibility? What were the motors in human material culture that allowed the tradition of the popular an ascendance in the Indian subcontinent? Dwivedi does not give answers to these questions. His commitment to the popular does reflect a mature understanding of society, but, curiously enough, he does not present the theoretical bases for positing the predominance of the popular in the Indic tradition. Dwivedi's project is subject to the limits of any project that considers the history of consciousness to be divorced from material circumstances, and from the processes and relations of production.

Defining the lens of history, Rajendr Kumar writes:

> History is never simply man-made but develops from the perspective of human potentialities. The historical lens is delineated by man's perspective on his ability to use his self-developed forces in one or several directions amidst the entire process of development, i.e. in all lands under temporally determined circumstances. In the core concept of literature too, if we do not accept the primacy of this historical lens, a literary-theoretical analytic presentation as such cannot qualify as the history of literature.[25]

It was only in the period of progressivism that the first serious attempts were made to understand class-based perspectives in literature. In the field of literary history, such perspectives were preferred in the writings of the progressives. Many critics who conceived of the cultural process as class-free greatly opposed this view. Some other critics found it acceptable to use the class perspective while studying works of modern and contemporary literature, but considered it an imposition when it came to literary history. From Dwivedi's viewpoint, literature has its own traditions that are constantly in motion. Therefore, literature is not fully contemporaneous with social change. Even Marxist theory agrees with the position that the base and the superstructure are not parallel to each other, but are in a dialectical relationship. It is never the case that with a change in the relations of production, there are immediate changes in the realms of ideas, politics, literature and art. Each of these superstructural elements possesses a relative autonomy as well as a genetic similarity, which in turn affect the production process. But in the final analysis, the superstructure is established on the base. Those who forget this clause, 'in the final analysis', misconstrue the relative autonomy of the superstructure as complete autonomy.

The critical thought of Gajanan Madhav Muktibodh represents the best forms of progressive thought in literary history. Just as critics who conceive superstructural forms to be completely autonomous of the base are devoid of the historical sense of literature, those who do not agree with the relative autonomy of superstructural forms, and mistake the final instance to be the first instance of determination, produce a vulgar sociology. Muktibodh launches an offensive precisely against this weakness of the progressivist argument. He sets up his historical lens by theorizing about the compelling twists and turns in the history of literature.

Another notable aspect of Muktibodh's criticism is commitment. The importance of commitment can be understood by the fact that the end-of-history arguments of postmodernity negate the very existence of such a thing. Such arguments declare that grand narratives of freedom cannot be written any more. History-writing, however, needs a specific commitment, a vision and a perspective. It is this philosophy of history that is the primary target of postmodern thought. In his criticism, Muktibodh uses a form of historical sociology according to which society is class-differentiated and history is the history of the struggles between these classes. Therefore, for Muktibodh, history does not have an end and the historical sense is an intellectual tool for devising a way out for the exploited man: 'the aim of this intellectualism is the independence of man – and not the philosophical independence of a disembodied humanism – i.e. the economic and cultural independence of people subjugated in society'.[26]

The value of commitment to historical sense can be also gauged from the fact that despite being a modern writer, Ramchandr Shukl wrote the first systematic literary history in Hindi, in support of forces of historical regression. In this context, despite being a votary of tradition, Hazari Prasad Dwivedi appears progressive in his orientation. A special and apposite relation is visible between commitment and historical sense in the thought of Muktibodh, which articulates commitment as a strong ideological proposal. On this basis, he considers history, society and psyche to be interconnected within literature, and thus lays emphasis on the historical analysis of theory and creativity. Some of Muktibodh's exemplary writings in this regard include his essays '*Madhyayugin bhakti andolan ka ek pehlu*' [An Aspect of the Medieval Bhakti Movement], '*Nayi kavita ka aatmasangharsh*' [Internal Struggle of New Poetry] and '*Naye sahitya ka saundaryashastr*' [Aesthetics of New Literature], and his critical writings on *Kamayani* and *Urvashi*. Apart from these, the literary vision of his poems and short stories, and his political writings such as '*Bharat: itihas aur sanskriti*' [India: History and Civilization], also reveal his historical sense. I examine these writings below, in an attempt to describe Muktibodh's historical sense of literature.

An Investigation into the Failures of the Bhakti Movement

Muktibodh's essay on the Bhakti movement attests to his deep interest in Bhakti poetry in particular and in historical debates in general. The predominance of the class aspect of power within a cultural movement and the extent to which it transforms into hegemony are the high points of Muktibodh's conception of the Bhakti movement. He conceptualizes the inner contradictions of the Bhakti period through the lens of caste and articulates the attributeless–with-attributes [*nirgun–sagun*] dichotomy as a metaphor for two different classes. He proposes:

> Any literature should be conceived from three perspectives. First, what are the social and psychological forces that give rise to it? That is, the workings of which particular forces is it a product of? In which socio-cultural processes is it an element? Second, what is its inner form? What kind of imaginations and feelings have shaped its inner substance? Third, what are its effects? Which social forces have used or misused it, and why? Which psychic elements of the common–popular has it developed or destroyed?[27]

Muktibodh criticizes the tradition of Ram devotion, and, in particular, the pervasiveness of caste, religion and orthodox conventions in Tulsi's poetry:

> For the common people Kabir's message of true action was more revolutionary than Tulsidas's message. Tulsi had to accept the basic element of devotionalism [*bhakti*], that everyone is equal before Ram, but since Ram is the progenitor of the entire society, therefore the Vedic stations of life [*varnashram dharm*] and caste must be accepted. Pandit Ramchandr Shukl's excoriation of belief in the attributeless had a reason. Behind this was his consciousness based on puranic belief.[28]

Raising questions about the very basis of the Bhakti movement, Muktibodh further writes:

> Is it not an important fact that within the Ram branch of devotion, there is not a single influential and important poet from the low-caste *shudr* classes? Is it not an important fact that within the Krishn branch of devotion there always were large-hearted Muslim poets such as Raskhan and Rahim, but within the Ram branch of devotion not a single Muslim or *shudr* poet was able to bring out his poetic intelligence in any significant or substantial way, when it is a generally established fact that such people were held in great importance in the branch of attributeless [devotion].[29]

On the above basis, he concludes:

> A *bhakti* movement that begins from among the common people and within which the cultural desires of the common people spoke against social fanaticism, within which 'human truth' spoke, that same movement was recast by the upper classes in their own image, and, strategically compromising with it and then establishing their dominance over it and afterwards removing the popular elements from it, they established their complete hegemony.[30]

In search of the contradictions of the Bhakti movement, Muktibodh's essay identifies the historic hegemonic forces operating in the social realm. He believes that 'no literature can be properly analysed until we do not properly understand the cultural history formed by the basic social forces in movement in that period'.[31]

Differentiating between the Brahmin and non-Brahmin saint-poets of the Marathi poetic tradition, Muktibodh writes:

> The poetic sensibility of the non-Brahmin poet was more democratic, ecumenical and humanistic. In that age of self-assertion of the lower castes, due to their oppression at the hands of fanatical followers of puranism, the life of fiercely accomplished saints [*sant*] such as Gyaneshvar became intensely empathetic, difficult and fiercely resolute. His famous [work] *Gyaneshvari* remained hidden for three hundred years. The illustrious history of this work begins when it was rediscovered. It is quite clear that the fanatics in society caused misery to these saints.[32]

He then goes on to address the political and social milieu of eleventh-century Maharashtra:

> From the political standpoint, this populace was suffering under the feudal upper classes of both the Hindu and Muslim varieties. The saints' humanistic voice empowered them. Devotional singing brought the circulation of emotional sap [*ras*] in their lives. Gyaneshvar, Tukaram and other saints broadened the path of the immiserated peasants and other groups.[33]

But the arrival of Ramdas made Marathi saint literature a prey to Brahminical dominance. Shivaji, whose coronation was conducted by Ramdas, was a Maratha *kshatriya*, and on this pattern, while martial power and political power remained with the army leaders from the exploited and poor classes, in the social sphere a compromise was reached between the old and new feudatories. The army leaders were the new feudatories who came from disadvantaged castes such as Kunbi, Dhangar and Maratha. The result of this compromise was that while the Peshva was Brahmin, the martial power remained with the new feudatories.

'On the other hand, in the socio-cultural sphere, the people-centric message of the lower-caste devotional movement was blunted. These saints achieved recognition among all classes, but their message received a deathly blow and the caste-based religion of the Purans was re-established without fear.'[34] In this way, the Bhakti movement, which had expressed the people's hardships and sufferings and their aspiration to be rid of these, in the end came to stand on the side of the dominant and fanatical elements of the old social structure.

Tulsidas holds the same significance within the Bhakti movement in the Hindi region as Samarth Ramdas in the Marathi Bhakti movement. But 'the surprising thing is that today, whatever is being written about Tulsidas in progressive circles is at the expense of deliberately ignoring the socio-historical process of which Tulsidas was a part'.[35] At the end of his essay, Muktibodh repeats the point: 'No realistic assessment of literature can take place unless we understand the social forces in movement, which manifest themselves on the bedrocks of science and culture. This is particularly crucial for the study of saints such as Kabir and Tulsidas. I want to draw the attention of progressive circles in this direction.'[36]

In response to Muktibodh's position, Namvar Singh writes in *Dusri parampara ki khoj* [In Search of Another Tradition]:

> Muktibodh's main position is that the Bhakti movement arose as a revolutionary movement in the form of devotion to an attributeless divine through saints born into the low castes, but with time, the upper castes recognized its force and adopted it and systematically recast it according to their ideas, and gave it the form of devotion to Ram and Krishn, the deities with attributes. . . . In the transformation of devotion to Ram, even the remnants disappeared. Is it not an important fact that within the Ram branch of devotion, there is not a single influential and important poet from the low-caste *shudr* classes? 'Is it not an important fact that within the Krishn branch of devotion there always were large-hearted Muslim poets such as Raskhan and Rahim, but within the Ram branch of devotion not a single Muslim or *shudr* poet was able to bring out his poetic intelligence in any significant or substantial way . . . What is the reason that Tulsidas was the last poet of the Bhakti movement [in the Hindi region]?'
>
> The answer to these questions takes us to the view that the dominance of the elite upper castes is responsible for this, and, ultimately, they are responsible for the attenuation and termination of the Bhakti movement. From this analysis, we can also derive the reason for the rise of *riti* poetry after the Bhakti period. If we attend to the transformation of the early ecumenical poetry for the attributeless divine into sectarian devotion to the divine with attributes, then we can relate the spread of *riti* poetry to the resurgence of codified knowledges.[37]

Manager Pandey takes exception to Namvar Singh's acquiescence to the Muktibodhian position and writes, in his essay '*Bhaktivad aur Hindi alochna*' [The Bhakti Idea and Hindi Criticism]:

> At one end of Marxist criticism stands Ramvilas Sharma, for whom there is no contradiction between devotion to the attributeless and to the divine with

attributes. He is not ready to accept any note out of harmony in the music of Bhakti poetry. At the other end stands Muktibodh, according to whom: 'The struggle between the view of an attributeless divine and its opposite was the struggle of the elite, cultured, leisured class against the lower orders.' Namvar Singh elaborates Muktibodh's view to a final conclusion. If Ramchandr Shukl found the devotion and poetry of the attributeless divine to be anti-popular, Namvar Singh considers the devotion and poetry of the divine with attributes to be indifferent to the people and anti-popular.

In this controversy between two kinds of devotion, Muktibodh's argument based on caste and lineage is strange and Namvar Singh's acquiescence to it is surprising. In reference to Hazari Prasad Dwivedi, Singh writes: 'It is "vulgar sociology" to identify any writer's vision with the caste, class or community that gives birth to it.' If this view is to be accepted, then not just in Hazari Prasad Dwivedi's context, it should be true for Kabir, Sur, Mira and Tulsidas too. In which case, any attempt to determine the vision of the poets of both branches of devotion based on their lineage and caste should also count as 'vulgar sociology'. In such a sociology, caste and class become synonymous. Also, this sociology is based less on fact than on approximations. Who does not know that the spiritual master of the saints of the attributeless path, such as Kabir, Raidas, Sen, Dhanna, etc., was Ramanand, the devotee of the god with attributes! Alongside, it is a fact that several Muslim and low-caste devotees were a part of the latter stream of devotion.[38]

In the same essay, Pandey goes on to write:

In order to determine the limits of the stream of poetry about the divine with attributes, Muktibodh poses the following question: is it not an important fact that within the branch of devotion to Ram, not a single influential or significant poet emerged from the lowest *shudr* groups? This is a fact. But what does it prove? It is a fact all the same that in the modern period, in the progressive movement too, no poet emerged from the lowest *shudr* groups. Would it then prove that the major poets of progressivism are products of the domination of the elite, upper castes? There are other facts that are important too. Premchand has written such short stories as '*Thakur ka kunva*' [The Thakur's Well] and '*Sadgati*' [Deliverance], and Nagarjun a poem like '*Harijan gatha*' [The Harijan's Tale]. The writers of these literary works are not from the *shudr* community and therefore do they have no significance? Why has no significant writer emerged from the lower castes in the modern period of Hindi literature? This is a crucial sociological question. To answer it, a deep excavation of the composition of Indian society and the temperament of its cultural traditions is necessary. It will not suffice to condemn other writers and settle the matter. This tendency is not useful in comprehending the complex totality of the Bhakti movement either.[39]

A few significant points emerge from this long passage quoted from Manager Pandey. In the medieval period, to which belongs the literary movement that Muktibodh has in mind, i.e. the Bhakti movement, the interweaving of caste and class was greater than in the modern period. Second, Muktibodh does not consider the attributeless–with-attributes polarity to be the apogee of the opposition between the creative tendencies of the lowest and highest castes, respectively. Gyaneshvar was Brahmin by birth but, for Muktibodh, he paved the way for the poor peasant populace. By highlighting the social bases of Bhakti poetry, Muktibodh wants to correlate the transformations of the Bhakti period with the momentum of the social forces of that time in their dialectical opposition. The context within which he raises the issues of the labouring classes being a part of the 'attributeless' stream of the Bhakti period, of Muslim poets being a part of the Krishn devotionalist stream and of the absence of both groups of poets from the Ram devotionalist stream cannot be compared with the case of the absence of poets of low-caste origins in the progressive poetic stream. The entire epochal milieu is different. Not just within progressivism, poets from these groups are also absent in other modern poetic streams, while this was *not* the case during the Bhakti period. In the oral tradition, the poet could have been unlettered too. With the coming of the printing press, illiterate poets had little role to play in modern written literature. As the 'lower castes' fought for the right to education, they secured a place for themselves in modern literature. Giving the reasons for the failure of the anti-caste 'attributeless' stream of the Bhakti movement, Muktibodh writes:

> The main reason for this is that in that period, the revolutionary capitalist forces that could have ended the old social order did not develop. The material base for indigenous Indian capitalism was established by foreign imperialist capitalism. With the rise of indigenous capitalism, Indian nationalism and reformism were also born, and it ended the basis of the feudal social order, i.e. the mode of production based on professional castes.[40]

Thus, Muktibodh stresses the necessity of radical Indian capitalist forces for the destruction of the feudal social order, and he considers the non-development of these forces to be responsible for the failure of the Bhakti movement in the literature of the past. In this critical view, things are not determined by opinions, but on the basis of the laws of dialectics.

After the removal of literature of the *riti* period from the literary canon,

almost all subsequent attempts at establishing a canon for Hindi take the
Bhakti movement as the basis for arriving at the idea of a canon. Each
attempt has a different agenda, and thus different criteria for evaluation.
It is possible that Muktibodh does not subscribe at least to the agenda of
centrally establishing some writer within not just Bhakti literature but also
Hindi literature, or to do right by some poet. The issue of class difference is
missing from all the heights that Hindi criticism had reached in the work
of Muktibodh's predecessors. A complex formation comprising classes
that were discriminated against in the social form of caste was present in
the Bhakti period too and exists even today, but class distinctions within
castes have proportionally increased. Despite the increased momentum in
the formation of class differences within castes, class is not the sole reason
for this increase and caste too is not the only factor in this process. This
problem comes into being because 'theorists' consider class to be a 'static'
category which cannot be transformed. Muktibodh identifies the reasons for
the failures of the Bhakti movement with the changes in its contemporary
balance of class forces. His critical vision attends to hegemonic culture and
the processes of formation of hegemonic ideas, and studies the dialectical
movement of the driving forces of history for a particular period so that
a theoretical understanding of historical phenomena becomes possible.
Therefore, Muktibodh does not consider any of the poets of the Bhakti
movement to be canonical, but it is clear that his affinities lie with the saint-
poets of attributeless devotion. This aspect of the Bhakti movement is the
ground of his civilizational critique. Thus, his criticism of the different ways
of canon formation is made from this particular perspective.

'New Poetry'

But what has taken place? Our vanguardist cultural centres, if they
exist at all, have been unable to comprehend the current developments
in Hindi literature. From the beginning they have excluded this new
stream of Hindi poetry and continued its exclusion even when this
new stream was maturing and was strengthening its foundations.[41]
(From a letter written to the then General Secretary of the Communist Party
of India, Comrade Shripad Amrit Dange)

Later, when the progressive argument was opposed for its defence of new
poetry, the concept of the parallelism of life and poetic feeling was set in
stone. . . . Behind this concept, which looks self-evident from the outside, lies
a clear–unclear political motive, which is that the continuity and fundamental

unity between poetic life and real life is to be obscured. This principle is a very dangerous belief. This is a deliberately produced mental distraction by the rule-makers who launch a cold war from the ramparts of new poetry.[42]

Both the quotations above represent the struggle within Muktibodh's criticism. The problem that faced him was to simultaneously defend new poetry in the name of progressivism and to free it from the snare of intellectuals who wanted to push it into the abyss of the other side in the cold war, i.e. the first world. Decidedly his own side leaned more towards progressivism in terms of ideology.

With the passing away of 'romanticism'/*Chhayavad*, progressivism makes its appearance in Hindi literature. Within a brief period after this, experimentalism takes root with the emergence of *Tarsaptak* (High Octave), and with this, 'new poetry' [*nayi kavita*] begins. Muktibodh identifies new poetry from the same point of view. According to him, the development of a romanticist [*chhayavadi*] aesthetic philosophy and nuance, in opposition to the gross aestheticism of Braj poetry, was relatively more modern, but the former soon became detached from its times. The imagination turned away from this world to the other world. This process may be seen in Bal Krishn Sharma Naveen, Ramdhari Singh Dinkar and Harivansh Rai Bachchan. While this stream of poetry was more realist than 'romanticism', it did not escape romanticist trappings. Muktibodh locates in these poets' work an 'actualism' [*vastav-vad*] rather than 'realism' [*yatharthvad*], whose basis is emotion and not the intellect. Following this, Muktibodh opposes these poets' shallow nationalism based on 'Indian culture'. On the other hand, within the progressive stream of poetry, he notices a desire for a path of convenience. He recognizes a tendency to cut corners in the depiction of the infinitesimal parts of life in poems which generalize in the name of the life of the masses, and an inability to connect the particular with the general. On this ground of critique, experimentalism takes over. Muktibodh defines experimentalism as a form of revolt of the contemporary middle-class subject caught up in social circumstances and unable to express opposition because of 'romanticist' poetic language and structure of feeling:

> One result of this trend was that poetry was clad in the garb of intellectual prose. Due to the lack of harmony in society, and in opposition to it, a stark intellectual individualism took shape. Within some an inner awareness became prominent, while in others an external awareness became more realistic: whether it was inward-looking or outward.[43]

These became the intellectual conditions for new poetry.

According to Muktibodh, new poetry is poetry of the modern structure of feeling. This structure is different from both the medieval religious and the 'romanticist'–emotionalist, imagination-centric structures. It recognizes real social relations through an awareness of reality and delivers sympathetic reactions. This realism is born from the challenges facing the middle class. This is a realistic individualism as opposed to the romantic individualism of *Chhayavad*. New poetry accepts a realist self-awareness for the sake of intellectualism and is self-centric for the sake of individualism. Since the scientific understanding of progressivism had not matured by this time for it to induce heart-felt and soulful conviction, writers did not share a consensus within the ideological realm. This lack of consensus only contributed further to the self-centredness.

Nevertheless, Muktibodh notes two perspectives from which to theorize the notion of reality in new poetry:

> These poets are divided across two camps from the ideological viewpoint. The first camp is actively against progressivism, in which the most prominent writers are Mr Vatsyayan and Dharmvir Bharti *et al*. The other camp is in favour of progressivism, among which the important writers are Girirajkumar Mathur, Nemichandr Jain, Shrinaresh Mehta, Bharatbhushan Agraval *et al*.[44]

On the basis of the imagery, Muktibodh divides new poetry into two groups: the art-for-art's sake group and the group that versifies internal symbols. But it seems that the first grouping is more concrete.

Muktibodh focuses on a stream of new poetry that is more proximate to Marxism. He feels greater affinity with Afro–Asian and Latin American countries – for example, with Algeria and Egypt, Congo and Cuba, Sri Lanka and Japan, Indonesia and Argentina – than with the west. He enters this poetry through an externalization of its interiority and an internalization of exteriority. It appears that he is talking about contemporary poets such as Shamsher Bahadur Singh. The other stream considers Europe and North America as the paragons of modernity, and ascribes India's fragmentariness to the former. According to this stream, man is exploited within capitalist society but even more so in socialist society. Therefore, the artist must preserve his creativity through individualism. Muktibodh expresses the effects of this stream within new poetry in the following way:

> Excessive pessimism and the tendency to remain cut off from people and society, i.e. individualism, both take on a philosophical role, and by attaining the form of an ideology, have become quite popular in the domain of new

poetry and in Hindi literature at large. The mental state arising from the unfortunately enervating situation of Indian middle-class life today absorbs this Euro–American intellectual trend.[45]

In response to the allegation of intellectualism by proponents of romanticist poetry, the new poets hold that they are not intellectual in their outlook. Muktibodh situates this declaration in the appropriate context by noting that these poets really do not show any intellectual excellence; what is visible in their poetry is a banalization of whatever strikes the poetic sensibility. He highlights here the absence of a worldview. Rather than becoming a strength of new poetry, the 'personal' has turned into an ossified aesthetic pattern. Even poets do not comprehend other poets' work. This is because the personal turns into a personal solitude, and is fragmented due to its disconnection with human affairs.

Within the inner struggle of new poetry, Muktibodh notices the influence of the Cold War. The same struggle was playing out on a world scale between the polarity of the United States and the Soviet Union. Apart from being an economic and military issue, the politics of the Cold War divided culture worldwide into two opposing viewpoints. Muktibodh is alert to this:

> You may remember that from 1951–52 onwards, to dislodge progressive ideology from the literary field, in particular in poetry, Cold War sallies were made from the ramparts of new poetry. According to me, this Cold War was the literary branch of the political Cold War taking place in the world. . . . These circumstances were prepared by a special group in an almost organized manner.[46]

By 1955, when this essay was written, the concept of the 'insignificant man' was emerging under the auspices of Agyey. For Muktibodh, the concepts of the 'insignificant man' and 'modernist thinking' cut off the writer from the palpability of life and were thus condemnable. He remarks that within this modernist structure of feeling, the life-experiences undermined by imperialism and capitalism and those of combative oppositional forces are considered untouchable.

In order to resolve this problem, Muktibodh reaches to its roots. He raises the issue of the process of poetic creation. His essay, 'Nayi kavita ka aatmasangharsh' [The Inner Struggle of New Poetry] is relevant in this regard. His critical writings regularly address the relations between art and materiality. He acknowledges that new poetry aims to express 'the sharp dialectical interaction between the knowledges of the sensible and knowledge-based sensibilities.' Thus, Muktibodh lays down the construction of the 'triadic struggle' against this challenge:

> The poet of today must struggle on three fronts. The triadic form of his struggle is, or should be, this: 1. Struggle to attain the substance; 2. Struggle to make expression effective; 3. Struggle to develop perception. The first relates to the maximally effective uncovering and scrutiny of human actuality. The second relates to competence in representation, and the third relates to theory, or the development of a worldview, or the interpretation of actualities. This is the triadic struggle.[47]

In order to grapple with the problems of new poetry and the challenges facing it, and, in the process, to define and characterize it, we can now turn to the writing process behind new poetry. Muktibodh's thesis of the 'three moments of art' was derived from this process. When the poet faces his inner realities, it inaugurates his awareness, knowledge and imagination. The first moment of this uncovering is also the first moment of art. In the second moment, this imagination or awareness is in a dialectical unity, in opposition with life-value and experience. This produces fantasy. The struggle between fantasy and social discourse takes place in the third moment, which leads to the expression of the work of art.

Through this description of the process of writing, Muktibodh establishes, first, that self-uncovering or self-manifestation is not an inanimate but a continuous process. In this way, the poet can connect his particularity with generality and thus transform his particularity into a new generality.

> It appears to him that his particularity – which is no more his particularity – produces a very everyday affective glow, affective rays. What does this particularity consist of? They are the life-values, viewpoints regarding life, which the poet encounters in the expanse of his external life. In other words, the life-value and life-vision lodged within the interior are the psychological representation of the external world.[48]

Here Muktibodh also introduces the important question of aesthetic involvement, through which he points to the class basis of the entire process of the production of art. In the third moment of art, when the struggle between fantasy and expression takes place, the artist is pushed towards a special model of expression by his aesthetic involvement. This model is not based on individual preference but, rather, is constructed from the aesthetic engagements of a particular class. The standards of beauty of upper middle-class poetry and those of the lower middle class are starkly different. In this way, Muktibodh prepares the ground for discussing the logic underlying claims made by new poetry for the significance of the individual. He identifies the ossification of aesthetics to be the overriding danger of new poetry. It is clear that in the crosshairs of his criticism is the intellectual stream exemplified by Agyey. Muktibodh writes:

> If the new models of aesthetics placed before us by some important persons from the region of the new verse tendencies, thanks to their class-based aesthetic engagement, are not amended, we will not be able to represent fully or effectively our own life-experiences. The poetic personality that produces a closed system ('You cannot pervade it; that which pervades you, only carry on with it') can only present an ossified aesthetic engagement.[49]

In effect, Muktibodh not only feels the need to specify new models for poetry in his time, but he also goes on to formulate some of these models. Investigation of the class bases of new poetry becomes the basis for proposing his own Hindi canon. He struggles against the double-edged dangers of new poetry, and by referring to its writing process, he saves new poetry, embedded in its time and place, from 'somnolence due to poisonous misinterpretation'.

Civilizational Critique

Muktibodh uses the term 'civilizational critique' in the sense of a keyword. According to him, all of civilization develops from the dynamic of struggles between classes. If we were to ask why Muktibodh is drawn to civilizational critique, the answer lies in his poetic universe. He reveals the relation between his philosophical outlook and civilizational critique in his poem 'Chakmak ki chingariyan' [Sparks of Flint]:

> That in my incomplete short poem,
> All the lofty idols of the questionnaire
> I bring down and smash with a hammer.
> Since all those questions are artificial and
> The answers even more deceitful.
> The question is the one –
> In my civilized cities and villages
> When will each man become beautiful, contented and free from exploitation?[50]

His impatience with the exploitation of man by man draws Muktibodh towards the conceptual business of civilizational critique. This was Bhagat

Singh's imagination as well. Faced with the deep paradox of questions being deceitful and the answers even more so, Muktibodh feels compelled to sift through the entire history of civilization; i.e. this civilizational critique is a response to the coopting of voices of opposition by the regime, and to the issue of the rights of the dispossessed and the marginalized in post-independence India. It is to Muktibodh's credit that he proposes to re-evaluate civilization from the standpoint of people marginalized in history.

Madhup Kumar contends that civilizational critique is not an ideological project, and advocates viewing it against the backdrop of the exigencies of civilization: 'Civilizational critique is produced by the necessity of examining literature through codified principles against the backdrop of civilizational exigencies. . . . It is not simply a protocol to comprehend the work and its criticism but a way of paying one's dues to the entire civilization.'[51] The point of emphasis in Kumar's formulation is that he wants to evacuate civilizational critique from the literary domain and situate it within the broad dimensions of the humanities. In Muktibodh's formulation, civilizational critique is more an expression of the prominence of politics in literature than an illustration of the cultural forms of civilization in literary form. The idea of civilizational critique is a product of thought from the 1950s and 1960s. Recommending the responsibilities of critique, Muktibodh writes in his essay 'Navin samiksha ke adhar' [The Principles of New Critique]:

> Objectively, the task of the critic or analyst is more engrossing and creative than the artist's or the writer's. He must immerse himself in the experiences of life's ocean of actuality and then learn to surface from there so that the waves do not overwhelm his vision. The critic who embarks on evaluating the patterns of the reflection of life without evaluating the life of his class, society or status within his own life, can never do real criticism. While he may cloak intellectual immaturity arising from the absence of truths derived from actual life-experiences as close attention to detail, his criticism will never be creative.[52]

The dangers elucidated above by Muktibodh for the critic correspond to the critic's class location, and even more so to his class-based point of view.

Among the definitions that emerged and transformed in the struggle between feudalism and capitalism was also the definition of civilization. Namvar Singh holds the view that it is only with modernity that the concept of civilization has attained its current sweeping meaning. He writes in an article in *Pahal*:

> With the development of civilization, the work of the poet becomes perilous, and I add to this that the work of criticism becomes even more perilous.

Now, at the end of the twentieth century, civilization only means capitalist civilization. The economic development of civilization, its technological development and the social system that pertains to it, i.e. its economic system, all these are what is known as the development of civilization.[53]

In Muktibodh's thought, within the terminology of civilizational critique, the word 'civilization' is a carrier of the efforts to set up a new idea of civilization within capitalist civilization. He is an expert in formulating such terminology, establishing new definitions and elaborating their meanings. Several critical terms such as fantasy, knowledges of the sensible and knowledge-based sensibilities, and the pain of truth-in-consciousness have been given to Hindi criticism by Muktibodh. Today, in an era of privatization, marketization and liberalization, we notice again the transformations in 'civilization' under the leadership of imperialist nations such as the United States. These nations ascribe the murderous cycles of capital and the exploitation of nations to the backward state of civilization. We may note here two connotations of civilization that have surfaced in world politics after 1990. One pertains to third world civilizations, civilizations of people crushed by imperialism. The second refers to the controllers of multinational corporations, imperialists and the indigenous comprador class. Civilization is not a ubiquitous concept; the concept of civilization turns into a class-based perspective. For Muktibodh, civilization is a counter to capitalist civilization as the civilization of the underclasses.

In the essay mentioned above, Namvar Singh writes:

> The crisis of the twentieth century has been turned into their bread and butter by some people, and there is no gainsaying that such stories and poems are also being written. . . . You would remember that at one point many films were made on the lives of the aboriginal people and about Naxalism. These films were making money out of the Naxal revolution and the class against which these films were made was enjoying them as entertainment. . . . Muktibodh used to say that the greatest problem today is how to recognize the camouflaging of the work of art. Therefore, critical work is becoming more difficult to practise.[54]

The twentieth-century crisis as mentioned by Namvar Singh cannot be simply associated with civilizational critique, but it can be said that a disaggregated picture of the movements of the foundational classes among the people enters literature through middle-class carriers of the petit-bourgeois ideology. Class becomes a critical category for the first time in Hindi criticism through Muktibodh's civilizational critique. The issue of seeing beyond the camouflage of art and criticism, which Namvar Singh points out through Muktibodh, is impossible without a class-conscious point of view.

The second important proposition that establishes the basis of civilizational critique, besides the class-conscious viewpoint, is historicism. Muktibodh affirms his belief in the continually forward-moving motion of time, which he visualizes as a spiral. According to him, a truly historicist viewpoint is one that assimilates not just external situations and conditions, but also the psychological facts of literature into the form of expression of society's historical processes of development, and gives a dynamic account of them. He disagrees with and considers erroneous the idea that the economy determines literature in a straightforward manner or that the latter changes in relation to the former. He argues that more than situating literature in its social circumstances, we need to compare psychologism within literature with the processes of historical development.

In his essay 'Samaj aur sahitya' [Society and Literature] Muktibodh writes, again:

> The implication is that until we give a sociological explanation for the psychological–aesthetic analysis of literature under review, we cannot accomplish a complete analysis and evaluation of its inner aspect, its potentialities and limits. . . . Today's variegated life is discordant, today's civilization is gripped by decline. Therefore, it is natural for tension to exist in today's poetry. Poetry in any age is either situated in a relation of opposition to its milieu or in harmony with it.[55]

Thus, Muktibodh articulates questions of civilizational critique through a sociological analysis of the psychological reception of beauty and art. Clearly, in his own time, it was in the light of the broken spell of the Nehruvian model and the sharpening of the regime's class character that the need arose to critique once more the entire civilization, so that history could signal towards the path of progress.

In order to establish the claim to civilization by people pushed to the margins by the developmental process of the civilization, Muktibodh raises the question of the people's claim to history. Before including writers in his canon, it was necessary to establish its theoretical bases. Towards this end, he tries to give new critical readings of contemporary literary works which were aligned with the agenda of canon formation based on common consent by the dominant class and its culture.

Evaluating Kamayani: *The Rules of Canon Formation*

As a part of his project of civilizational critique, Muktibodh prepares a critical analysis of Jaishankar Prasad's *Kamayani* and Ramdhari Singh Dinkar's *Urvashi*. The analysis of *Kamayani* was important because of the poem's interest in historical investigation. In search of reflections of its meaning in *Kamayani*, critics regularly revisited the reawakening-era discussion about the golden past. In his essay '*Kamayani: ek punar vichar*' [*Kamayani*: A Reassessment], Muktibodh writes:

> In an effort to think in the direction of comprehending the actual character of the intimately mutual relations between epoch and literature, two special kinds of literature present themselves in our view. The first in which there is a mere shadow of the epochal tendencies, i.e. in relative form, these epochal tendencies are not conceived in a conscious way but rather, in being overpowered by a distinctive mental inactivity, they are presented merely in shadows, well-made or deformed. The second kind of literature is one which transcends the present and waits upon humanity's future by consciously accepting the implication, connotation, and transformative and destructive purports of these epochal tendencies. This latter kind of literature doubtless aims at the refinement of human consciousness. But often it has been noted that the final judgements (whether these be universally acceptable or not, which is another matter) about life reached by the greatest of artists (such as Tolstoy), after pictorially critiquing the entirety of society, raise the alarming possibility that these judgements may be pernicious. Such alarm is only natural. Criticism is practised on vital truths alone. Therefore (despite pictorial critique enjoying a high position in literature), after the critique of the facts under review, the writer of literature makes a run for a generalization of those facts to the final judgements, overpowered by his own self-directed or other-directed tendencies, whether with courageous or foolhardy steps, and only then does it become absolutely essential to consider consciously and with care his ultimate decisions, and to analyse them appropriately. Literature is fundamentally based on all shapes of fruitfulness, along with the experiential expansiveness of the understanding of its own life, as well as on those truths which can be designated by the word 'perspective'. Since human awareness is refined not just by the writer of literature, but is accomplished also by the officials of the physical as well as social sciences (and it would be impossible without the cooperation of the latter), it is always essential for the critic to check whether the object of criticism, and the decisions, generalizations and final judgements of its producer, are not in opposition to today's purely theoretical and experience-rich science. (Since the refinement of awareness is related to

the rise, further transformation and development of the human condition, therefore) the critic's obligation is not confined to being just, sympathetic and generous to the writer, but exceeds far beyond this. Therefore, in the current situation in the country and in the world, the critic's vision attempts to not vest itself in the inner aesthetic of the work under analysis, but to penetrate the destination of the final judgements of the writer of literature so as to assess whether the destination accords with justice, is useful and beneficial! Critical endeavours of this kind are highly appropriate for *Kamayani*, whether they are successful or not. The judgements which Prasad arrives at about Ida, Shraddha and Manu, their domain is quite extensive. Issues such as man, woman, the individual, society, civilization, liberation, etc., are all within the ambit of Prasad's analytically weighted poetic sensibility.[56]

Through this long quotation we may note that one of the fundamental bases of civilizational critique is the productive tension between contemporaneity and history. All writers tend towards a revaluation of their past based on issues in their present. It is impossible to scrutinize the past by returning to the past or by becoming the past. But similarly located in the present, a journey into the past carrying the additional burdens of the present creates dissonance. Muktibodh saves himself from this dissonance and, using Prasad's hero Manu from *Kamayani*, he not only critically investigates the past and deploys class as a category in the determination of its character, but also formulates the contemporary historical bases of Prasad's epic as a struggle between modernity and feudalism. In this way, Hindi criticism witnesses a new conceptual discussion in which the dialectic of time moves towards both poles of temporality, the past and the present. This dialectic is worked not simply as an intellectual tool but rather as the inner movement of life. Although Prasad's Manu resides in the primeval times of *Kamayani*, in Muktibodh's '*Kamayani*: A Reassessment', he is released from the world of fantasy and the qualities concretized by this entire process of exclusion are: perception of the deep crisis in the modern heart, a style of interpreting tradition that is proposed by Prasad himself, which is at heart an element in the project of historical revision from the period of the reawakening. In this project, the entire past is taken to be golden. The early nationalist intellectuals reread history under the auspices of the reawakening. Historians of the Subaltern school describe this dissonance in the project of nationalism, which we have mentioned earlier. The antiquarianism in nationalist thought that the Subaltern school of historians point towards was being constructed in culture by thinkers such as Jaishankar Prasad. Muktibodh not only extricates *Kamayani* from this cultural dynamic but concomitantly, with the alibi of reading *Kamayani*, reveals a hitherto unexplored aspect of the politics of criticism.

Namvar Singh: The Search for Criteria

Namvar Singh's critical endeavours stretch from studies in Apabhransh to contemporary literature, but his main works are *Chhayavad* [Romanticism], *Kavita ke naye pratiman* [The New Criteria for Poetry] and *Dusri parampara ki khoj* [The Search for Another Tradition]. Apropos the discussion on canon-making, Singh's *Dusri parampara ki khoj*, written around the figure of Hazari Prasad Dwivedi, is the key point of discussion in the section on Dwivedi in Chapter Two. The most important figure in Singh's canon is Muktibodh, or new poetry under his name. In this section, I will discuss Namvar Singh's other major work, *Kavita ke naye pratiman*, in relation to Muktibodh's place in poetry and Singh's critical writing on him. It will be instructive to see how, on the same issue, one critic's opinion differs from that of another critic who is included by the former in his proposed canon.

As we have noticed in the discussion so far on the processes leading to the formation of the Hindi canon, with the advent of Ramvilas Sharma on the critical scene, the axis of criticism began to turn around Marxism. Muktibodh and Ramvilas Sharma engaged with Marxist criticism in divergent ways. Whereas Sharma developed Marxist thought in the direction of anti-colonialism, Muktibodh primarily employed it to conduct a deep investigation into the process of writing. The ground on which the two critics sparred and debated was 'new poetry'. Any future Marxist critic will need to go through the terms of the debate between Sharma and Muktibodh before thinking of, or rethinking, the Hindi canon. On the other hand, under the leadership of Agyey and the Parimal group (of modernist critics), new poetry was precisely at the heart of all critical debate. The agitation to find and establish the criteria for new poetry is found in the critical writings of this entire period. In Muktibodh's words, on both sides of the Cold War new poetry provided an adequate ground for canon formation. Namvar Singh accepts these double-edged opportunities, as seen in his controversial and most prominent work *Kavita ke naye pratiman*. Against such a background, in comparison with his other works, this work is most relevant to a discussion on canon formation.

Written in 1968, Namvar Singh's book announces Muktibodh to be an undisputed part of the Hindi canon. The book is also dedicated to the poet. In the introduction to its first edition, Namvar Singh writes: 'At the centre of new criteria for poetry stands Muktibodh. Muktibodh is exceptional in that he did justice to both poetry and criticism.'[57] In the discussion below, we will assess whether Muktibodh objectively occupies the same place in the canon as claimed in Singh's book or if 'new poetry' is established by the book's argument. What is its relation to other schools of thought that aim to establish 'new poetry' in the canon, and does it reshuffle previous canons of Marxist criticism?

Singh's book is divided into three parts; according to its own criteria, the structure of the book is consolidated around organic parts. The first part comprises criticism of existing criticisms. This part of the argument is foundational in establishing the necessity for new critical criteria. The third part builds towards the new criteria for 'new poetry', and the coda to the third part is a critical reading of Muktibodh's poem, *'Andhere mein'* [In Darkness].

Singh begins his argument in the book by referencing Vijaydev Narayan Sahi, not with regard to the criteria for judging new poetry but for poetry itself. He explains the writing process of new poetry as a movement inwards from the outside, through the notions of fact becoming truth and the impersonality of experience. Against individuation in *Chhayavad* poetry, whence does this impersonality arise? On Sahi's evidence, Namvar Singh's answer to this question is 'construction' or 'composition'. The construction of 'new poetry' makes it impersonal. Precisely due to such construction, 'new poetry, through its "inner weave", sets forth the principle that poetry does not so much produce a "statement" of some "generality" (general thought, feeling or belief) as the dramatization of a singular situation'.[58] Following Muktibodh's example, Singh puts the aesthetics of 'new poetry' on trial, but he fails to make class his primary category of analysis after Muktibodh. Commenting on this tendency, Muktibodh had situated it in the hopelessness of the western world and the middle-class location of the writers of 'new poetry'. He located the concrete bases of this ossified aesthetic within this class position itself.

By considering Nagendr's theorization of *ras* in juxtaposition with *Chhayavad*'s romantic theory, Namvar Singh characterizes the *Urvashi* controversy as integral to the processes of canon formation in Hindi criticism. The facts of this controversy are the following: in 1964, Bhagvatisharan Upadhyay published an article on Dinkar's verse play *Urvashi* in the journal *Kalpana*. The review proved to be so intellectually stirring that almost all the major critics of the time wrote responses to it as well as on the original work. In truth, the controversy around *Urvashi* was a debate on the bases of canon formation in contemporary criticism. All the participants in the debate agreed with the view that 'for the criticism of a poetic work, extra-poetic criteria should not be used'.[59] In other words, the *Urvashi* controversy brought out the fact that the critical principles used by nationalist and early Marxist critics were exhausted in the study of literature. In the analysis of a literary work, a preponderance of critical principles over the work itself means staleness of criticism. Namvar Singh draws attention to two aspects of this controversy. The writers who supported Upadhyay's position as stated in his article found it to be useful, honest and authentic, albeit not very complete. The other camp opposed the article 'in the name of good taste, restraint, balance and civility'.[60] Singh identifies an underlying contradiction between the viewpoints of the two sets of writers, but the list of writers reveals that this categorical distinction is not so clear. Within 'new poetry' itself there were different streams in operation, which could not be delineated simply by contesting the use of 'externalities' in establishing the criteria for poetry. It is precisely where Singh views a distinction based on aesthetic positions that Muktibodh locates the contradictions within 'new poetry' on a wider horizon. According to Muktibodh, the causes for the contradictions within 'new poetry' are the inability of the 'special' to become 'general', the narrowness of its world vision and an ossified aesthetic. He elaborates:

> Something else is required. Something else completely! – That which could express the organicity of life with all its characteristics. . . . Some people believe in the 'search'; there are enough people who swear by continuous discoveries, continuous research, but they stop at merely the theorization of their discoveries and research. At most, it remains at the level of self-discovery or research of the self with a zeal which may produce five to ten poems, but it loses steam after that. And in such poems we get repetitions, re-repetitions, repetitions–re-repetitions. The same vicious cycle begins . . . in which our material elements are burnished by first corroding them with the harsh chemical fluids of our language, our history, our culture and literature. . . . We must conclude that the main issue is of the consciousness of life, and not the discovery of the treasure of expression.[61]

Turning the lens on the evaluative criteria in Ramvilas Sharma's criticism of new poetry in the *Urvashi* controversy, Namvar Singh remarks:

> The view of 'new poetry' developed by Ramvilas Sharma was formulated keeping the 'realist' stream of poetry in mind. Under the influence of socialist political leaders, he signposts 'new poetry' as the work of writers producing anticommunist propaganda. He considers the emphasis on form in the dialectic of form and content to be an obfuscation of material reality. For him, Kedarnath Agraval and Nagarjun are the most accomplished poets of

the realist stream of poetry, whom some people want to dismiss in order to harm the realist stream. He views 'new poetry' as a part of neo-mysticism and existentialism.[62]

It becomes clear here that Ramvilas Sharma does not distinguish between 'new poetry' and individualism, and that he finds at its core a foreign thought. We have already discussed this in detail.

In *Kavita ke naye pratiman*, Namvar Singh brings into comparison the *Tar saptak* moment and the Nehru era, in a discussion of the milieu around 1950–51. The fertility of experimentalism is reflected in the harmony between Nehru as the discoverer of India and the poets in search of the truth of the self and its individuality. The feebleness of this link could be a point of debate. Namvar Singh argues that poets free of the illusions of the Nehru age were the most successful, and, citing Muktibodh albeit in subdued tones, he confirms the links between 'new poetry' and the Cold War and middle-class opportunism during that period.

But by the second part of the book, in which new standards for poetry are proposed, Muktibodh's two axioms mentioned above prove to be weak as used by Singh. In this part of his argument, he presents the creativeness of poetic language, poetic imagery and flatness of expression, poetic structure, the complexity and tension in experiencing, sincerity and authentic perception, as well as milieu and value, as the new criteria for poetry.

In his discussion of the productivity of poetic language, Namvar Singh alludes to the concept of 'poetry on the page'. Thus, he considers the poem to be an objective reality and holds its verbal architecture to be essential for its analysis. He spars with his predecessors' criticism in these terms: 'If language is the vehicle for the poet's experience and knowledge, then with the analysis of this language we can gauge the truth of that experience.'[63] In this way, it is the productivity of poetic language that attains objectivity which brings any new category of experience into knowledge. Singh is also not unaware of the dangers of reducing signification [*kathya*] to verbality [*kathan*]:

> To exhaust signification into verbality is clearly a danger arising from a formalism within criticism, as some critics mistake the analysis of the linguistic particularities of verbality to be the analysis of the poetic work in its entirety. But the sensitive critic, who believes in the spread of meaning outside the precinct of the word, will evaluate poetry *in toto* only on the basis of poetic language by capturing all the meaning emissions from the word according to context, in which an ethical evaluation is also inherent.[64]

The danger of formalism spoken of by Singh needs further explanation. A far greater danger lies in the collapsing of signification into verbality than in the collapsing of verbality into signification. What, then, should be the way out? The way proposed by Singh, i.e. capturing the spread of meaning outside the precinct of the word and therein locating the productivity of poetry, itself does not lead to 'logically sound conclusions'. This path is more in the direction of the processes underway in the three moments of art proposed by Muktibodh. Muktibodh underlines the fertility of poetic language that emerges from the dialectic of language and psychical fantasy. Therefore, it becomes essential for the critic to investigate this dialectic within the poetic work and bring it in line with his epistemological awareness. Through such a reading, the path to the poem's implicit meanings is opened. In sum, without an analysis of the process of writing, it is impossible to determine the characteristics of a poetic work.

The critic Ashutosh Kumar addresses the same issue in these words:

> But the analysis of the process of writing cannot be confined to the study of one work alone. Marxist criticism demands that each work should be seen as an element in a larger socio-cultural process. This process should then be treated from a Marxist-historicist viewpoint. Only then can the individual work's relation with the general process be discovered. Based on this discovery alone can the singularity of a specific work of art be formulated.[65]

In a letter written to Jankivallabh Shastri, Nirala discusses the composition of 'Todti patthar' [She, Breaking Stones] in the same vein. Namvar Singh situates 'new poetry' within the same discussion and points to the limits of poetic imagery. It is his view that the yardstick of iconicity is a part of the *Chhayavad* structure of feeling. If imagery is taken to be the central object in poetry, Singh argues, two corollaries follow. First, the image is rendered stock; on this issue, Singh discusses at length Nagendr's notion of imagery. Second, he discusses the conventional tropes based on the 'borrowed capital of images' employed by lyricists claiming to make new songs. From within 'new poetry', two kinds of links emerge with this image tradition. Some poets chase after scintillating poetic imagery and the critics become transfixed by these images. Singh contends that in this way the poem comes to be seen as a soldering of images. Other poets, in opposition to this tendency, practise flatness of expression.

> The corollary is that poetry is not synonymous with imagery. Ordinarily poetry can be written without that which is called imagery. And such poems cannot be considered inferior to image-heavy poetry. In poetry, the composition of

images does not always iconize reality but sometimes de-iconizes reality too
(although the words 'iconize' and 'de-iconize' are used quite loosely). Imagery
in poetry is not just a sign of the manifestation of reality; rather, it can be a
means to escape reality too. The image scheme has generally affected poetic
language for the worse. Due to imagery, poetry moves away from everyday
spoken language. It disrupts the easy rhythms of spoken words. It disrupts the
power of syntax; it makes invisible the internal verbs of language; adjectives
grow in weight; and poetic connotation loses ground. To remove these
weaknesses poets are adopting flatness of expression.[66]

But the change alluded to in this analysis is strongly related to the world
of contemporary politics. It is more than coincidental that at the end of
his essay, Singh remembers an essay written by Krishnanarayan Kakkad in
1967 – known as the year of Naxalbari. It is well known that the Naxalbari
movement did not just attract one branch of 'new poetry', but also left
a deep impression on poetry at large. If the dynamics of this movement
is considered along with the transformations in poetic language, then we
can surmise the material considerations behind the flatness of expression.
This was a movement built up by the anger of dispossessed peasants and
it also had an effect in the field of culture where it tried to change cultural
distinctions. It posed a challenge to the old canons. In this background,
the poets from a non-middle class background who wrote 'new poetry'
expressed a different kind of class sentiment in their poetic language.

Namvar Singh acknowledges that in the making of poetry, logical
derivation is not the only kind of derivation in the reading of a poem.
He writes apropos older critics such as Nagendr, who considered logical
derivation to be of prime importance:

> If it becomes essential to ascribe a value, then logical derivation in poetry is
> relatively a vulgar derivation. . . . It appears like the theorems of geometry,
> the main assumption at first, the construction and then the proof at the
> end, in which when the critic witnesses the repetition of poetic rhyme, the
> words tumble out of the mouth: 'this is what had to be proved' or *quod erat
> demonstrandum.*[67]

Singh holds that in the other kind of poem which uses logical derivation,
the derivation does not appear in the form of interpretation. Objectively,
the construction of such poems is crystalline. Apart from these two kinds of
poems, there are poetic compositions called long poems. In contrast with
the self-centric lyric, these compositions are based on the sociality of theatre.
This should remind us of Muktibodh's words in the second edition of *Tar*

saptak, where he asks himself: 'Why did all this happen? Why was there an increase in imagery? Why did the themes expand? Why did poems shrink in size?'[68] The answers too come from himself in the process of explaining the changing composition of his poetry. As may be expected, he connects this with the changing situation in social and class circumstances:

> Political hopes and aspirations, their socio-ethical dreams, began haunting me. My circumstances broadened. . . . In one go I was free and liberated. This was a new living actuality. Within this actuality there were numberless circumstances, psychological states and material states of the struggling man. There was a need to cast them in some comprehensive normalizations and give them poetic form. In this direction I have tried my forceful best. The extra-long poem was a result of that. . . . In truth, the main issue facing me today is not about the shortage of content and the excess of form, but the orgy of content and the insufficiency of form.[69]

It is precisely this that Namvar Singh attempts to signpost as a part of the compositional process, and he posits a 'search for identity' as the central problematic in Muktibodh's work. It is clear that while Muktibodh lays emphasis on content for long poems, Namvar Singh argues in favour of form. Singh does not enquire into the origins or conditions of this search for identity in his critical writing.

Singh posits contradiction and irony in the composition of 'new poetry', and treats them as fundamentals of poetry. He contends that at the heart of a poet's creativity and experimentalism, there is the unity of the true sentiment of play and the sentiment of symbolic play [*lila*]. This leads, on the one hand, to a realization of the 'realness' of life as opposed to 'seriousness', and on the other, it can give rise to fraudulence. At this point, Singh distinguishes between the activist sentiment and cynicism. A great poet grapples with his living circumstances and only thereby achieves dramatic irony in his poetry. Thus, the sentiment of play in his poetry is not there simply for effect. Singh explains: 'But due to poetic qualities such as the tightness of composition, the austerity of words, the irony-derived complexity of sentiments, passionlessness and the acuity of thought, etc., this kind of poetry is said to deserve an important place in verse.'[70]

Muktibodh, in contrast, looks for the reasons for the importance of this poetry through an analysis of class. The perception of irony that was widespread at that time among the middle class took the form of irony within poetry. Muktibodh delineates 'new poetry' against *Chhayavad* poetry by raising the question of complexity of experiences. Singh develops this line of thought and considers the complexity of inner states of mind and experience within the ecology of the context and context-derived sentiments. Through Nagendr's inventory of states of consciousness and I.A. Richards' penetrative and exclusivist poetic criteria, Singh expands the extent of the discussion and bases the complexity of poetic experience on the dialectic between states of communication and non-responsiveness. This dialectic is also, according to him, the basis of the structure of perception in 'new poetry'. He seems to agree here with Sahi's formulation of the *Chhayavad* epoch as defined by a 'theatrics of balancing'.

Objectively speaking, behind the dialectic of poetic perception in 'new poetry' is the intellectualism of the new poet. This intellectualism is a product of those social circumstances of the new poet whose roots can be traced to middle-class antinomies. Namvar Singh addresses this intellectualism thus:

> If new poetry wants to establish opposition and tension as the standards of poetry, then it is only developing the glorious tradition of Hindi. From the historical viewpoint too, it would not be amiss to stress today the values of opposition and struggle in poetry. Today, only they will be disturbed by struggle who think, along with the ruling class, that after the winning of independence, the need for struggle is over. Such people can struggle as hard as they can for improving their status or preserving their power, but they consider struggling for others unthinkable – whether this struggle be in life or in poetry. . . . Muktibodh has moved struggle and opposition one step ahead to the point of critical tension.[71]

The key question here is the analysis of this tension. Muktibodh describes an environment of tension or siege within 'new poetry' and uses this to articulate the contradictions of middle-class life. The overwhelming desire to enter the domain of the upper classes and access the conditions of life available there contribute to the building of this tension in inverse proportion. At the other end, the conditions are always ripe for the downward slippage of the lower middle class into the vast underclass of society. With this knowledge, the poet stuck in middle-class thought and conditions of life looks for a way out with the help of ideology. In this task, a world vision comes to his aid. The struggle between the inner and the outer becomes fiercer in this process. If we accept this interpretation of tension, very few of the 'new' poets would be able to produce writing that corresponds to this tension.

Namvar Singh moves on to investigate the process by which sincerity becomes a poetic value, through a comparison of the context of sincerity in 'new poetry' with preceding reactions of the progressive movement. He quotes Raghuvir Sahay to argue that sincerity as a value is higher than a preconceived partisanship and personal taste, and that through it, a true measure of the actuality of things is derived. Using Muktibodh as the authority, he writes: 'One meaning of personal sincerity is – the specific proportion or specific quantity in which a feeling or thought has come up, it should be presented in the same measure.' Muktibodh, however, considers this to be quite inadequate. According to him, 'the significant point is whether these feelings or thoughts are in harmony with some material element'.[72]

The definition proposed by Muktibodh differs from the definition given by the 'new' poets. The latter take a different route which leads towards 'the authenticity of perception'. This route opens up the parallel between life and poetry, which Muktibodh is at pains to contest. So what does sincerity mean? Namvar Singh relates sincerity to the poet's 'wisdom'. Without guaranteeing the objectivity of sincerity as a value of ethical judgement, its acceptability is reduced not just in poetry but in other realms as well. Then, the outward form of sincerity may change in accordance with the socioeconomic conditions of the writer. Namvar Singh addresses this problem thus:

> The history of the past fifty years in poetry shows clearly that in every flowering at the core there is the sound of sincerity, but sincerity in each epoch speaks a different tongue. If sincerity in *Chhayavad* is 'self-perception', then post-*Chhayavad* it becomes 'intention'. For progressivism sincerity involves 'class consciousness', and for the experimentalist 'new poetry' sincerity is 'authenticity of perception'. . . . The question that arises is whether an objective outline of sincerity emerges in this order and can become the basis for the evaluation of poetry. Alongside, the question also remains whether sincerity is a category at all for the evaluation of poetry.[73]

This is a difficult question. Namvar Singh tries to derive his definition of sincerity from a reading of contemporary poetry. Apropos Muktibodh, according to the structure of Singh's argument, this sincerity refers to a 'search for identity' – in which case, the question arises, can 'search of identity' be applied to all of 'new poetry' as a standard of evaluation? For Sahi, Bharti, Shamsher, Raghuvir Sahay and others, sincerity does not mean a 'search for identity'. Indeed, each poet can have a different understanding of sincerity. We can extrapolate from this that each poet will derive his sincerity from his class-positioned values. Then, if we consider the differentiation of poets made by Muktibodh within the middle class, we may see the class basis of sincerity, just as he established the class bases of aesthetics. It may be said that sincerity is a relative concept. In that case, the objectivity of sincerity is the only condition of its authenticity. Only on meeting this condition can the concept be put to use.

With reference to all the critical criteria discussed above, Namvar Singh proposes a movement from the inside outwards; that is, a poem's evaluation in terms of its composition, structure and language is obvious, and this is in opposition to the influential sociological aspect of Marxist criticism and becomes an attempt to develop it in another direction. The milieu and value as criteria not only point towards the complexity of the discussion, but also attest to the fact that Singh wants to work within the Marxist purview. In view of the difficulty in using sincerity as a critical concept, he proposes actuality as the basis of authenticity in poetry. This actuality pertains to the milieu that manifests in the poem sometimes as dramatic and self-centric symbols, and at other times as historical realities. He writes:

> In discussions of poetry today references to an autonomous 'universe' are being made once more, which is why it is essential to recognize the wrong aestheticist turn intrinsic in the phrase 'poetic universe'. It is ironic too that from the moment the demand for the knowledge of milieu has increased in poetry, the sounds of 'poetic universe' have become dominant.[74]

In summary, while including Muktibodh the poet in his canon and in the process establishing the 'new' principles of criticism, Namvar Singh ends up leaving behind the principles of the critic Muktibodh. Muktibodh uses class as a fundamental category in studying the process of writing for initiating the study of 'new poetry'. Singh uses the criteria discussed above and tries to move towards the category of class. The methods of these two critics are thus inverted in relation to each other. However much Namvar Singh acknowledges the influence of Muktibodh on the new criteria for poetry, the fact remains somewhat smaller than the assertion. It is no coincidence that on reading *Kavita ke naye pratiman*, we find that Vijaydev Narayan Sahi is the critic quoted most often in the book. Namvar Singh uses formalist weaponry to oppose formalism, but with that weaponry comes an entire stream of thought. Therefore, in an attempt to preserve and develop Marxist criticism, the 'criteria' of criticism fall outside the basic principles of Marxist criticism.

NOTES

[1] On the issue of the economic downturn, in his essays Stalin analysed the reasons for the Soviet Union being saved from it. Overproduction and continuous enfeeblement of the workers' labour power are a part of the regular crisis of capitalism. In order to recover from the economic crash of 1929, capitalism developed the concept of the welfare state. Marx gives a detailed analysis of this irresolvable crisis of capitalism in *Capital*. In order to overcome the current economic downturn, economists have

turned once again to Marx. In the 1930s, the reason for the destruction of the Indian peasantry was that the British had reduced India to a market of raw materials. With the crisis in the world economic system, the consumption of raw materials fell and the crop prices also plummeted, but the revenue demand did not decrease; rather, the drive for revenue collection became more oppressive. The achievement of 'dominion status' and the formation of Congress ministries in the British Indian provinces should be situated in this background. The British government found the Congress useful in dampening the enthusiasm of expected popular rebellions, and with that indefinitely postponed the demand for independence.

[2] Gyanendra Pandey, who has conducted a detailed study of the peasant movement in Avadh, contends that it was delinked from the Congress-directed independence movement and was led by the masses. See Pandey (1995), pp. 129–82.

[3] Jain (1998), pp. 67–68.

[4] Sharma (2002), p. 14.

[5] Stalin (1913).

[6] Stalin (1953), p. 315.

[7] Sharma (2008), p. 240.

[8] Ibid., p. 260.

[9] Talwar (2005b), p. 92.

[10] Krishn (2008), p. 132.

[11] Pandey (1981), p. 31.

[12] Mishr (1987), pp. 55–56.

[13] Talwar (2005a), pp. 257–58.

[14] Talwar (2002), pp. 396–404.

[15] Sharma (2003), p. 27.

[16] Ibid., p. 58.

[17] Ibid., p. 23.

[18] Nilkant (1985).

[19] Quoted by Manager Pandey in special article on D.D. Kosambi; see Pandey (2007), p. 18.

[20] Dwivedi (2000), p. 20.

[21] Pandey (1981), p. 138.

[22] Pandey (2007), p. 18.

[23] Marx and Engels (1977), p. 35.

[24] Ibid.

[25] Rajendr Kumar (2009), p. 102.

[26] Pandey (2005), p. 17.

[27] G.M. Muktibodh, 'Madhyayugin bhakti andolan ka ek pehlu', in Muktibodh (1998), Vol. 5, p. 293.

[28] Ibid., p. 292.

[29] Ibid.

[30] Ibid.

[31] Ibid., p. 289.

[32] Ibid.

[33] Ibid.

[34] Ibid., p. 290.

[35] Ibid., p. 294.

[36] Ibid.

[37] Singh (1982), pp. 84–85.

[38] Pandey (2002), p. 25.

[39] Ibid., p. 26.

[40] Muktibodh (1998), Vol. 5, p. 293.

[41] Letter to Shripad Amrit Dange, in Muktibodh (1998), Vol. 6, p. 397.

[42] G.M. Muktibodh, '*Nayi kavita ki prakriti*', in Muktibodh (1998), Vol. 5, p. 319.

[43] G.M. Muktibodh, '*Prayogvad*', in Muktibodh (1998), Vol. 5, p. 287.

[44] G.M. Muktibodh, '*Hindi kavya ki nayi dhara*', in Muktibodh (1998), Vol. 5, p. 318.

[45] G.M. Muktibodh, '*Nayi kavita aur adhunik bhavbodh*', in Muktibodh (1998), Vol. 5, p. 30.

[46] G.M. Muktibodh, '*Nayi kavita ki prakriti*', in Muktibodh (1998), Vol. 5, p. 324.

[47] G.M. Muktibodh, '*Nayi kavita ka aatmsangharsh*', in Muktibodh (1998), Vol. 5, p. 328.

[48] Ibid., p. 330.

[49] Ibid., p. 333.

[50] G.M. Muktibodh, '*Chakmak ki chingariyan*', in Muktibodh (1998), Vol. 2, p. 243.

[51] Madhup Kumar (n.d.), p. 102.

[52] G.M. Muktibodh, '*Navin samiksha ke aadhaar*', in Muktibodh (1998), Vol. 5, p. 83.

[53] Namvar Singh's speech, published in *Pahal*, 53, p. 46.

[54] Ibid., pp. 47–48.

[55] G.M. Muktibodh, '*Samaj aur sahitya*', in Muktibodh (1998), Vol. 5, pp. 70–71.

[56] G.M. Muktibodh, '*Kamayani*', in Muktibodh (1998), Vol. 4, pp. 341–42.

[57] Singh (2003), introduction to first edition, p. 8.

[58] Ibid., p. 40.

[59] Ibid., p. 66.

[60] Ibid., p. 68.

[61] G.M. Muktibodh, '*Nayi kavita: nissahay nakaratmakta*', in Muktibodh (1998), Vol. 5, pp. 337–38.

[62] Sharma (1997), introduction to second edition, pp. 5–6.

[63] Singh (2003), p. 105.

[64] Ibid., p. 209.

[65] Ashutosh Kumar (2009), p. 95.

[66] Singh (2003), p. 131.

[67] Ibid., p. 136.

[68] G.M. Muktibodh, '*Aatm-vaktavya*', in Muktibodh (1998), Vol. 5, p. 269.

[69] Ibid., p. 270.

[70] Singh (2003), p. 165.

[71] Ibid., p. 181.

[72] Ibid., p. 189.

[73] Ibid., pp. 191–92.

[74] Ibid., p. 210.

CHAPTER FOUR

The Counterpositions to Marxist Criticism

Vijaydev Narayan Sahi: The Pressures of Contemporaneity

In the introduction to Vijaydev Narayan Sahi's book *Jayasi*, Kanchanlata Sahi writes: '*Jayasi* is significant for the light it sheds on [Malik Muhammad] Jayasi, but perhaps also because it sheds light on Sahi himself.'[1] This is a strong claim because Sahi arrives at Jayasi's work after going through all the major intellectual disputes of the 1960s, and gives a critical account of Jayasi's poetry. He invests all the energy derived from the disputes about 'new poetry' in order to produce a reassessment of Jayasi.

Sahi notes a 'roar of silence' in the criticism around Jayasi; that is, he establishes that Jayasi was a forgotten poet in the literary world prior to Ramchandr Shukl. What were the reasons for this? In search of an answer, Sahi notes the allegorical weight placed on Jayasi's *Padmavat* and discusses the issue of Sufism in the poem. He is of the view that an ideology from outside the text damages the composition. He writes: 'It has become next to impossible to discuss Jayasi by distancing him from Sufism [*tasavvuf*]. This misunderstanding hides from view not only Jayasi's poetic personality, his creative acumen and to some extent his originality, but it also makes him a victim of double injustice and neglect.'[2] Sahi believes that instead of such a reading, the poem's affectivity should be captured through its own warp and woof. His book on Jayasi is a testament to this view. Taking his cue from the structure of Hazari Prasad Dwivedi's *Kabir*, Sahi first uncovers the personality of Jayasi by removing the layers of Sufism cloaking the poet. What remains is this: 'An ordinary but emotional human being, a friend who joined hearts, and an intensely talented, imaginative and intellectual poet.'[3]

A comparison of Dwivedi's *Kabir* with Sahi's *Jayasi* reveals a huge difference between the portrayals of the two characters. Kabir appears to be a personality from the medieval era, while Jayasi appears to be a poet from among Sahi's own Parimal associates. Turning to Sahi's treatment of the canto on Nagmati's separation from her husband in *Padmavat*, it is well known that Shukl considers the description of this separation to be of utmost significance and the centrepiece of the entire poem. Shukl opines that Nagmati forgets her queenliness, or, more accurately, Jayasi forgets that Nagmati is a queen. He presents her as an ordinary housewife, and her pain does not remain a queen's pain but becomes an experience of ordinary women. Locating this transformation in the verse, 'I am husbandless, who will repair the hut's roof?' Shukl writes:

> He visualizes human beings and all flora and fauna to be bound by the same thread through an ordinary heartfelt element's universe-expansive feeling. . . . Nagmati's state of separation extends not just to the human race, but can be seen among the flora and the fauna too. . . . In this state Nagmati completely forgets her queenliness and sees herself in the form of an ordinary woman.[4]

Sahi agrees with Shukl, but it is important to read his own views on the matter:

> It was the description of Nagmati's separation that made Shukl transport Jayasi from anonymity to the Hindi triumvirate. I want to chime my voice with Shukl's in utter humility. But this description does not simply communicate the sharpness and lyricality of feelings; it adds new perceptions to our sensorium. The entire description of separation from the beloved, in the *barahmasa* mode, takes form in Nagmati's voice. In the first few verses, Nagmati's mortal body and the women attendants of the palace are shimmeringly visible. Suddenly, with a jerk, the imagination is freed and we come face to face with a voice, and a voice alone. Slowly, the shimmering mortality is sloughed off. All mortality slowly disappears. The women attendants disappear. The Chittor fort, the royal palace, all disappear, so much so that even Nagmati's mortal body disappears. A voice pierces through the wilderness, forests, groves, hills, fields – a clear but disembodied voice. This voice continuously swims across the heart-touching essence of space and of passing time. Space and time both drop off like an unnecessary outer covering – only essence remains as essence. . . . This voice has a transcendental impersonality which leaves even Nagmati far behind.[5]

Recalling Nirala's memorable expression about Tulsidas, 'pierced by the arrow of space and time, the poet of infinite beautiful imagery awoke', let us look at the implicit meanings of Sahi's formulations. He begins by announcing his agreement with Shukl's views. This means that he accepts the transformation of Nagmati into an ordinary woman and as a representative image of great suffering. But he does not actually hold this view. He strips Nagmati's separation of realism. Whereas Shukl searches for the foundation of Jayasi's poetic world, in the context of the description of Nagmati's separation, Sahi attempts to delink that poetic world from Shukl's evaluation. Sahi delinks the separation from the beloved, first from its immediate context, then from space and time coordinates, then from historical conditions, and finally from the human speaker Nagmati as well. It is a relief that he does not extend this further, which could have led to a delinking of the poem from Jayasi himself. What then remains? Is it pure separation, or pure sadness, or pure pain? Heartfelt essence is what remains. In consequence, impersonality appears and that too as transcendental. Only after this transformation does pure suffering attain the status of a voice in the historical world. Matters are further confused as even after this formulation Sahi claims to be following Shukl's thought.

Does this mean that in order to reach the essence of poetry, we must get rid of all the signs of the real world from its presence? Is it not an ideological proposition to turn past events into a contemporaneity divested of history, when it is precisely ideology that Sahi considers pernicious for poetry? In the debates around 'new poetry', the autonomy of the individual was the important issue. Stress was laid on the authenticity of experience in order to elaborate Agyey's theory of the 'moment' of creation. But Sahi advocates forgetting even the immediate present in the reading of the poetic work. The issue for the reader is how to experience this impersonal essence. The reader can only attempt to access this essence that lies close to 'pure poetry' through spatio-temporal coordinates. In which case, what is the role of material reality in this poetic and critical method? Only by separating this separation, grounded in time and place, from the latter does Sahi make it pervasive in all of time and space. But what is the need for such critical moves?

Muktibodh addresses the same problem when he writes: 'The fantasy which is severed from all personal suffering of experience, i.e. that which becomes neutral and through the sensibilities within experience itself is emitted and thrown out, is in one sense personal while at the same time being eternally impersonal.'[6] For Muktibodh, this issue relates to generalization and representativeness, while for Agyey and Sahi, it relates to the fundamental autonomy of the individual. Secondly, it is only after the severing of any other poetic feeling from its throbbing, hurting core that fantasy is formed for which generalization and representativeness are essential. But the process does not end here. The dialectic of the third moment in art does not allow it to remain formless. Sahi is able to install *the* poetic work on the high throne of impersonality only after severing it from its social milieu, quite apart from and in contrast with Muktibodh's impersonality within the writing process itself.

In the context of his discussion of *Padmavat*, Sahi includes the Nagmati separation episode within the ambit of this artistic viewpoint. In this manner, the 'emotive experience' of Jayasi's poetry as identified by Sahi comes into opposition with the 'emotive experience' as formulated by Shukl. The spatio-temporal character of the 'emotive experience' gets lost in the process of becoming 'essence'. Perhaps it is for this reason alone that Sahi considers Jayasi to be a modern poet. The implication is that he becomes a poet only after his rediscovery by Shukl. In Sahi's words: 'I had said in the beginning that even if Jayasi was a writer from the sixteenth century, he was invented by Ramchandr Shukl only in the twentieth century. In this sense alone he is a poet of the twentieth century. But his creativeness is modern in a deep sense.'[7]

What is modernity according to Sahi? He wants to identify the poet in Jayasi outside the precinct of medievalism. He repeatedly disconnects Jayasi from other medieval saint-poets, and stresses that the latter is a poet and a poet alone. Towards this end, Sahi finds it imperative to remove the cloak of Sufi thought from Jayasi's poetry. He contends that Jayasi's point of departure is man, and not a god or divinity:

> His thought is mainly focused on man – man as he is in ordinary life learns things, falls in love, runs the household, shows bravery or cowardice in war, establishes political states, behaves ignominiously and deceitfully, establishes communities, shouts slogans to mobilize people – and after all this, is gripped by the deep tragedy of his incompleteness.[8]

In Sahi's formulation, it is this representation of man in Jayasi's work that makes the poet modern. This is what contributes to his intellectual depth and freedom from ideology.

It is somewhat surprising that despite the presence of Kabir and Tulsi in Sahi's book, which deepens the colour of 'modernity' in Jayasi, Surdas is almost never mentioned. Is it the case that all the parameters of modernity applied to Jayasi could well be applicable to Surdas as well? If we ignore the question of the deep tragedy of modernity, as mentioned above, man is also the centre of Sur's poetic imagination. The tragedy in the description of the *gopis* in separation from their beloved is no less tragic. But it is well known that Sur belongs to a pastoral economy, historically speaking. Will this not require a closer examination of modernity as defined by Sahi in his study of Jayasi? Man as described in the quotation above from Sahi looks suspiciously similar to Muktibodh's 'insignificant man'. As we have already discussed, for Muktibodh, this insignificant man is a product of the tensions and contradictions in post-independence middle-class life.

In Muktibodh's writings, the framework of modernity is discussed in the essay '*Nayi kavita aur adhunik bhavbhodh*' [New Poetry and the Modern Sensibility]. The underpinnings of Sahi's modernity can be understood in relation to Muktibodh's formulation. The latter writes:

> Today, for the educated middle class, the situation in India is not favourable. . . . The value of money has increased, the value of human beings has fallen. . . . The western fashion of civilizational critique holds that man is petty, man is hollow, he is by nature selfish. . . . Man is at heart petty. Therefore suffering is primeval. There is no way to get past suffering.[9]

Now we can compare the 'tragic' in Jayasi with Muktibodh's formulation. Sahi repeatedly refers to Jayasi's 'tragic' vision, in which nothing remains at the end but suffering. This is the content of the 'essence' discussed above.

In this way, Sahi identifies his own historical middle-class situation in the realm of *Padmavat*. If this were not the case, a sinuous critic like Sahi would never have conflated man of the medieval age with the man who 'shouts slogans to mobilize people'. In the same order of thought, Sahi posits deep intellectualism in opposition to intellectual commitment. He defines the former thus: 'With the introduction of the non-apparent meaning, intensification, undulations of thought and the unity of emotions are brought together within the contextual meaning.'[10] As for intellectual commitment, he defines it as 'a situation where the non-apparent spirit becomes meaning-heavy and the concrete emotional context of the story becomes secondary.'[11] That Sahi uses his contemporary historical consciousness to assess Jayasi's poetry is one thing. The larger issue is that he uses his own historical consciousness as a criterion to evaluate the medieval period. This anachronism is noted by Satyaprakash Mishr: 'It seems to me that just as T.S. Eliot views Shakespeare and Dante and brings criticism to its true critical potential, Sahi too, in comparing Jayasi with Tulsi, Kabir, Khusrau and others, establishes Jayasi as the standard for his criteria of criticism.'[12]

Muktibodh too is interested in a similar critical project. It is more than mere coincidence that the two influential critics from the two streams of 'new poetry', the Marxist and Parimal groups, return to the Bhakti period in order to establish their canons of literature. Muktibodh writes about large chunks of the Bhakti period, while Sahi confines himself to Jayasi criticism. Sahi's propositions cannot be applied to the entire Bhakti period. Secondly, in trying to derive questions of identity in Jayasi's poetry through the criteria for new poetry, Sahi ends up countering his own position. Reproaching those who are ensnared by history from a position of being conscious of the present, Sahi writes: 'The allure of changing the past according to one's wishes and applying it to contemporary reality is not easily overcome. Who would want to write poetry in imitation of the sensibility of Tulsidas? But everyone wants to claim to be a descendant of that tradition.'[13] If the allure of changing the past according to one's wishes and applying it to contemporary reality is what is wrong with Tulsi criticism today, the same should apply to Jayasi too. Sahi carries on his argument without any acknowledgement of this contradiction.

Painting a baleful picture of his intellectual contemporaries, he writes:

> The contemporary intellectual and artist is surrounded by darkness; despite being full of courage he is made hopeless by indecision, yet he is unvanquished in his effort, grappling with questions that have no answers, but an opponent of false answers, he is limited by temporal truths, and yet he opposes pomposity; he accepts the existence of sorrow, but he remains a fighter for independence. His intelligence is his faith, his indecision his sincerity, his courage the totality of his personhood and his smallness his success.[14]

What are the other identifying marks of the intellectual–artist, immersed in his independence? After much critical effort, Muktibodh establishes the class location of this intellectual–artist. He decisively delineates the lower middle-class tendency within 'new poetry' of feeling broken down by its reduced socio-economic conditions, and of considering communism to be a repressive system antithetical to freedom following the Cold War logic. The insignificant man is unable to recognize the consolidation and the might of the people. This self and this moment in criticism turn contemporaneity into an eternal yardstick. His foundation for fighting a single fight against all injustices is revealed when this yardstick is put into practice. Fighting all injustices at one go means fighting against nothing. This is so because the rationale for the fight is not millions of poor people but only one's personhood.

In his much-quoted poem on Kabir, Sahi demands 'speaking truth with a whip crack'. This is a truth which could benefit anyone; Sahi advises against asking who the beneficiary is of this truth. Whence this irresponsibility? Does truth make the artist irresponsible? How valid then is that truth which is gleaned from the lives of others? Thirdly, if this truth is person-specific, then no definition of it would be possible; each person would have his own truth, whether he be communist or progressive. In this regard we should remember that Sahi's political guru, Ram Manohar Lohia, established the 'truth' of the religiosity of the people, and subsequently the Janata Party was caught in the web of communalist politics.

Muktibodh presents the insignificant man in the following way:

> This much is clear that within this 'modern sensibility' there is no comprehension of those forces of harassment which we call exploitative, or capitalist, or imperialist, and those forces of opposition are also not known to it which we know of as the people or the exploited class. . . . In short, among the Indian middle class those fellow feelings connoting progressive politics are not part of the 'modern sensibility'. We are merely the insignificant man, not the common people. Among the common people there is an irrepressible revolutionary power for transforming the world. But in the writings of those rule-givers, it is merely a blind force. The awareness of actuality is the richness of the individual's interiority. Therefore, the unit of the individual is important. This unit is the insignificant man, since it is not associated now or any more with the painful and fierce efforts to attain the highest levels of great ideals. The age of great souls, great geniuses and great men has passed. . . . If we become ordinary people, we would become targets of leftist tendencies and become a part of the blind force of the people, we would lose our sense of individuality. Therefore, we should leave the ordinary people and become insignificant man.[15]

As contrast, this recalls Sahi's essay in which he associates communism with Christianity and criticizes both: 'this is the altar of futurity on which the present is to be sacrificed'.[16] He notices a particular regimentation of the individual's autonomy in both communism and Christianity. He believes that in the name of a long distant future, both violate man's independence. In his essay quoted above, Muktibodh attacks this view with sarcasm:

> Individual autonomy is a holy principle (even if it comprises pillage, impropriety, corruption, selfishness, wantonness, worship of wealth, exploitation). If there are social ills, they will be removed only glacially. There are those who are scared of this autonomy because of their smallness. Those who accept demands made from the outside are inartistic. This Communist Party which primarily emphasizes man's awareness or self-consciousness and enslaves him, works through *regimentation* [in English]. . . . Some intellectuals and some people are foolish enough to come under their influence. It brings western influences to bear on India, it enslaves the minds of the people. Western influence is in

fact also an Indian influence, and the American legal order is in fact Indian. International communism is an enemy of India, international capitalism and imperialism are blood-brothers of India![17]

Muktibodh has in mind the entire stream of 'new poetry' which begins with Agyey and reaches its full form in the Parimal critics. The theorization of an eternal presentness is also a step in the same process.

We can now return to Sahi's literary work-based criticism. Working with his principle of harmony between two extremes, he produces a reading of *Padmavat* in which between the 'Singhal island' and the 'Chittor fort', 'Padmavati' emerges in vibrant colours.[18] He comes up with similar polarities in trying to understand poetic perception in the poet Shamsher. In Shamsher's reading, the opposition of Singhal island and Chittor fort turns into a dialectic between Marxism and extreme realism.[19] Sahi holds that man's desire to transcend time draws him towards utopia. In the discussion on Shamsher, utopia refuses to sacrifice the present on the altar of futurity but rather contemporizes both the past and the future. Therefore, according to Sahi, a tragedy is born from this opposition which is the emotive core of poetry. This poetic essence is present equally in Jayasi, Shamsher and Mallarmé, he argues.

Ashutosh Kumar takes issue with this criticism and raises the following questions about its validity:

> It is one thing to search for the world vision embedded in poetry. This world vision is not coterminous with poetry. . . . In Muktibodh's words, it is the embedded 'knowledge of the sensible and knowledge-based sensibility' in poetry. There is no objection if Sahi wants to call it 'intellectual depth'. But how valid is it to see it every time as man's existence-based irony, which is another name for modernist angst?[20]

We have already seen Muktibodh's class-based interpretation of this tendency.

We shall now attempt a final formulation regarding the tensions underlying Sahi's viewpoint. The first point is embedded in Sahi's contemporary milieu. In our discussion of two other critics of the same period – Muktibodh and Namvar Singh – we noted how Cold War politics affected the process of canon formation in their work. That is, how the debate between formalism and materialism was amplified in Hindi criticism. Neither critic ever claims that the opposing side has no substantial point to make. The challenge facing these critics was to learn from the principles of counter-thesis and to develop their critical project by attacking its points of weakness. This, undoubtedly, had to be achieved by neither abandoning one's own bases nor by allowing a free run to the opposing side. Sahi conducts his critical project on the same ground.

The second issue is also based on historical conditions. The search for Indianness was an important part of the anti-colonial effort. But the relations between Indianness and modernity were never simple or straightforward. In Chapter One above, we encountered Partha Chatterjee's argument about 'the home and the world' within Indian nationalism. Similarly, the quest for Indianness was pertinent to both Lohia and Sahi. Lohia reached the Hindu divinities of Ram, Krishn and Shiv in this quest. In search of a modernity that matched their vision of it, Lohia arrived at reinterpretation of myth while Sahi reached Jayasi's poetic corpus. Ashutosh Kumar comments on this critical turn:

> The question was how to become modern without abandoning or questioning tradition. And if it wasn't possible to exist without becoming modern, what was one to make of one's Indianness which itself was impossible to forget, abandon or ignore? The desperation to get rid of the colonial heritage could posit Indianness only as a negation of the west. And if modernity belongs to the west, then we have need of it. We must find our own, separate modernity. The concept of history, the idea of progress, are both forms of western thought. The west has a special concept of time – a linear one.[21]

Sahi builds his criticism precisely on this one point – in his essay 'Marxvadi alochna ki communist parinitiyan' [Communist Conclusions to Marxist Criticism], for example. In the canon proposed by this counter-thesis to Marxist criticism, the same point is developed later in the work of Nirmal Verma. In the final section of this chapter the discussion will turn to Verma's canon criticism.

NIRMAL VERMA: IN SEARCH OF INDIANNESS

Vijaydev Narayan Sahi's view of 'the sacrifice of the present on the altar of history and futurity' re-emerges in Nirmal Verma's discussion of the unitary temporality of Indianness. Verma asserts that the human-centric European intellectual tradition gave birth to history, and this concept of history became an enemy of unified temporality. He overturns all earlier historical forms of the nation-state to posit this unified temporality as a cultural unit. He deploys this category of the cultural unit as primeval and unchanging, and considers colonialism to be a schismatic force in Indian culture.

Verma's 'search for Indianness' is primarily a venture in opposition to colonial power, through which emerges the possibility of negating what one sees of oneself in the mirror of colonialism, as well as of beautifying the past and thereby opening up the possibility of mysticism. Therefore, the search for Indianness can be made by examining contestations within society as well as through meditation in solitude. Through these means one can reconstruct historical consciousness as well as become free of it. This should not be taken to mean that the 'search for Indianness' can lead the researcher to a particular place. Verma does not consider this search to be ideological. In his view, our attitude towards society and ourselves will determine the outcome of our search for Indianness.

In his own search for Indianness, Nirmal Verma turns towards the past. In Ashok Vajpeyi's words, this quest is an 'agitation for India': 'Nirmal Verma imagines wholeness by focusing on the fissure caused by the experience of colonialism in Indian thought and the mutual otherness between east and west resulting from it.'[22] But the point of recovery that Verma arrives at in his search for (or invention of) Indianness is an aggregation of the ideas of historical time and space in which there are no living people, nor a trace of their struggle. What remains at that point is only 'man shivering in accursed, kinless alienation'. If the outcome of the search for Indianness is this kinless man who displaces from the nation the man fighting against living conditions that are 'one level below humanity', then for sure his India would be plagued by no other sorrow but the pangs of spiritual alienation. The scars of deep feudal exploitation cannot disperse the indivisibility of his consciousness. Even if, in Ashok Vajpeyi's words, Nirmal Verma appears to be standing on 'the bloodied ground of history', this ground is determined by the critic after his own heart. In this bloodied reality, no trace of pre-modern blood is in sight. From the same vantage point, one needs to question Verma about the Bhakti period, for example, in particular about Kabir. If Kabir does not represent a fissure (à la post-colonialism) in his thought, why then is the man in his poetry fragmented?

Verma identifies this wholeness in Buddhism and orthodox Hinduism:

> [A]mong the religions, only two appear to me to be completely true and validated in themselves – the first is the Upanishadic–Puranic religion which says that the singularity of the earth can be subsumed under a truth which is indivisible. And the second, at the opposite pole, is the Buddhist faith in which even the self is considered to be illusory.[23]

In other words, the orthodox faith settles sorrows by making them indivisible and dissolving them into the void, while Buddhism, in contrast, does the same by positing itself as illusory. Although Verma does not specify the underlying bases of this definition of Buddhism, it is difficult to agree with his elucidation. It can be safely said that the creation of an inner world which can dissolve sorrows into the void did not work in the past nor does it work today.

Verma argues that the Hindus did not write about other cultures or the west because they had no shortcomings, whereas the Orientalists were full of a cultural emptiness. The Hindus possess a civilization that is primeval, which found no need to debate with history-bound civilizations. Verma establishes this as the basis of tradition which is founded on memory [*smriti*]. It goes without saying that this tradition is more or less unchangeable, without history and complete in itself. It was later destroyed by colonialism and industrialization. What then is the way out? Can we return to our pre-colonial past? Jaidev identifies the antiquarianism in Verma's propositions and writes: 'we may not be able to return to the pre-colonial past but our art based on ancient values is alive in our brahmins, ascetics and saints.'[24]

In Agyey and Verma's cultural thought, the delineation of colonialism takes place around the conception of time. Both the critics locate separateness from the culture of the west or Europe in the separateness of the concept of time. Verma writes: 'The most baleful effect of British rule in India was not that we became economic and political slaves, but that history forced us for the first time to legislate our consciousness through the categories of past, present and future.'[25] He considers history to be the antonym of memory or tradition. Memory or tradition is a sempiternal present in which the divisions of past, present and future do not obtain. The past lives on in the present and never passes away. Similarly, the future does not hold any special significance besides the present. The indivisibility of time arises from memory which is where art originates.

In his essay '*Bharat aur Europe: pratishruti ke kshetr ki khoj*' [India and Europe: In Search of a Region of Echos], Nirmal Verma writes:

> Europeans would have had a more harmonious and restrained knowledge of Indians had they come into direct contact with Indian culture, and not through the distorted vision of British colonialism. This distortion worsened due to the historical context in which they had to understand Europe and face its realities. This context was not available to them through their tradition, but rather through the European categories of knowledge, science and philosophy. Indians had to acknowledge Europe in a language that was not their own, through categories of thought that were European in provenance, with a social milieu that was colonial in character. It is not surprising, therefore, that the picture of Europe that India made for itself was as fragmentary and prejudiced as the European conceptualizations of India.[26]

Verma gives a cultural or civilizational reading of alienation and dispersal. He considers the 'self-dispersal' or alienation of the west to be the alienation of the human from the non-human world. The non-human world *is* nature. In the colonial period the Indian mind was similarly alienated, but not completely so. The mythical space–time is the key to the relationship between the human and non-human worlds with which pre-colonial India was always in touch, although Europe was delinked from this mythical consciousness from the time of the Enlightenment, as was India under the rule of colonialism. Nature lies both within the human and outside of it. The internalization of nature does not allow nature outside to become a cause for violence. There is no opposition therefore between man and nature. Besides being the living memory of the relation between man and nature, the mythic is also the dream of subconsciousness. If, in the eyes of Europe, India was 'gripped by sleep', then the mythic was the dream of that sleeping culture. Europe awoke and lost that dream of 'unconsciousness', and fell into the nightmare of history. Rather than a clash of two civilizations, Nirmal Verma describes a more complex process:

> Now it is no longer the clash of two civilizations, Indian and European, which represent two separate ideals; rather it was internalized by the Indian and European civilizations, wherein one aspect of European civilization, romanticism, clashed with another aspect of the same civilization, scientific progress and positivism, just as the traditionalism of Indian civilization was opposed to another of its aspects, i.e. western liberal ideology.[27]

The spiritual crisis through which Verma visualizes the fortunes of man and nation is applied by him to the study of literature too. In this regard he raises the questions of genre and form, and emphasizes their distinction. He also makes controversial statements about Premchand as a writer in several of his essays. I will discuss below Verma's notion of Indianness, in particular its manifestation in the form of the novel, and finally, his assessment of Premchand's work.

In the keynote speech at a Sahitya Akademi seminar in 1999, Verma declared that the western form of the novel had delimited and harmed the multilayered Indian reality. European novels of the eighteenth and nineteenth centuries were produced by an autonomous sensitivity about the building of an individuality, whereas in India, the novel form was made available on the basis of a previously given typology. At the time, the process of individuation in India had not reached the state in which it was in Europe. Verma concluded that there is an urgent need to give an account of the various kinds of oppositions in Indian ethical thought. Even if the genre of the great epic had exhausted itself, the great epic sensitivity was not dead.[28]

It is ironic that the collective ethical epic sensitivity that Verma posits as Indian, against the individualized consciousness of the European novel, became an object of enquiry and attention in European thought as it turned to myth and archetypal symbols in literature. This raises several questions. Is the rise of the novel in India due to the fragmentation of our sensibility? Do indigenous traditions of storytelling lend more creativity to our novelistic narratives? Does the social-realist novel constrict the expression of Indian reality?

Marxist critics have chosen to answer these questions from the fortress of sociology. Manager Pandey grapples with the issue of Indianness or foreignness of the genre of the novel in his essay 'Upanyas ka samajshastr' [Sociology of the Novel]. He throws light on the historical conditions underlying the origin and development of the novel:

> For the birth and development of the novel, i.e. for its existence, there is a need for certain material and ideological conditions which emerged only in the modern period. If the essentials for the existence of the novel, i.e. the printing press, publication and a journal or magazine culture, are the fruits of scientific development, then its authorship and readership centred in the middle class were the result of a capitalist social formation. Alongside these material preconditions, the ideological forms of individualism, a secular viewpoint on life and a realist world vision are essential, which are the products of modern intellectual thought. Human freedom, the importance of the individual and the dignity of human relations could become central features of the process of creation of the novel only when the human mind became ready to not accept the power of any other-worldly force besides its own experience and rationality. This was not possible in the medieval period. The novel is the literary form that expresses the revolt of modernity against medievalism.[29]

In contrast, Verma holds the epic-heroic sensibility to be essential for Indian reality, while criticizing the western form of the novel: 'For our narrative prose we chose such a "genre" as the "novel" which emerged and developed from the absolutely different cultural experience of Europe. . . . From Premchand to the contemporary novelists no one may cast any doubt on the novel genre, leave alone a re-examination based on one's experience.'[30]

Verma was engrossed for a long time in consolidating a special form of Indianness using memory and tradition. He found a deeper affinity between Indianness and the epic-heroic sensibility than with the novel. His dream novel is presented by himself thus:

Freeing ourselves from the precinct of the European novel, the novel whose rebirth we envision will exhibit all those scars of injuries on the human body which the person bore in a previous birth, but now that pain will be not directed at another but rather get connected with the totality of the existence of creation in whose happiness we are happy, in whose sadness we are sad. In that state, vision, being, experience cannot be divided into separate categories.[31]

Manager Pandey rebuts this position:

The novel is considered to be the epic of the modern age, therefore it is the inheritor of the ancient memory of the nation. But the nature of the novel is different from the epic. The epic is an encomium to the past of national life, whereas the novel is about contemporary social processes which contest the homogeneity and univocality of the ideology of the ruling class. Besides this, the novel form disrupts the collectivizing ideology of nationalism by presenting different communities, classes and identities amid the imagined communality of the nation. The history of the novel from around the world proves that the form is immensely malleable, dynamic, multi-dimensional and innovative. Therefore, Mikhail Bakhtin warns theorists of the novel that every principle of the novel form is prone to complication that wants to be tied to some static quality or ideological connection. Even nationalism is an ideology, which the novel resists being tied to. Social-realist novels are permanently pitted against the kind of nationalism nurtured by historical and individualist romance novels. In the work of the romantic novelists, memory of the past and imagination of the future overwhelm any understanding of the present. This entire tradition of narrative assists revivalist nationalism, while the social-realist novel faces the realities of time and society, and thus fashions an emancipatory and vanguardist national consciousness. In the latter we get an articulation of the actualities of life and of democratic aspirations, and we can hear the voices of the people living in the margins of nationalism.[32]

In the same essay, Manager Pandey shows that nationalism is not always emancipatory or radical. The nationalism of India's independence movement did not accommodate most peasants, workers, women and Dalits. The Subaltern school of history militates against this tendency of elite nationalism in which the people are a faceless and voiceless mass. Premchand's novels present the realities and struggles of peasant life against this very idea of the faceless mass.

Verma's views on Premchand have been thoroughly questioned by Jaidev. In a rebuttal of Verma's treatment of Premchand the novelist, Jaidev writes: 'Godan is a great literary text not because it portrays the helplessness and deception in Hori's life, but because it shows that a man can never attain peace, not even after death, unless he gifts a Brahmin priest a cow.'[33] Premchand's novels present the independence struggle as much more than the biography of its great leaders. The struggle for Indian nationalism was initiated by peasants, workers, women and Dalits, who were not simply a faceless mass. This fact is revealed in the works of Premchand, and not in the works of nationalist historians or Nirmal Verma. Many decades before the Subaltern historians, Premchand tore to shreds the alleged indivisibility of nationalist consciousness and unravelled its relations of power. There was no doubt in his mind about the tragedy of Surdas in *Rangbhumi* [The Arena of Life], and the betrayal of the great peasant movement by its leadership through a compromise with the ruling class. The class composition of Indian nationalism is revealed by the ongoing class struggle within it. Raja Mahendra Pratap, the nationalist in *Rangbhumi*, declares Surdas's struggle to be a disturbance; Amarkant in *Karmbhumi* wavers and compromises easily; in *Godan* the feudal–capitalist nationalism of Rai Sahib and Khanna foreshadows the class bases of political power in post-colonial India.

In Premchand's *Gaban* [Fraud], Devidin Khatik, who has lost two of his sons to the independence struggle, asks a nationalist leader: 'Sir, tell me truly, when you say "independence", what form of it appears before your eyes? Will you too draw huge salaries, live in bungalows like the English, retreat to the hills, walk about in English style? What good would this independence do to the country?'[34] In *Godan* [Gift of the Cow], Mirza Khurshed announces, 'When we say "democracy", in practice it is the rule by big merchants and landowners and nothing else. Whoever has money, wins at the ballot.'[35]

In the globalizing India of today, if Ravibhushan identifies lakhs of farmer suicides with Hori's death, it is not without reason.[36] Premchand was one of the first to expose the anti-farmer tendencies of the market supported by the landowning, capitalist powers on a national and international scale. Premchand's Indianness is not based on memory or dreams. It is a vivid picture of the nation seen through its complex contradictions. Hazari Prasad Dwivedi writes: 'If you care to know about the manners, language, ways of living, hopes and desires, feelings and thought of the people of north India, then no better introduction can be had than Premchand.'[37] If the real Indian peasant as portrayed in Premchand's novels is a colonial peasant, what would a pure 'Upanishadic' peasant look like? Nirmal Verma is in search of a Hori who worries not about his land and exploitation, but only about faith, memory and Propriety (not propriety).

In truth, it is difficult to argue with Verma because within his notion of tradition no value is given to historical events. He only has faith in timelessness (as opposed to history) and in belief (as opposed to rationality). In this way, he discards the realm of rational analysis. For him, this is a matter of pure faith which transcends reason, intellectual curiosity and realism. In this struggle, the purity of the Hindu faith wins and becomes the core of a great civilization. Thus, it becomes a point of mobilization for patriotism and nationalism. Jaidev calls it political deceit and raises the issue of the other benighted classes 'within this tradition':

> He was dismissive of those who spoke of other, alternative, little cultural traditions. In his thought there is only one tradition and nothing else. I am unable to dive into tradition so spectacularly because I fear that I would be beaten and shut out. This is likely because I plan to ask, first, what relief does this tradition offer to the lowest castes and child widows? I would be kicked twice: for asking the question in the first place, and then for sullying this pure world by asking such a profane question.[38]

For a stream of thought invested in upholding both the worldly and spiritual foundations of the individual, it is ironic that the question of social location, expressed as identity, is never broached by Verma. Critics who are anti-Marxist desire to transcend actually-existing society as the basis of writing and talking about experience.

In order to carry forward this discussion about canon formation and critical standards into our present, the next and final chapter discusses the contemporary conjuncture of canon and criticism in Hindi through two exemplary instances of identity politics: the feminist and the Dalit streams of criticism. This well help us locate the Hindi canon in its current moment of contestation and reconstruction by drawing on the historical debates we have seen so far in this discussion.

NOTES

[1] Sahi (1983), Introduction.
[2] Ibid., p. 23.
[3] Ibid., p. 22.
[4] Singh (1998), pp. 122–25.
[5] Ibid., p. 111.
[6] G.M. Muktibodh, '*Tisra kshan*', in Muktibodh (1998), Vol. 4, p. 85.
[7] Sahi (1983), p. 106.
[8] Ibid., p. 62.
[9] G.M. Muktibodh, '*Nayi kavita aur adhunik bhavbodh*', in Muktibodh (1998), Vol. 5, p. 307.

[10] Sahi (1983), p. 70.

[11] Ibid.

[12] Mishr (1993), p. 61.

[13] Sahi (2007a), p. 146.

[14] Ibid., p. 163.

[15] G.M. Muktibodh, '*Nayi kavita ki prakriti*', in Muktibodh (1998), Vol. 5, p. 326.

[16] Sahi (2007b), p. 161.

[17] G.M. Muktibodh, '*Nayi kavita ki prakriti*', in Muktibodh (1998), Vol. 5, p. 326.

[18] See the chapter '*Padmavat ka vishleshan*' [An Analysis of *Padmavat*], in Sahi (1983), pp. 80–112.

[19] See Vijaydev Narayan Sahi, '*Shamsher ki kavyanubhuti ki banavat*' [The Composition of Shamsher's Poetic Perception], in Sahi (2007a), pp. 194–219.

[20] Ashutosh Kumar (2009), p. 140.

[21] Ibid., p. 136.

[22] Ashok Vajpeyi, 'Introduction', in Vajpeyi, ed. (2001), p. 7.

[23] Interview with Nirmal Verma, in ibid., p. 27.

[24] Lal, ed. (2001), p. 128.

[25] Nirmal Verma, '*Shatabdi ke dhalte varshon men*', in Verma (2000), p. 65.

[26] Nirmal Verma, '*Bharat aur Europe: pratishruti ke kshetr ki khoj*', in Verma (2000), p. 136.

[27] Ibid., p. 132.

[28] Ramakrishnan, ed. (2005), p. 12.

[29] Pandey (2002), p. 48.

[30] Singh (1980), p. 2.

[31] Quoted by Dhruv Shukl in '*Adhunik manushya ke aatm ka naya chhand*', in Vajpeyi, ed. (2001), p. 131.

[32] Pandey (2002), p. 148.

[33] Jaidev (2001), p. 128.

[34] Premchand (2004a), p. 203.

[35] Premchand (2004b), p. 97.

[36] Ravibhushan (2006), pp. 16–18.

[37] Dwivedi (1988), p. 250.

[38] Jaidev (2001), p. 128.

CHAPTER FIVE

Questions of Identity and Decanonization

Feminist Criticism: Questioning Literary Criteria

In the final decades of the twentieth century, discussions around feminist and Dalit consciousness became important. Both these streams of criticism posed fundamental questions about the canons proposed by Hindi criticism. They highlighted how gender difference and caste stratification play both a clear and a hidden role in the process of canon-making. This meant questioning the common sense of Hindi canon criticism. Neither aesthetic excellence nor the class basis of criticism was left unchallenged. Before these two movements, the most prominent debate in Hindi criticism had been between aestheticism and realism. After their advent, these two categories were put into question; indeed, the terms of the debate changed.

If the literary value of a work is owing to its artistic quality, then does the latter arise from its aesthetic self-awareness? And is this self-awareness class- and caste-bound? Can aesthetics also belong to the marginalized groups of society? Our contemporary period has witnessed sharp rebuttals to the universalist claims of this elitist argument. Alongside, questions have been raised about the realist school of writing and criticism that used to claim to represent the excluded classes. The counter-argument was that realism was produced by those who were far from the experience of social reality, who had not even a nodding acquaintance with realism on the ground. Such literature cannot speak to those who are at the receiving end of this reality. Feminist and Dalit critiques entered into a debate with Marxist theory, pointing out that the latter's primary category of class ignored the special conditions of Indian society, and was unable to take into account caste- and gender-based experiences of oppression. This debate was also situated in the context of worldwide debates on Marxism by identity-based movements. At one time, this debate was conducted by the Blacks in North America. In the present discussion, I now turn to the feminist and Dalit criticisms of the Hindi canon which argue for the reinvention of the canon, at one end, and at the other, for a re-examination of the literary tradition itself.

Although women have expressed their disquiet in their creative writing, little work has been done in relation to the canon and literary criticism. Some feminist writers themselves have pointed to this problem:

> In English literature, feminist criticism is a popular and well-recognized term. But it has little popularity in Hindi. It would be more accurate to say that Hindi critics feel no attraction towards this term. . . . It is a fact that not even a rudimentary understanding has emerged in Hindi about feminist criticism. . . . Feminist criticism means adopting a point of view on the evaluation of women's writing and woman-centred writings by men.[1]

Feminist criticism primarily works with the categories of anti-patriarchy and female emancipation. The women's movement and feminist ideology also draw on these categories. Sudha Singh writes on the question of woman as an identity:

> Feminist women writers view the identity of being a woman as multidimensional. The identity can be expressed along several lines: gender, body, psyche, or experience. . . . The politics of female identity involves taking the woman out of male contexts and placing her within a female one. This means countering patriarchy as an ideology.[2]

Despite the proliferation of women's creative writing since the time of the reawakening, the canons proposed by Hindi criticism do not include women in any real measure. Women's writing does not become a serious object of criticism until the 1990s. This was a time of not just fiction-writing by women, but also of the establishment of feminist literary criticism and its foundational principles, and the production of translations of feminist writings from across the world.

Historically speaking, the women's question was first posed by the reform movements of nineteenth-century Bengal. The main voices of this early feminist moment were Raja Rammohun Roy, who campaigned against widow immolation, and Ishwar Chandra Vidyasagar, who fought for widow remarriage and similar movements against the practice of polygamy in elite and upper-caste families. The so-called 'disappearance' of the women's question from the agendas of social reform and nationalism has been a point of contention among historians. Partha Chatterjee, among other historians, has analysed this issue.[3] He argues that much before the nationalist project stood up to the colonial state and demanded political rights through a mass movement, a prior autonomous arena of cultural pre-eminence was posited by the nationalists. While, in the early part of the nineteenth century, the elite social reformers appealed to the colonial law and power to achieve their ends, by the end of the century, the new middle class established a cultural inner domain which they ruled to be autonomous and free from colonial intervention. Thus, social institutions and practices were divided into two domains: a profane outer realm and a spiritual inner realm. The former included the economy, politics, science and technology, while the latter was a domain of cultural identity in which India was assumed to be superior to the west. As proficiency in living in the outer domain increased, the need to protect the inner domain became pressing. Chatterjee argues that the nationalists resolved the women's question by placing it within the inner domain of spirituality, so that it ceased to be a political question. Taking a metaphor from Rabindranath Tagore, he sees this as a division between the home and the world.

From the Hindi viewpoint, Pranay Krishn gives an analysis of the women's question based on Chatterjee's thesis:

> Formal education was not only granted to the new middle-class woman, but became a condition for being middle class. For women's emancipation and 'the nationalist scheme for self-liberation, women and men had to participate equally'. The new bourgeois values of disciplining: e.g., orderliness, thrift, cleanliness, realization of personal responsibility, literacy, account-keeping and healthy practices, household management techniques based on new worldly and economic circumstances related to the outside world, these were on the agenda of 'women's education'. Towards this end, the woman had to acquaint herself with the outside world, and therefore the rules of women's seclusion were made lax, and society and culture determined different models for feminine and masculine behaviour.[4]

In the Hindi public sphere, Bhartendu's *Balbodhini* is an early example of articulation of the women's question. Balkrishn Bhatt wrote an article titled '*Striyan aur unki shiksha*' [Women and Their Education] in favour of women's education. Bhatt writes:

> Do not make empty protestations that women are being oppressed today, and that they deserve it because of their reduced state and feeble minds. Be assured that if you want to stuff into their reduced state foreign freedoms, even if you consider it to be desirable in your hearts, there could be no greater violence

against them. Something that is not understood by someone who is made to do it will surely cause anxiety and distress. Therefore I entreat you not to mention the comforts enjoyed by women in other countries in the context of women here.[5]

We notice here a clear tension between the women's question and the national question. Women are expected not to look western but to appear modern nevertheless: this was the fundamental contradiction in the culture of the time. A deep patriarchy was silently embedded within anti-colonialism which was more complex than the simple home–world binary. Even while women increasingly participated in the nationalist movement, this basic contradiction played itself out even in the arena of political struggle.

The contestation between the identity of woman and nation was visible in the works of the *Chhayavad* period. Sudha Singh identifies this struggle in the following words: 'The opposition between love for women and the nation should not be read as an opposition between personal and nationalist love as it was construed between 1916 and 1936 in the *Chhayavad* period, in particular in Prasad's oeuvre.'[6] Jaishankar Prasad's short story '*Puraskar*' [Award] becomes relevant here. Although the story is set in the medieval period, its binaries are modern. The heroine Madhulika is ready to sacrifice herself in love for Arun. She loves him boundlessly. But her love for the nation surpasses her personal love and she ends up getting Arun imprisoned. Arun is given the death penalty while Madhulika is rewarded. Prasad makes this opposition more acute as Madhulika asks for the death penalty as her award. Death appears to be the only solution to this binary opposition, especially from the woman's standpoint. But Prasad too, in order to portray the basic opposition of his society, must show the sacrifice of the smaller identity in favour of the larger identity. We will notice this structure again in the Dalit argument, especially in the example of the Poona Pact.

Namvar Singh shows that in *Chhayavad* poetry, woman is presented in the states of 'goddess, mother, companion, soul'. Thus she is not a subject in her own right. This is despite the fact that an excellent story writer, such as Mahadevi Varma, was grappling with this tendency, and struggling to shore up women's claim to subjecthood and authorship.

In his analysis of Mahadevi's essays in the collection *Shrinkhla ki kadiyan* [Links of the Chain], Manager Pandey situates her essays on women's awakening within the development known as the 'Indian reawakening'. In her writing, Mahadevi expresses the validity of the woman's voice. Unlike Prasad, she does not obfuscate the question of identity in relation to nationalism. She posits three layers of the identity of woman in her time:

The end point of the ideas of the Indian woman is that society may not corral them inside Indian culture in order to confront the challenge of the modern age. . . . The second view belongs to the middle-class woman who believes in making Indian cultural values the foundation of modern society. . . . The third and the largest class of women is still not awakened, and is not expected to think beyond its immediate world.[7]

Mahadevi argues for a confluence of the two classes of women; she wishes to harmonize the ancient and modern images of femininity. But her project is significant in that in her search of culture, she reaches matriarachal societies and highlights women's oppression after their downfall. Secondly, she identifies the market and personal independence as factors in the making of modern femininity. Mahadevi thus moves beyond the opposition of the home and the world. It is significant that the third class of women mentioned by her is present in her writing in a developed form, and this is what distinguishes her feminism from that of her contemporaries.

Bhaktin, Bibiya and Gungiya belong to the third strata mentioned by Mahadevi, and she gives them a voice for the first time in literature. Pranay Krishn observes:

They are not imaginary women who represent the nation or the national community. Mahadevi knew from her own experience that the new patriarchy established by the renaissance or the reawakening, while honouring women in spirit, had taken away so much from them. . . . These women from the lowest castes who were deprived of the light of the reawakening had been saved from being colonized by nationalist feminism.[8]

Premchand too wrote enthusiastically about the women's question in his novels. He was being read from a feminist angle. Critics such as Virendr Yadav have attempted to reread Premchand from the viewpoint of the politics of identity. Sudha Singh observes in her essay, 'Strivadi Premchand' [The Feminist Premchand]:

Premchand's entire oeuvre rejects the hegemonic mindset. This is the point at which Premchand crosses the limits of the ideology of the reawakening and proposes a new programme for women's emancipation. He is one of the first Hindi writers to betray a scientific understanding of women's issues. For him, women's problems are national and gendered problems. Considering the extent to which he discusses women's problems, no other group has received similar attention in his works.[9]

Further, Premchand wrote about almost all the major problems faced by women in his time: child marriage, inheritance, birth control. However, we need to take into account feminist critics who argue on the basis of women's own experience in literature. Katyayini, for example, writes:

> It is my view that the sympathies and sensibilities of the most honest of male feminist writers on the question of women's equality cannot be the same as that of a woman writer. The former can bear witness to the tragedy of a woman or be a sympathizer, but he cannot be an authority on her. Thus, he can theorize philosophically and politically on the women's movement, but at the level of literary writing, his creativity, perception and, to an extent, his conception cannot be that possessed by a woman writer.[10]

In post-independence fiction we begin hearing women's voices. Sudha Singh explains the reasons for this:

> While personal experiences are expressed in poetry, the writing of poetry, because it is a densely symbolic form of cultural expression, demands training and a constant social interaction. . . . The novel too is a part of the social sphere. But as a genre it does not demand much from the writer. . . . Being an open genre, entry can be gained at several points and many exits are available too. Therefore, on a worldwide scale, women adopted novel-writing.[11]

Krishna Sobti, Mannu Bhandari, Shivani, Chandrakiran Saunrexa, Usha Priyamvada, Mridula Garg, Chitra Mudgal, Nasira Sharma, Prabha Khaitan, Mamta Kaliya, Alka Saraogi and Maitreyi Pushpa have been the leading feminist voices in Hindi fiction. The fictional worlds of these writers address the questions of the status of women in the family, patriarchal oppression, changes in gender relations, economic pressures and the freedom of the body.

An aspect of feminist criticism that is salient in respect of the canon, and which shook up views on the canon, is the body. An exemplary novel in this regard is Krishna Sobti's *Mitro marjani* [To Hell with You, Mitro], whose protagonist Mitro refuses to accept any curbs on her freedom despite repeated attacks on it. Mitro's characterization is diametrically opposite to the pre-independence nationalist bourgeois woman. Her existence does not pay heed to the demands of another – whether those demands are big or small, pure or impure, ethical or unethical. In Mitro, Sobti constructs a frankness of women's self-expression that has been lost to the middle class. Mitro in Hindi literature matches the female characters memorably created by Ismat Chughtai in Urdu who may well be shattered by poverty, but do not concede to patriarchal violence and masculine outrageousness. It is precisely restrictions on the body that express the idealization of women favoured by patriarchy and nationalism. Under such conditions, it is not possible to speak of authentic female characters in writing without restoring the corporeality of women. Pranay Krishn declares Mitro to be a powerful example of 'the embodied presence of women in Hindi fiction'.[12]

If we try to construct a feminist canon on the basis of prose literature, then a fully embodied tradition emerges which posits several aspects of women's lives with acuteness, but the field of criticism is not as well developed. This seems to be the reason why, despite expressing women's issues in depth and with gravity, feminism has not be able to make a mark in debates on the Hindi canon.

Finally, we must address the point raised by the feminist critic Katyayini: that in view of our contemporary situation, the capitalist system poses new challenges to feminism in India. On the other hand, there is an urgent need for liberation from a half-baked, male-dominant Indian feminism. Third, feminism needs to guard itself against several western postmodernisms. And fourth, Indian feminism needs to affiliate itself with women at the lowest rungs of society, with women in villages and women who labour.[13]

DALIT THOUGHT: THE NEED FOR AN ANTI-CANON

The process of canon formation was jolted by Dalit thought. Rejecting all hitherto existing canons, Dalit thinkers argue that these were produced by Brahminical critics. An entire social group that was excluded from the canon is now staking its claim. In the words of Sharankumar Limbale, this group comprises 'all the untouchable castes living outside the village boundary, the aboriginals, the landless cultivators, labourers, the mass of agriculturists, the nomadic castes'.[14]

In Hindi literature, Dalit thought emerged in the decades of the 1980s and 1990s. Unlike the Marathi context, this was not inspired by an active political movement. Dalit thought in Marathi literature emerged concomitantly with the intellectual tradition of Phule and Ambedkar, and related social movements. In Hindi, Dalit thought is associated with a point of view that speaks for an independent Dalit claim to politics. Limbale describes the political conditions of its emergence in the 1980s and 1990s:

> Vishwanath Pratap Singh's 'blow of the Mandal hammer' brought together these scattered forces. Everyone got together, not just on the issue of social equality and social justice, but on the demand for a share in political power. . . . The remaining push was provided by Kanshi Ram and Ms Mayawati and their slogan of 'share political power!'.[15]

However, problems arise when this political context meets the question of identity in Dalit thought. Some Dalit thinkers point to the dangers of using the Dalit movement as a means of attaining political power. Kanwal Bharti observes: 'Dalit politics . . . was not controlled and regulated by the social force of the Dalit movement. In a stark inversion, Dalit politics controlled and regulated the Dalit movement, because of which the latter scattered, went astray and weakened.'[16] At its heart lies the Dalit middle class's interest in sharing power. The same middle class is active in literary writing and therefore the cry emanates from within Dalit thought: 'represent the downtrodden Dalits!'.

The criteria for canonization came under discussion with the advent of Dalit writing. The 'validity of perception' in the *Chhayavad* and 'new poetry' versions fell away as a criterion, and emerged situated in the content of concrete living experience. Muktibodh had proposed the linking of perception with reality. This became a point for further development. Following the idea from feminist criticism, Dalit thought emphasized self-perception against sympathetic observation, i.e. only Dalits can express the condition of Dalits and no one else. On this basis, Kanwal Bharti divided Dalit thought into three streams:

> The first stream comprises Dalit writers born into Dalit families who hold a vast universe of self-perceptions. The second stream consists of Hindu writers, in whose creative universe Dalits are portrayed as objects of aesthetic satisfaction. The third stream belongs to progressive writers who view Dalits in the status of the dispossessed.[17]

The discussion turned towards the importance of lived experience. Consequently, the Dalit autobiography became the most significant achievement of Hindi Dalit literature.

Critics responded with the question, can the experience of a single person represent the experiences of an entire community? Limbale answered as follows: 'The Dalit writer's assertion is that the life that I have lived, suffered and seen, I express the same in writing. Since experience is expressed in Dalit literature as an aspiration for freedom, its forms resemble a "we" more than an "I".'[18] Some exemplary autobiographies in this regard are Omprakash Valmiki's *Juthan* [Leftovers], Mohandas Naimisharay's *Apne apne pinjre* [Cages of Their Own] and Kaushalya Vaisantri's *Dohra abhishap* [The Double Curse]. These autobiographies are not simply the writers' personal stories, they articulate the gamut of Dalit life-experiences of their times. Kanwal Bharti marks the newness of this writing: 'Autobiographies such as *Apne apne pinjre* and *Juthan* were published in Hindi, which presented to us a completely new social reality.'[19]

As has been pointed earlier, in debates around the limits of 'self-perception', critics observed that Dalit autobiographies are the life-stories of those writers who have already achieved a position in middle-class and educated walks of life. While these autobiographies articulate the socio-cultural discrimination experienced by the whole community, they do not give an authoritative picture of the lowest among Dalits and the sufferings of the class of landless cultivators. This issue relates to people who are ground down by the double mill of caste and class. The question of representative expression is central to any argument based on identity. Giving a synopsis of this debate, Pranay Krishn writes: 'The debate around which class is the most prominent in the expression Dalit identity seems to be an attempt to assess aesthetics in the light of the processes of class differentiation within the Dalit community.'[20]

Debates around class and caste and their interrelationships have taken place regularly in Dalit criticism. These debates have also meant reflecting on the relations between Marxism and Ambedkarism. There have been attempts to unify the categories of caste and class, but it was necessary to deploy caste as a fundamental category for its self-definition. Dalit intellectuals have responded severally on this question. Pointing to the Brahminical leadership of the communist parties, they argue for a Dalit leadership, which is as important as the demand for livelihood and respect. A large stream of these intellectuals also argue for the joining together of the leftist and Dalit movements. Kanwal Bharti considers the leadership of Marxist and Dalit politics to be distanced from Marx and Ambedkar, and argues in favour of the radical form of both politics as essential.[21]

In the chapters above, we have noticed that with Dalit identity politics taking shape, its clash with nationalism became inevitable. At one time, Phule declared colonialism to be beneficial for Dalits. Ambedkar's struggle from within the nationalist movement is also a case in point. But the Dalit movement at that time was conducted under the leadership of a middle class which was itself a product of colonial modernity. Similarly, the leadership of the national movement rested with the middle and business classes, which too had been produced by colonial processes. Several commentators use a value-based rather than a factual vocabulary to talk about these processes, which inevitably reduce their historicity. There is a need for an objective analysis of nation and identity. If these are decontextualized from their time and place, Phule and Ambedkar would be read unilaterally as supporters of colonialism. In response to this problem, Pranay Krishn writes:

In Phule's time, the leaders of social reform set their hopes on the British rule. Phule stood at a historical crossroads where only the mere rustlings of an emergent nationalism could be heard, which were made up of the thought of the middle and business classes. Research has yet to be conducted to investigate how modern thought redefined the fact of the traditional caste system under colonial British rule. In any case, by the time Dr Ambedkar began an independent Dalit movement, the national movement was at a mature stage. The main flashpoint between nationalism and the Dalit movement is considered to be the issue of separate electorates and the Gandhi–Ambedkar Poona Pact.[22]

Dalit criticism adopted a two-pronged strategy: on the one hand, it underlined the difference between literature depicting Dalit lives written by non-Dalit writers and Dalit literature; on the other, it conducted a thorough rereading and rehabilitation of Dalit writers and literary works from the period before the rise of the Dalit movement in order to extricate them from aestheticist tendencies. Three writers were at the centre of this discussion: Kabir, Premchand and Nirala. It was necessary to conduct a thorough revision of Kabir in order to delink him from later Vaishnavite–Vedantic interpretations. Thus it was also necessary to question the powerful canonical formulations of critics such as Hazari Prasad Dwivedi in order to demolish canons based on hegemonic readings of Kabir and to establish Kabir within the tradition of Dalit thought. This challenge was met by Dr Dharmvir, who wrote six studies on Kabir in response to the dominant stream of Kabir criticism: *Kabir ke alochak* [Kabir's Critics], *Kabir ke kuchh aur alochak* [Some More Critics of Kabir], *Sut na kapas* [Neither Yarn nor Cotton], *Kabir: Dr Hazari Prasad Dwivedi ka prakshipt chintan* [Kabir: Dr Hazari Prasad Dwivedi's Secondary Thought], *Kabir aur Ramanand: kinvdantiyan* [Kabir and Ramanand: Apocryphal Legends] and *Kabir: baj bhi, kapot bhi, papiha bhi* [Kabir: Falcon, Pigeon and Brain Fever Bird]. This series of books initiated a debate which is considered to be the most intellectually vibrant debate in the history of Hindi criticism. Dharmvir aims at nothing less than the restitution of Kabir in the Dalit intellectual tradition by arguing against the whole tradition of modern Kabir criticism, led by Hariaudh, Shyamsundar Das, Ramchandr Shukl, Hazari Prasad Dwivedi, Parshuram Chaturvedi, Ramnivas Chandak and other progressive critics, and extricating Kabir from the Brahminic–Vaishnavite, Hindu, Jain, Buddhist, Nath–Siddh and progressivist–popular traditions. Almost all the major critics in Hindi participated in this debate with Dharmvir; the latter's serious accusations against Dwivedi made the discussions even more heated.

Veer Bharat Talwar, as a participant in the Kabir debate, wrote an essay on it, 'Kabir par kabze ki ladayi' [The Fight over Kabir's Appropriation].[23] Ashuthosh Kumar observed that Dharmvir provided a new dimension to criticism by deploying postmodern deconstruction. 'He relied heavily on deconstruction in his critical writings. A prime example of this is Dr Dharmvir's "deconstruction" of the critics of Kabir. . . . Dr Dharmvir shows that critics who praised Kabir prepared their own special readings of the poet. These "readings" were based on the critics' own Brahminical prejudices.'[24]

The other strand of Dalit criticism debated the literary works of humanist and progressive non-Dalit writers. In recent years, attempts have been made by Dalit critics to reread the works of Premchand and Nirala. The idiom of sympathy versus self-perception is usually used to characterize the writings of non-Dalits about Dalits and Dalit autobiographies. But new readings have also tried to signal the undertones of opposition to Dalit consciousness in the works of non-Dalit writers who are otherwise considered to be sympathetic to Dalit lives. In this regard Dharmvir's book *Premchand: samant ka munshi* [Premchand: The Feudal Lord's Scribe] is significant. Following his treatment of Kabir, Dharmvir presents a rereading of Premchand's short story 'Kafan' [The Shroud], in which he tries to give an interpretation of the 'absence' that lies between the narrative and the outside. Dharmvir critically reconstructs the story using Premchand's other writings and Shivrani Devi's book *Premchand: ghar mein* [Premchand: At Home]. Using an assumption along the lines of 'if this had happened, what would have happened', he writes:

> In truth, in Premchand's much discussed story 'Kafan' about *chamar*s [an 'untouchable' caste], only 'one-ninth' of the truth is spoken. Eight-ninths of 'Kafan' is left unsaid and remains in Premchand's belly. Only Dalit criticism of literature can unearth the whole iceberg. The entire story could have made new sense had Premchand written the truth about Dalit life in the last sentence, that Budhiya was pregnant with the child of the village zamindar. He had raped Budhiya in a field. Perhaps then light would have fallen, and everything would have been revealed and understood.[25]

Dalit critics have been engaged with Premchand's works both before and after Dharmvir. This criticism was based on placing the entirety of Premchand in his own tradition. Objections were raised against 'Kafan' in that no Dalit could be so inhuman that he is busy eating potatoes while his wife is dying and that he spends the money for her shroud on alcohol. The implication is that Premchand has knowingly represented Dalits as inhuman and deformed human beings. Kanwal Bharti confirms this view:

'Premchand creates the conditions that deform the characters of Ghisu and Madhav.' But Bharti's evaluation of Premchand's entire oeuvre is as follows: 'The progressivism of Premchand may not have been Ambedkarite, but was close to it.'[26] Dharmvir does not agree with this statement. Through his reading of the short story he enters Premchand's private life and associates his confession about two liaisons with illicit relationships. In this way he reveals the contents of 'Premchand's belly'. He implies that it could only be rape at the hands of some feudal personage or his scribe that impregnated Budhiya, and that neither Ghisu or Madhav have any sympathy for the mother and child. Bharti and Dharmvir criticize 'Kafan' as being anti-Dalit for almost diametrically opposite reasons. Bharti finds fault with Premchand's dehumanization of the Dalit person, while for Dharmvir that question does not arise and he corners Premchand on his caste identity instead. But on the question of self-perception (against sympathy), both writers concur.

Rajendr Kumar intervenes in this debate by stating that 'while it is true that the Dalit experience is missing from the writings of non-Dalit, progressive writers, if their work is read in the context of the tradition of Hindi literature, then, in comparison with other writers, their work reflects a clearer Dalit viewpoint.'[27] He appeals for an evaluation of Premchand and Nirala, taking into account their place within the entire tradition. In this debate the key questions are as follows. What should be the Dalits' attitude towards the non-Dalit tradition? What should be their stand on progressivism? One stream of Dalit criticism argues that the question of self-perception should be made central; the other argues that the shortcomings of writers sympathetic to the Dalit position should be revealed and they should become a part of Dalit literature.

Another important question confronting Dalit thought is the need to change the canon. The canon of Dalit thought, based on the criteria of self-perception, is disrupted when another voice of opposition emerges from *within* it. Dalit women's identity is one such challenge before Dalit thought. Sheoraj Singh 'Bechain' argues for the participation of Dalit women in the development of Dalit thought in his book *Stri vimarsh aur pehli dalit shikshika* [Feminist Thought and the First Dalit Woman Educator]. The Dalit women's question becomes critical when it is relegated to second-order importance, or sacrificed as the smaller for the larger cause. These problems recall the early debates about Dalit identity, such as the acrimonious debate between Gandhi and Ambedkar on national politics. My intention here is not to make an analogy between Gandhi's attitude towards Ambedkar and Dalit criticism's treatment of the Dalit women's question. The point here is, can smaller claims be ignored in the name of bigger identitarian claims?

The eminent anti-caste thinker Kancha Ilaiah opens a new vista in this debate in his book *Why I Am Not a Hindu*: 'Among the Dalit bahujans political relations within the family or community setting are basically democratic. In terms of the parent–child relationship, politics operates in what might be termed a "patriarchal democracy".'[28] According to Ilaiah, Dalit families are more democratic than upper-caste ones. But is this universally true? Both words in the phrase 'patriarchal democracy' are mutually negating polarities. No true democracy can be patriarchal, and no true patriarchy can be democratic in nature. Against this conception, Vimal Thorat characterizes the 'triple oppression' of the Dalit woman by the patriarchal establishment both within and without Dalit thought. In an interview, Sushila Takbhaure elaborates this position further from her own standpoint as a Dalit woman writer:

> When a part of my autobiography, *Shikanje ka dard* [The Pain of the Vice] was first published in the journal *Hans* in November 2009, I received many phone calls. They wanted to know why I was still living with my husband. Some Dalit writers accused me of defaming my husband. Others said that in order to prevent other Dalit women from writing, they were opposed to my writing. Some others made fun of some of the anecdotes in the autobiography. They humiliated me in front of other people in public. There was opposition against me both at home and outside. Despite all this I did not give up my courage. My autobiography speaks of women's emancipation along with the liberation of Dalits. It is a message for the emancipation of humankind.[29]

In summary, even if Dalit criticism is emergent in debates on the canon, it has successfully questioned some of the bases of canon formation. This may not have resulted in a decisive change, but the Dalit position has impacted other processes of canon formation.

Notes

1 Sudha Singh (2008), p. 94.
2 Ibid., pp. 11–12.
3 See Chatterjee (1993).
4 Krishn (2008), p. 261.
5 Bhatt (2004), p. 41.
6 Sudha Singh (2008), p. 251.
7 Varma (2004), p. 82.
8 Krishn (2008), p. 277.
9 Singh and Chaturvedi, eds (2004), p. 245.
10 Lal, ed. (2001), p. 156.

[11] Sudha Singh (2008), p. 59.
[12] Krishn (2008).
[13] Lal, ed. (2001), pp. 157–65.
[14] Limbale (2000), p. 38.
[15] Ibid., p. 19.
[16] Bharti (2002), p. 129.
[17] Ibid., p. 102.
[18] Limbale (2000), p. 40.
[19] Bharti (2002), p. 124.
[20] Krishn (2008), p. 308.
[21] See the chapter 'Punashchah: Dalit aur vam: gairzaruri saval' [Postscript], in Bharti (2002). He clarifies in the introduction itself that the chapter is written with a view to compare Dalit thought with Marxism. He declares the question of identity to be key to the imagination of movements against social injustice.
[22] Ibid., pp. 309–10.
[23] Talwar (1997).
[24] Ashutosh Kumar (2009), p. 169.
[25] Dharmvir (2005), p. 17.
[26] Bharti (2002), p. 129.
[27] Rajendr Kumar, 'Dalit chetna: Hindi sahitya mein uske kuchh aks, kuchh andeshe', in Rajendr Kumar (2009).
[28] Ilaiah (1996), pp. 39–40.
[29] Interview with Sushila Takbhaure, in Ram (2013), pp. 102–03.

Bibliography

Ahmad, Aijaz (1994), *In Theory: Classes, Nations, Literatures*, New Delhi: Oxford University Press.

Ambedkar, B.R. (1993), *Sampurn vangmay*, edited by Vasant Moon, translated by Radheshyam Bandhu *et al.*, Vol. 3, New Delhi: Dr Ambedkar Pratishthan.

Ambedkar, B.R. (2014), *Annihilation of Caste*, in *Dr Babasaheb Ambedkar: Writings and Speeches*, Vol. 1, edited by Vasant Moon, New Delhi: Dr Ambedkar Foundation.

Amin, Shahid and Gyanendra Pandey (1995), 'Preface', in *Nimnvargiy Prasang*, Vol. 1, New Delhi: Rajkamal Prakashan.

Ashutosh Kumar (2009), *Samkalin kavita aur Marxvad*, Aligarh: Department of Hindi, Aligarh Muslim University.

Bharti, Kanwal (2002), *Dalit-vimarsh ki bhumika*, Allahabad: Itihas Bodh Prakashan.

Bhatt, Balkrishn (2004), '*Striyan aur unki shiksha*', in Sudha Singh and Jagdishvar Chaturvedi, eds, *Stri asmita: Sahitya aur vichardhara*, Kolkata: Anand Prakashan.

Chandpuri, Qa'im (1965), *Kulliyat*, edited by Iqtida Hasan, Lahore: Majlis-e-taraqqi-e-adab.

Chatterjee, Partha (1993), 'The Nation and Its Women', in *The Nation and Its Fragments: Colonial and Postcolonial Histories*, Princeton: Princeton University Press.

Chauhan, Shivdan Singh (2002), *Alochna ke maan*, edited by Vishnuchandr Sharma, New Delhi: Swaraj Prakashan.

Cuddon, J.A. (1981), *A Dictionary of Literary Terms and Literary Theory*, Malden: Wiley-Blackwell.

Dalmia, Vasudha (1997), *The Nationalization of Hindu Traditions: Bharatendu Harischandra and Nineteenth-Century Banaras*, New Delhi: Oxford University Press.

de Tassy, Garcin (1953), *Hindui sahitya ka itihas* (Hindi translation of *Histoire de la littérature Hindoui et Hindoustani*, Vol. 1, 1839 and 1870; Vol. 2, 1847), translated by Lakshmi Sagar Varshney, Allahabad: Hindustani Akademi.

Dharmvir (2005), *Matrsatta, pitrsatta aur jarsatta*, Vol. 3: *Premchand: Samant ka munshi*, Delhi: Vani Prakashan.

Dwivedi, Hazari Prasad (1988), *Hindi sahitya: udbhav aur vikas*, New Delhi: Rajkamal Prakashan.

Dwivedi, Hazari Prasad (2000), *Hindi sahitya ki bhumika*, New Delhi: Rajkamal Prakashan.

Dwivedi, Hazari Prasad (2007), *Hazari Prasad Dwivedi Granthavali*, New Delhi: Rajkamal Prakashan.

Faruqi, Shamsur Rahman (2007), *Urdu ka arambhik yug: Itihas, vishwas evam rajniti*, New Delhi: Rajkamal Prakashan.

Gilchrist, John (1802), *Oriental Linguist: An Easy and Familiar Introduction to the Hindoostanee, or Grand Popular Language of Hindoostan, (vulgarly, but improperly called the Moors)*, Calcutta: P. Ferris.

Grierson, George A. (1889), *The Modern Vernacular Literature of Hindustan*, Calcutta: Asiatic Society.

Guillory, John (1993), *Cultural Capital: The Problem of Literary Canon Formation*, Chicago: University of Chicago Press.

Guillory, John (1995), 'Canon', in Frank Lentricchia and Thomas Mclaughlin, eds, *Critical Terms for Literary Study*, Chicago: University of Chicago Press.

Howatson, M.C. (1989), *Oxford Companion to Classical Literature*, Oxford: Oxford University Press.

Ilaiah, Kancha (1996), *Why I Am Not a Hindu: A Sudra Critique of Hindutva Philosophy*, Calcutta: Samya.

Jain, Nirmala (1992), *Hindi alochna ki bisvin sadi*, New Delhi: Radhakrishn Prakashan.

Keay, Frank E. (1920), *A History of Hindi Literature*, Calcutta: Association Press.

Keay, Frank E. (1931), *Kabir and His Followers*, London: Oxford University Press.

Krishn, Pranay (2008), *Uttar aupniveshikta ke srot aur Hindi sahitya*, Allahabad: Hindi Parishad Prakashan, University of Allahabad.

Krishn Kumar (2007), '*Viprit kalpanayen*', in *Mera Desh, Tumhara Desh*, New Delhi: Rajkamal Prakashan.

Lal, Chaman, ed. (2001), *Dalit and Woman in Indian Literature*, New Delhi: Saraansh Publications.

Lentricchia, Frank and Thomas Mclaughlin, eds (1995), *Critical Terms for Literary Study*, Chicago: University of Chicago Press.

Limbale, Sharankumar (2000), *Dalit sahitya ka saundaryashastra*, New Delhi: Vani Prakashan.

Madhup Kumar (n.d.), '*Sabhyata samiksha aur Muktibodh*', *Abhipraay*, Nos 24–25.

Martin, Montgomery, ed. (1836), *The Dispatches, Minutes and Correspondence, of the Marquess Wellesley, K.G.*, Vol. 2, London: W.H. Allen and Co.

Marx, Karl and Friedrich Engels (1977), *The Manifesto of the Communist Party*, Moscow: Progress Publishers.

Mishr, Satyaprakash (1993), *Alochak aur samikshayen*, Allahabad: Vibha Prakashan.

Mishr, Shivkumar (1987), '*Navjagarankalin sahitya ke charitr ka ek vishisht pehlu*', *Alochna*, July–September.

Mishr, Shivkumar (2002), 'Ramchandr Shukl', *Vartaman sahitya*, Vol. 19, No. 5, May.

Mishr Bandhu (1965), *Sankshipt navratn*, tenth edition, Lucknow: Ganga Granthagar.

Mishr Bandhu (1987), *Hindi navratn arthat Hindi ke nav sarvotkrisht kavi*, Lucknow: Ganga Pustakmala.

Muktibodh, G.M. (1998), *Muktibodh Rachnavali*, edited by Nemichandr Jain, New Delhi: Rajkamal Prakashan.

Murfin, Ross and Supriya M. Ray (2003), *The Bedford Glossary of Critical and Literary Terms*, New York: Bedford/St Martin's.

Naval, Nandkishor (1981), *Hindi alochna ka vikas*, New Delhi: Rajkamal Prakashan.

Neelabh (2005), *Pratimanon ki purohiti*, Allahabad: Sadanira Prakashan.

Nilkant (1985), *Ramchandr Shukl*, Allahabad: Lokbharti Prakashan.

Pandey, Gyanendra (1995), *Nimnvargiy prasang: kisan andolan aur bharatiya rashtrvad, avadh ka kisan andolan, 1919–1922*, New Delhi: Rajkamal Prakashan.

Pandey, Manager (1981), *Sahitya aur itihas drishti*, New Delhi: Vani Prakashan.

Pandey, Manager (2002), *Anbhay sancha*, New Delhi: Purvoday Prakashan.

Pandey, Manager (2005), *Alochna ki samajikta*, New Delhi: Vani Prakashan.

Pandey, Manager (2006), *Desh ki baat*, New Delhi: National Book Trust.

Pandey, Manager (2007), special article on D.D. Kosambi, *Prabhat Khabar*, Dipavali special issue.

Pant, Sumitranandan (2008), 'Introduction', *Pallav*, New Delhi: Rajkamal Prakashan.

Pradhan, Gopal (2009), *Hindi navratn: Hindi alochna ki pahli kitab*, New Delhi: Swaraj Prakashan.

Premchand (2004a), *Gaban*, New Delhi: Rajkamal Prakashan.

Premchand (2004b), *Godan*, New Delhi: Vani Prakashan.

Rajendr Kumar (2009), *Pratibaddhta ke bavujud*, New Delhi: Swaraj Prakashan.

Ram, Ramnaresh (2013), *Dalit strivad ki atmkathatmak abhivyakti*, New Delhi: Nayi Kitab Publications.

Ramakrishnan, E.V., ed. (2005), *Narrating India: The Novel in Search of the Nation*, New Delhi: Sahitya Akademi.

Ravibhushan (2006), '*Hori ki mrityu aur kisanon ki aatmhatya*', *Samkalin janmat*, Vol. 25, No. 1.

Sahi, Vijaydev Narayan (1983), *Jayasi*, Allahabad: Hindustani Academy.

Sahi, Vijaydev Narayan (2007a), *Nitant samsamayikta ka naitik dayitv – 1, chhatvan dashak*, Allahabad: Hindustani Academy.

Sahi, Vijaydev Narayan (2007b), *Nitant samsamayikta ka naitik dayitv – 2, chhatvan dashak*, Allahabad: Hindustani Academy.

Saraswati (1912), Vol. 13, No. 1, January–February.

Shah Nawaz, Mumtaz (1990), *The Heart Divided*, Lahore: A.S.R. Publications.

Shahi, Sadanand, ed. and trans. (1988), *Hindi sahitya ka itihas* (translation of Frank E. Keay, *A History of Hindi Literature*, 1920), Gorakhpur: Lokayat Prakashan.

Shambhunath, ed. (2004), *Samajik kranti ke dastavez*, Part One, New Delhi: Vani Prakashan.

Sharma, Ramadhar (1962), *Hindi ki saiddhantik samiksha*, Kanpur: Anusandhan Prakashan.

Sharma, Ramvilas (1977), *Mahavir Prasad Dwivedi aur Hindi navjagaran*, New Delhi: Rajkamal Prakashan.

Sharma, Ramvilas (1997), *Nayi kavita aur astitvavad*, introduction to second edition, New Delhi: Rajkamal Prakashan.

Sharma, Ramvilas (2002), *Bharatiya sahitya ke itihas ki samasyaen*, New Delhi: Vani Prakashan.

Sharma, Ramvilas (2003), *Acharya Ramchandr Shukl aur Hindi alochna*, New Delhi: Rajkamal Prakashan.

Sharma, Ramvilas (2008), *Bhasha aur samaj*, New Delhi: Rajkamal Prakashan.

Sharma, Ramvilas (2009), *Acharya Ramchandr Shukl aur Hindi alochna*, New Delhi: Rajkamal Prakashan.

Shastri, Vishnukant (1977), *Dwivediyugin Hindi alochna: Hindi sahitya ka vrihad itihas*, Part Nine, Varanasi: Nagari Pracharini Sabha.

Shukl, Ramchandr (1997), *Hindi sahitya ka itihas*, thirty-second edition, Varanasi: Nagari Pracharini Sabha.

Singh, Namvar (1980), editorial, *Alochna*, April–June.

Singh, Namvar (1982), *Dusri parampara ki khoj*, New Delhi: Rajkamal Prakashan.

Singh, Namvar (1990), *Chhayavad*, New Delhi: Rajkamal Prakashan.

Singh, Namvar (1998), *Ramchandr Shukl*, second edition, New Delhi: Sahitya Akademi.

Singh, Namvar (2003), *Kavita ke naye pratiman*, introduction to first edition, New Delhi: Rajkamal Prakashan.

Singh, Namvar (2005), *Dusri parampara ki khoj*, New Delhi: Rajkamal Prakashan.

Singh, Namvar, ed. (1998), *Ramchandr Shukl sanchayan*, second edition, New Delhi: Sahitya Akademi.

Singh, Omprakash (2007), *Ramchandr Shukl granthavali*, Part Four, available at http://www.hindisamay.com/alochna/shukla%20granthavali4/bhag7.html.

Singh, Sudha (2008), *Gyan ka strivadi path*, New Delhi: Granthshilpi Prakashan.

Singh, Sudha and Jagdishvar Chaturvedi, eds (2004), *Stri asmita: Sahitya aur vichardhara*, Kolkata: Anand Prakashan.

Stalin, J.V. (1913), 'Marxism and the National Question', available at https://www.marxists.org/reference/archive/stalin/works/1913/03.htm.

Stalin, J.V. (1953), *Collected Works*, Vol. 2, Moscow: Foreign Languages Publishing House.

Talwar, Veer Bharat (1997), '*Kabir par kabze ki ladayi*', *Pal pratipal*, October–December.

Talwar, Veer Bharat (2002), *Rassakashi: Unnisvin sadi ka navjagaran aur pashchimottar-prant*, New Delhi: Saransh Prakashan.

Talwar, Veer Bharat (2005a), '*Hindi navjagaran: adhyayan ki samasyaen*', in *Samna*, New Delhi: Vani Prakashan.

Talwar, Veer Bharat (2005b), '*Ramvilas Sharma ki vivechan paddhati aur Marxvad – III*', in *Samna*, New Delhi: Vani Prakashan.

Tripathi, Vishvanath (2010), *Hindi alochna*, New Delhi: Rajkamal Prakashan.

Vajpeyi, Ashok, ed. (2001), *Nirmal Verma*, New Delhi: Rajkamal Prakashan.

Vajpeyi, Nanddulare (2003), *Mahakavi Surdas*, New Delhi: Rajkamal Prakashan.

Vajpeyi, Nanddulare (2007), *Hindi sahitya: bisvin sadi*, Allahabad: Lokbharti Prakashan.

Varma, Mahadevi (2004), '*Stri asmita*', in Sudha Singh and Jagdishvar Chaturvedi, eds, *Stri asmita: Sahitya aur vichardhara*, Kolkata: Anand Prakashan.

Varshney, Lakshmisagar (2004 vikrami), *Fort William College (1800–1854)*, Allahabad: Hindi Parishad Prakashan, Department of Hindi, University of Allahabad.

Verma, Nirmal (2000), *Patthar aur bahta pani*, Bikaner: Vagdevi Prakashan.

Index